imple in Meals

SIMPLE IN MEANS, RICH IN ENDS
Practicing Deep Ecology

Bill Devall

PEREGRINE SMITH BOOKS
SALT LAKE CITY

92 91   6 5 4

Copyright © 1988 by Gibbs Smith, Publisher

Published by Gibbs Smith, Publisher, P.O. Box 667, Layton, UT 84041

Printed and bound in the United States of America

Design by J. Scott Knudsen

Cover photograph, "Dense Fog, Highwater Path, Winter 1985," ©Ron Finne

Library of Congress Cataloging-in-Publication Data

Devall, Bill, 1938-
   Simple in means, rich in ends: practicing deep ecology / Bill Devall.
         p.   cm.
   Bibliography: p.
   ISBN 0-87905-294-5
   1. Man—Influence on nature.
2. Human ecology—Philosophy.
3. Environmental protection.
4. Environmental policy. I. Title.
GF75.D5   1988
333.7'16—dc19

Contents

We shall not cease from exploration
And the end of all our exploring
Will be to arrive where we started
And know the place for the first time.

T. S. Eliot, "Little Gidding"

Introduction

Ihave taught college level courses on human ecology and the new philosophies of nature for the past two decades. During that time I have participated, in a modest way, in numerous conservation and environmental debates and in campaigns to save areas of wilderness and biological diversity. This book grew from many discussions I have had with students, environmental activists, and philosophers. During these discussions many people asked, "What can I do to practice deep ecology? I agree with the intuition of deep ecology but I can't practice clearly in this hyperactive civilization."

The term *deep ecology* was coined by Norwegian philosopher Arne Naess in 1972. Naess' approach and his methodology to building a new natural philosophy and the contrasts between reform environmentalism and deep ecology have been discussed in many books and articles (see Appendix A).

The primary focus of this book, however, is on practicing. Practicing, to me, includes many activities which are not usually labeled as environmental activism. In terms used by poet Gary Snyder, we are practicing on many levels, simultaneously. Some people focus on practicing through what Snyder calls the "real work"—personal, inner work which seeks clarification and insight. Others are practicing by developing sophisticated intellectual arguments justifying the protection of biological diversity and respect for nature. Others practice through their political activism. I highlight some of these practices in this book and provide some tentative guidelines and suggestions to further our practice. Throughout the book I prefer to use the active tense—practicing. To me this implies we become part of something larger than our narrow, egotistic self. Practicing may not make us perfect, but through practicing we test our theories and perhaps develop further insights from which more sophisticated theories develop.

One inspiration for this book was the life of ecologist Aldo Leopold. Leopold's famous *land ethic* is explained in only a few pages of his book *A Sand County Almanac,* but it expresses a lifetime of experience as a field ecologist. I see a similar interplay between practicing and insight in the life work of John Muir, the founder of the American conservation movement, and Henry Thoreau.

It is not just that we learn from experience, but rather how we are experiencing the world. That is the basis for authentic statements of our environmental philosophy. Even when we don't fully understand our experience in an intellectual sense, we can understand with our bodies.

I practice Aikido, a form of contemporary Japanese martial training. Many times our teacher (called *sensei* in Japanese) demonstrates techniques and watches students explore those techniques. He urges us to "keep practicing. Don't think about it. Just keep practicing. This is your experience."

My thesis in this book is that finding the right form of practicing helps us to cultivate our ecological self and makes a formal philosophy, or statement of environmental ethics, into a living, practical philosophy. Arne Naess provides, in my estimation, a methodology for clarifying and articulating our insights into a formal statement of philosophy. Each person can work through this process to articulate his or her own kind of deep ecology position. However, we still need practical suggestions for integrating what we say and what we do.

This integration occurs through exploring our ecological self. Finding our center and integrating from our center into the larger "body" of the world involves us in exploring aspects of reality which tend to be neglected in our society. There are ways to discover authentic, ecological self which are simple, though not necessarily easy.

Why focus on *self* in an age of ecological crisis? Perceptive writers including Wendell Berry, Gary Snyder, Theodore Roszak and Naess, suggest that there are social and economic reasons for the ecological crisis, but at its root it is not so much a crisis of the environment as a crisis of character and culture. A central thesis of this book is that as long as we think of our *self* in a narrow, "me first," self-serving way, we will suffer. When we put the vital needs of other beings above our narrowly conceived self-interest, then we discover that our broader and deeper needs are met in the context of meeting the needs of the "other," because we have broadened and deepened our self to include the other into ourself.

The deep, long-range ecology movement is a hope-filled movement. Philosophers who have articulated formal statements of deep ecology suggest it is a radical approach to being-in-the-world. It is radical in the sense of getting back to our roots. Through practicing we enrich our lives in ways which do not impoverish the habitat of other species.

This book is written not only for professional philosophers and social scientists but for interested, concerned citizens who feel what Aldo Leopold called the "wounds of the world." To be trained as an ecologist, Leopold wrote nearly fifty years ago, "is to live alone in a world of wounds." But today we do not live alone. Many people realize the importance of the environment. We live and work together. The deep, long-range ecology movement is both a movement among professional philosophers seeking a new philosophy of nature and a collective expression of our vital need to be *in* the world rather than to be just transients waiting for a ticket to somewhere else.

This is not intended as a systematic guidebook to solving our mental dis-ease, nor does it include a systematic review of all the philosophical literature on deep ecology. It is intended as a modest conversation with readers which will help us integrate theories and action, culture and person.

In structure the book moves from theory to practice. The first chapter contains an overview of the deep, long-range ecology movement and contrasts the types of arguments using a deep ecology perspective with those using reform environmental perspectives. In this chapter I suggest some of the reasons it is difficult for us, in political forums, to refer to deep ecology directly.

The second chapter is a discussion of ecological self. It includes a discussion of gender, eros and deep ecology and suggests ways of cultivating ecological self as process. Chapter three presents some of the literature, poetry and music expressed from a deep ecology position.

Chapters four, five and six concern lifestyles which are congruent with a deep ecology position, political activism and dwelling in mixed communities. The term *mixed community* was used by Naess to refer to relations between humans and other animals. I use it to mean what Aldo Leopold calls the "land community," the broader community of humans and other beings.

I have used practical examples throughout the book, many drawn from the American environmental movement. The deep, long-range movement, however, is found in many nations, especially Australia, Canada, Mexico, Norway, New Zealand, and Great Britain. I hope that readers in all countries will be able to correlate examples from their own cultures.

The Deep, Long-range Ecology Movement

T o every natural form, rock, fruit, or flower,
Even the loose stones that cover the highway
I gave a moral life: I saw them feel,
Or linked them to some feeling: The great mass
Lay bedded in a quickening soul, and all
That I beheld respired with inward meaning."
William Wordsworth, *Selected Poems and Prefaces* (1965)

Since Arne Naess introduced the distinction between shallow (reform) environmentalism and deep ecology in 1972, the distinction has gained general acceptance among philosophers and environmental educators (Miller 1988). In this chapter I discuss the relationship between reform and deep ecology. In practical political debates, arguments based on reform and deep perspectives are both appropriate in certain situations. But the weaknesses of reform arguments should also be noted. In particular I am concerned with the dilemma of environmental activists who feel they must use reform arguments in order to be understood by political decision-makers and who reject using deep arguments because they are seen as too subversive. In using reformist arguments, however, activists help to legitimate and reinforce the human-centered (anthropocentric) worldview of decision-makers.

Before launching into a discussion of the conceptual framework of deep ecology arguments, however, I want to digress with a short account of my personal intellectual and emotional development from reform to deep ecology. My story in a modest way shows some of the pain which environmental activists feel in attempting to articulate their arguments in political arenas. Since the theme of this book is practicing deep ecology, I want to show how arguments, conceptual theories, and testimony presented in political forums are related to our personal lives. Some philosophers define deep ecology as, primarily, a philosophical movement based on insight and reflection. In my experience, action came before reflection. Perhaps that is also true of many readers of this book. I want to show how to present arguments based on deep ecological intuition in political arenas. I also want to show the intimate relationship between action, intuition, and reflection. Reflecting on your own experiences, perhaps you can find personal turning points which deepened your experience and broadened your ecological awareness.

Like many people in the 1960s and '70s, I began my active involvement with the environmental movement over threats to a specific place. For me it was Redwood Creek in Humboldt County, California, and the political campaign leading to the creation of Redwood National Park to protect a portion of that watershed. During the 1960s, when I was in graduate school at the University of Oregon, I was aware of various environmental problems in an abstract and vague sort of way. I read about the problems of increasing human population, air pollution, and conversion of farmlands into suburban housing tracts. I majored in college in sociology and political science. I never saw a course listing in human ecology or environmental philosophy.

When I moved to Humboldt County in 1968, the first Redwood National Park Act had just been signed by President Lyndon B. Johnson, but many proponents of the national park were extremely dissatisfied with the political compromise which resulted in the park act. They were particularly distressed that the integrity of the Tall Trees grove (a grove including probably the tallest tree in the world) was not protected in the park act. Instead of thinking like a watershed, that is, thinking about the relationships among logging, road building, and sediment load of Redwood Creek, Congress had included only a narrow band of trees along Redwood Creek, up to the Tall Trees grove in the boundaries of the new park. Working with the Sierra Club and other environmental groups, I was soon hiking up Redwood Creek during winter flood stages, learning various theories of redwood forest regeneration and methods of measuring sediment load of stream beds, and arguing that the national park boundaries should be expanded from ridge to ridge in the lower eleven miles of Redwood Creek.

I began my relationship with redwood forests with a romantic view of wilderness. In rare moments, such as hiking alone in some relatively remote section of Redwood National Park on a fine spring morning or in late fall when the maple leaves have fallen along the creek, I still feel awe and mystery of the primeval forest. I imagine that I am the first person ever to experience the silent splendor of primeval redwoods.

In the early 1970s I did not have an elaborate philosophical argument to back my assertion that the Redwood National Park should be expanded. I only had my feeling that it was wrong to clear-cut such old trees. If I gave any reason for my position, in those years, I would say they had been inhabitating Redwood Valley for a long time. They should have their own space just as humans have their space.

I soon learned that some economists and foresters have elaborate arguments based on theories of private property rights, rates of return on investment, regeneration rates and future value which justify clear-cutting the last primeval redwood forests. I also learned that ecologists are still learning about the complex relationships between redwoods, fog patterns, vegetation, soils, and other aspects of the redwood biome. Primeval redwood forests are being rapidly converted to managed stands of new growth timber before we understand all those relationships. Worse than that, many people seem to be in such a hurry to cut the primeval forests for timber that they will never take time to respect them for their own sake.

I was angry, and felt physical pain, a kind of suffering, every time I saw a truck loaded with an old growth log rushing down the freeway to the lumber mill. I appreciated the need for jobs by loggers, but I also valued the sublime beauty of primeval forests.

The boundaries of Redwood National Park were expanded by Congress in 1978 as a result of a masterful political compromise by Congressman Philip Burton which included provisions for restoration of portions of the Redwood Creek watershed (Schrepfer 1983).

After passage of the Redwood National Park Expansion Act, I continued to be very active in reform environmental groups, working on a variety of issues—including wilderness preservation, coastal access and protection, and water policy. But I became less and less interested in short-term politics and more interested in the reasons why a whole civilization would become dedicated to bringing vast areas under intensive management for narrow goals such as production of commercial timber through monoculture tree farming.

Many experts in silvaculture, hydrology, wildlife management, forest ecology and geology presented results of their research on Redwood Creek to various congressional committees during the debate over expansion of Redwood National Park. Much of this testimony was useful in establishing the assertion that Congress should act to protect the integrity of the watershed. But I continued to feel that primeval redwood forests had a right to continue existing just because they were there.

I began reading John Muir, Henry David Thoreau, and Robinson Jeffers and discovered Aldo Leopold's *Sand County Almanac.* Not until I discovered the writings of Arne Naess did I find a label for my feelings. I began to understand more clearly my growing discontent with reformist arguments.

Even though Naess coined the term *deep ecology* in the early 1970s, by rereading the history of the environmental movement in North America we can see that the deep, long-range ecology movement has interwoven with the reform environmental movement for over a hundred years. If reform environmentalism and deep ecology seem to be diverging in the late 1980s, it is because of the increasingly conservative political stance of reform environmental organizations, their willingness to legitimate the institutions which exploit mountains and forests, and their lack of ecological vision.

I do not intend this chapter as a political history of environmentalism. That has been extensively documented in such books as Stephen Fox's *John Muir and His Legacy: The American Environmental Movement* (see also Hays 1987). Nor do I want to review the technical philosophical arguments pro and con over the major insights of deep ecology (see Appendix A: Further Reading). However, a brief look at the history of reform and deep ecology in the U.S.A. illustrates some of the reasons for the tensions and dilemmas in the lives of those acting from a deep ecology position. Clarification of the meaning of deep ecology may also clear away some of the confusion created by social scientists, such as Lester Milbrath, who misunderstand deep ecology (see Milbrath 1984).

A Brief History

The reform environmental movement began during the nineteenth century as more and more illnesses related to the growth of industrial civilization became clearly recognized. Reformers fought to alert decision-makers to the dark side of industrial civilization—air and water pollution, deforestation, destruction of nutrient cycles, toxic poisoning. George Perkins Marsh, in *Man and Nature* (1864), demonstrated that the fate of civilization depends, to a great extent, on how we treat natural resources. Deterioration of the land will result from ignorant disregard of nature's laws.

In the words of Arne Naess, the goal of reform environmentalism has always been "the health and affluence of people in developed countries." This objective is, of course, honorable, and many improvements in the health and well-being of citizens in the United States and other nations can be credited to environmentalists, but the objective is parochial and pragmatic (Naess 1973). Reformers rarely questioned the basic social and philosophical assumptions of urbanizing, industrializing civilization. In the early 1980s the political stance of many reform groups continued to be mildly liberal, that is, favoring government intervention to regulate business, and staying definitely within the parameters of philosophy, politics and acceptable social action defined by the dominant institutions in economically rich nations (Sale 1986).

Some small groups advocated a "green politics." A political party which included ecology as a plank in its platform was successful in elections in the Federal Republic of Germany in the early 1980s.

Many leaders of mainstream environmental groups in the U.S.A. espouse a political agenda that is not based on a new philosophy of nature nor on the premise that radical changes in politics and culture are necessary to solve the problems of this civilization.

In 1984 the executive directors of ten of the largest reform environmental groups began meeting to discuss the future of the reform environmental movement in the United States. This group, which I like to refer to as the Gang of Ten, included executive directors of the Sierra Club, Audubon, The Wilderness Society, Natural Resources Defense Council, Environmental Policy Institute, National Wildlife Federation, Environmental Defense Fund, Izaak Walton League of America, National Parks and Conservation Association, and Friends of the Earth. In the political context of the 1980s in North America, these professional environmentalists formulated an agenda that was limited in scope, vision, and politics.

Although their statement, *An Environmental Agenda for the Future,* was not submitted to the governing boards of their organizations, it is the closest we have to a consensus of thinking among reform environmentalists in the U.S.A.

The *Agenda* was published in 1985. In the introduction, these reformists state they "hope that this look at the larger picture will spawn fresh ways of thinking and new ideas to help in the pursuit of environmental quality." They state their belief that "a successful strategy for the future must appeal to the broadest spectrum of the American people" (Cahn 1985).

The *Agenda* consists of policy recommendations and summary statements concerning eleven topic areas. Policy recommendations are directed primarily to the United States Congress. The authors say that, if enacted, these recommendations will carry the U.S.A. into the twenty-first century with a growing economy and a more healthy environment for humans.

The tone of the *Agenda* is managerial. The underlying assumption seems to be that nature is a collection of natural resources and the primary users and beneficiaries of these resources are humans.

The *Agenda* is premised on three key principles: 1) sustained economic growth is necessary to achieve higher environmental quality; 2) government regulation benefits both economy and environment; and 3) environmental groups must use the same strategies for the rest of the century as have been successful during the past two decades.

The eleven topic areas covered in the *Agenda* are: nuclear issues, human population growth, energy strategies, water resources, toxins and pollution control, wild living resources, private lands and agriculture, protected land systems, public lands, urban environment, and international responsibility.

The authors of the *Agenda* avoid comments or questions concerning cultural and personal transformation. The authors do not call for a new worldview nor do they criticize human chauvinistic attitudes toward nonhuman nature.

In sum, the authors of the *Agenda* suggest that reform environmentalism is primarily a political movement within mainstream political institutions in the U.S.A. It continues a hundred-year tradition among progressive, reform environmentalists who have sought to change public policies, improve public health, and reconcile rapid economic growth with some protection of scenery and public green spaces.

Ecosophy and Deep Ecology

In contrast to the *Agenda,* a few visionary writers have sought a different way of seeing the earth. They have sought ecosophy. *Ecosophy* is a term combining *sophia,* the old word for *wisdom,* and *eco,* for *earth* or *land.* Therefore ecosophy is earth wisdom. When we have ecosophy we harmonize with the will-of-the-land.

Arne Naess consistently emphasizes that "what we modestly try to realize is wisdom rather than science or information. A philosophy, as articulated wisdom, has to be a synthesis of theory and practice. It must not shun concrete policy recommendations but has to base them on fundamental priorities of value and basic views concerning the development of our societies" (Naess in Tobias 1985, 258).

Since the deep, long-range ecology movement began in the richest industrial societies, the language used by supporters tends to reflect, Naess says, the "cultural provinciality of those societies."

Although ecosophy as a perspective or understanding was inspired, at least in part, by the science of ecology, it is not the exclusive property of the contemporary deep, long-range ecology movement. Ecophilosophical themes are found in many philosophies and religions, including Native American spiritual practices, Zen Buddhism, Taoism, some pre-Socratic Greek philosophies, the cult of the Bear, and in rituals and ceremonies of many gathering and hunting peoples in all historical eras on all continents.

Deep ecology themes are found in the writings of Dutch philosopher Benedict Spinoza, some American transcendentalists including Ralph Waldo Emerson and Henry Thoreau, and in the writings of John Muir. Twentieth-century writers taking a deep ecology-type position include D. H. Lawrence, Aldous Huxley, Robinson Jeffers, Gary Snyder, Marston Bates, Aldo Leopold, and Rachel Carson.

Ecosophy is not just abstract theory, not philosophy in the usual academic sense, nor only action. It develops from our action and reflection on action, from theory and practice.

The deep ecology *movement* is one which cultivates ecosophy. Writers have suggested other terms to refer to this movement, including panecology (after the ancient European god), foundational ecology, spiritual ecology, and radical ecology. *Spiritual ecology* is useful for some people, but spiritual suggests the old dualism in western philosophy—mind versus body, spirit versus matter.

The term *deep ecology* refers to finding our bearings, to the process of grounding ourselves through fuller experience of our connection to earth. Naess says "the term 'deep' is supposed to suggest explication of fundamental presuppositions of valuation as well as of facts and hypotheses. Deep ecology, therefore, transcends the limit of any particular science of today, including systems theory and scientific ecology. *Deepness of normative and descriptive premises questioned* characterize the movement" (Naess in Tobias 1985, 256).

Deepness is felt in the way we are experiencing our lives. Deepness of thinking means articulating basic priorities, or more or less intuitive beliefs. Deepness means exploring our dreams to recognize our archaic unity with all life and basic symbols. Some people find

Jungian archetypes especially relevant in this work. Deepness implies an attitude of dwelling-in-the-moment, meditating; letting one's own rhythms and perceptual room open up; respecting and including what is there, what comes, involving the flow of actions from the level of the unconscious that Wilhelm Reich calls 'eros'.

Deep ecology is also a metaphor. Deepness is settling into the stream of things as they are. It means moving down into cooler, more profound waters. It involves us in a quality of openness to the flow of change. Transformation in a fluid state can occur in a quiet, slow-moving stream or a swift-moving mountain river. Deep ecology is ecological realism.

What Naess calls "shallow ecology," and I call "reform environmentalism," is not a label placed on individual persons. There are no "shallow ecologists" versus "deep ecologists." The terms refer to different ways of experiencing the world and to different types of whole argumentations in political discussions rather than to arguments taken in isolation. Sometimes I base my arguments presented to colleagues or public officials on considerations of human health or economy. These are shallow but appropriate arguments for the political arena within which I operate. There are many excellent arguments for species preservation, for example, which are persuasive to many people, but which *only* concern the short-range well-being of some humans.

The deep ecology movement is not a new religion or cult, nor does it fight any religions. Supporters of deep ecology are fighting against thoughtlessness and mindless behavior.

Different intellectual arguments for deep ecology are found in the thinking of theoreticians from several religions and philosophical traditions. Different religions, such as Christianity and Buddhism, may have different "first premises" or beliefs. The important process is to work from these ultimate norms to a deep ecology position.

Table I is a modification of a schematic presented by Arne Naess. It consists of four levels. Level one includes philosophical-religious systems or explanations. Level one statements are basic beliefs, religious and philosophical, from which a person derives his or her point of view in deep ecology. Level two statements are ultimately derived from level one. Not all level one statements belong to deep ecology as such. That is, we might disagree on fundamental beliefs as between Christian, Buddhist, or Islam religions. Many statements on level one are more or less incommensurable but are compatible with a deep ecology philosophical position on level two. Some interpretations of these systems are anthropocentric. Other interpretations lend themselves to reaching a deep ecology position intellectually within the theoretical tradition on the top level. For example, St. Francis of Assisi has been called the patron saint of ecology, and some suggest that working from the teachings of St. Francis one can reach a deep ecology position in the Christian tradition. The "New Road" project of the World Wildlife Fund illustrates the cooperation and dialogue currently occurring between religious leaders and members of environmental movements.[1]

Similarly some ecofeminists state a position which can be developed into a second level, deep ecology position (See Hallen 1987).

TABLE 1

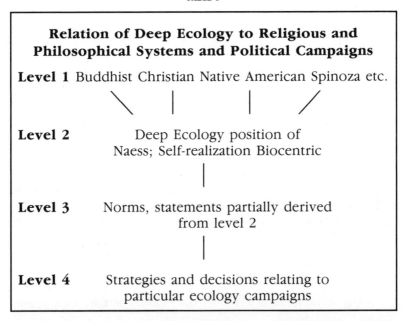

Relation of Deep Ecology to Religious and Philosophical Systems and Political Campaigns

Level 1 Buddhist Christian Native American Spinoza etc.

Level 2 Deep Ecology position of Naess; Self-realization Biocentric

Level 3 Norms, statements partially derived from level 2

Level 4 Strategies and decisions relating to particular ecology campaigns

Third-level statements form platforms for various political movements, such as the Green movement, appropriate technology, Earth First!, and various bioregional movements. Deep ecology positions and arguments are found in all these movements. In each movement there are anthropocentric and biocentric tendencies.

Fourth-level statements refer to decisions concerning specific strategies for specific situations, such as the worldwide rain forest action campaign and the Save the Grizzly Bear campaigns in North America. Many single arguments used in these campaigns are based on a deep ecology position, but, depending on the circumstances and situation, effective human-centered arguments are advanced by activists. The campaigns occur within specific political and social contexts; and reasonable people, all committed to a deep ecology position, can, of course, disagree about which campaign strategies are most effective.

In 1984 Naess and George Sessions articulated a platform consisting of general, neutral level-two type statements of deep ecology. They felt the need to formulate this platform, or set of principles, as some people interested in deep ecology have been confused, being confronted with very different philosophies or religious beliefs among the supporters of deep ecology. Questions were asked such as, "What is the essence of deep ecology? What makes you feel it is *one* movement?"

One set of wording cannot be expected to appeal to all supporters of deep ecology. In the following version, I would substitute 'worth' for 'value'. To me 'worth' implies worthiness in and of itself. 'Value' as commonly used in America, implies 'dollar value', or 'human value'.

Naess insists that his formulation of his deep ecology platform is "without great pretensions" and has a limited function of stimulating dialogue—both between supporters of deep ecology and between supporters and critics of deep ecology.

1. The well-being and flourishing of human and nonhuman life on Earth have value in themselves (synonyms: inherent worth; intrinsic value, inherent value). These values are independent of the usefulness of the nonhuman world for human purposes.

2. Richness and diversity of life forms contribute to the realization of these values and are also values in themselves.

3. Humans have no right to reduce this richness and diversity except to satisfy vital needs.

4. The flourishing of human life and cultures is compatible with a substantial decrease of the human population. The flourishing of nonhuman life requires such a decrease.

5. Present human interference with the nonhuman world is excessive, and the situation is rapidly worsening.

6. Policies must therefore be changed. The changes in policies affect basic economic, technological, and ideological structures. The resulting state of affairs will be deeply different from the present.

7. The ideological change is mainly that of appreciating life quality (dwelling in situations of inherent worth) rather than adhering to an increasingly higher standard of living. There will be a profound awareness of the difference between big and great.

8. Those who subscribe to the foregoing points have an obligation directly or indirectly to participate in the attempt to implement the necessary changes.

Each reader can examine these statements and write interpretations, elaborations or qualifications. The platform is not dogma but consists of suggestions. The following paragraphs include my qualifications on Naess' platform.

1. 'Inherent value', 'intrinsic value', or 'inherent worth' are sometimes used synonymously by philosophers. As used here, 'inherent worth' means that the value of a natural object is not dependent on a human observer of that object nor on the monetary value of the natural object to some human.

This statement refers to the ecosphere, not just to life as defined by biologists. *Life* or *living being* is defined broadly in the deep ecology movement. It means flourishing of ecosystems, rivers, mountain systems, and the Earth as a whole. It is implied in expressions such as "Let the river live!" Some writers, such as Warwick Fox, prefer the term *ecocentric,* meaning Earth-centered, rather than biocentric to refer to a deep ecology understanding of living beings.

2. This statement refers to complexity and diversity. In ecological theory all species have a function for the system and are valued in themselves. They are not just supporters of higher life forms.

Ecocentrism means rejecting the position that some life forms (such as humans) have greater inherent worth than other life forms. Richness and diversity of life forms are being undermined by many common practices of humans in our era.

Complexity is not synonymous with complication. Contemporary civilization exhibits much complication but is not more complex than the multifaceted reality manifested by some primal tribes.

3. Vital needs are biological, social, and spiritual. Needs are satisfied within environmental, technical, and cultural contexts. There are several ways to fulfill each vital need. For example, we might suggest that humans have a vital need for leisure, but they don't have a vital need to use off-road vehicles in delicate desert environments

to fulfill their leisure needs. Vital needs are discussed extensively later in this book, but as a general principle we can assert that lifestyles based on deep ecology principles seek to satisfy vital needs with the most simple, elegant, and least environmentally destructive means.

4. Human population of the Earth reached five billion in 1986. Many experts on human population expect it to reach six billion by the year 2000. Most of the growth will occur in so-called developing nations of Africa, Asia, and Latin America. In Western European nations population has stabilized and may even decline without in-migration. Some experts estimate that half the annual population growth in the U.S.A. comes from in-migration, mostly from Latin America. Each nation has a population problem which can be addressed within the cultural system of that nation (see Kammeyer 1986; National Research Council 1986; Repetto 1987; Van de Kaa 1987; Catton 1987).

Population is not an issue of the rich against the poor or rich nations against poorer nations. But it is a fact that 80 percent of the Earth's population lives in developing nations and most of the women in these nations are of childbearing age.

Population growth, of course, is only one factor in the current environmental crisis. Increasing per capita consumption, poor land use practices, military operations and preparations which destroy landscapes (nuclear weapons testing, etc.), and inappropriate government policies are interrelated.

Migration to virgin territories or new worlds is not a viable approach to solving the problem of a growing population. Especially inappropriate are government-sponsored programs in Brazil and Indonesia to move large numbers of their inhabitants into tropical rain forests in those nations. Large-scale farming is not feasible in the Amazon rain forests or eastern islands of Indonesia.

Many commentators favor funding contraceptive programs for those people who want contraceptives. While there are moral and economic questions concerning certain birth control techniques, such as abortion, these problems should be resolved within an overall commitment to reducing the birthrate, especially in third world nations.

In 1987 Naess defended the proposition that "the flourishing of human life and cultures requires that human population is substantially smaller than at the present time."

He classifies his "ultimate goals of mankind" as individual, social (communal), and cultural. Ultimate goals do not have an instrumental aspect. Richness of culture—literature, art, music, compassionate human relationships—does not require a large population. He says, ". . . looking back some thousand years, and imagining some futures, the conclusion seems to me rather certain: on the average no very great population is required in each culture. On the contrary, huge numbers tend to reduce the manifold."

Humans live in communities that provide a basis for their attempts to have pleasure, happiness, and perfection. Achieving these goals does not require a huge population. Support for this position is found in the work of a number of anthropologists (see Stanley Diamond 1974).

Naess concludes that realization of ecologically sustainable communities within which humans are achieving ultimate goals requires a smaller human population than at present and "there are no ultimate goals of mankind the realization of which needs reduction of the richness and diversity of life on Earth" (Naess, "Population Reduction," 1987).

5. This statement is mild, given the serious environmental crisis we are experiencing. Destructive and widespread interference by humans is well documented. For a realistic overview see various *State Of The World* reports published by Worldwatch Institute, Washington, D.C. It is likely that combined effects of acid deposition, ozone layer depletion, rising species extinction rates, human-caused desertification, deforestation, and toxic waste pollution are changing world weather patterns and causing irreversible changes on large areas of the Earth (Worldwatch 1984, 1985, 1986, 1987; Pawlick 1984; Holdgate 1982; London 1984).

Only zoning massive areas of the Earth as "wilderness" (including protective treaties for air and ocean areas) and forbidding large-scale technocratic developments in these areas will protect what J. Lovelock calls the "vital organs" of Gaea (the Earth Organism) (Lovelock 1979).

Humans, of course, will continue to modify some ecosystems, as do many other organisms, to suit their own vital needs. The issue is not human interference versus pristine nature but the rate, extent, and scale of modification.

6. Many excellent principles which would change the direction of national economic policies are contained in the World Charter for Nature (U.N. General Assembly 1982) and the World Conservation Strategy.

Some conventional economic development policies, such as building big dams, have been shown to be counterproductive to sustained economic growth and to be environmentally destructive. Critics of the World Bank have asked for radical reforms in World Bank guidelines on funding development projects. Some nongovernmental organizations have been more effective in encouraging constructive changes in developing nations than have agencies of the United Nations.

The appropriate technology movement encourages realistic, community-based development processes.

7. "Quality of life" as used here does not need to be quantified. It refers to social, psychological, and ecological well-being. Conventional definitions of "standard of living" used by economists are misleading. Living in deep relationship with wild nature is rarely included in scales of standard of living.

8. The way I interpret this last point, we have an obligation to change our lifestyle, help influence public opinion and public policies on environmental issues, and think and act more deeply. Of course there are legitimate disagreements over priorities for action. Such disagreements are healthy for the movement, and full discussion in the spirit of mutual respect can bring out added dimensions of our dilemma and reveal creative approaches to the crisis of self and culture which is ultimately an environmental crisis.

Scientific and Subversive Ecology

There are two types of ecology as perspectives leading to a deep ecology position. Both are useful to the deep, long-range ecology movement. 'Scientific ecology', as summarized by Paul Ehrlich in *The Machinery of Nature,* provides theories explaining relationships between organisms and their habitats. But the science of ecology thus conceived cannot answer all our questions concerning nature's habits. There are other ways of knowing. However, Ehrlich says this "does not diminish the absolutely crucial role that good science must play if our over-extended civilization is to save itself. Values must not be based on scientific nonsense. . . . Given the present level of human overpopulation only a combination of changes in basic values *and* advances in science and technology seems to provide much hope for avoiding unprecedented calamities" (Ehrlich 1986, 18).

The second ecology has been called the 'subversive science'. As Theodore Roszak says in a much quoted section of his book *Where the Wasteland Ends,* "Its sensibility—holistic, receptive, trustful, largely non-tampering, deeply grounded in aesthetic intuition—is a radical deviation from traditional science. Ecology does not systematize by mathematical generalization or materialist reductionism, but by the almost sensuous intuiting of natural harmonies on the largest scale. Its patterns are not those of numbers, but of unity in process; its psychology borrows from Gestalt and is an awakening of wholes greater than the sum of their parts. In spirit, discipline is contemplative and therapeutic, a concernful listening with the third ear" (Roszak 1972, 367).

The subversive insight of ecology is that not only is everything connected with everything else but there is a literal intermingling of person and Other, of mind-in-nature.

Donald Worster concludes that the science of ecology has not taught us very much new in the organization of nature, but it has reawakened in us intuitions long suppressed in the era of scientific reductionism (Worster 1977).

The philosopher J. Baird Callicott in an article on the metaphysical implications of ecology evokes these deeper meanings of ecological consciousness by suggesting that there are no logical connections between ecological premises and metaphysical conclusions but that "ecology has made plain to us the fact that we are enfolded, involved, and engaged within the living, terrestrial, environment—i.e., implicated in and implied by it" (Callicott 1986, 301). Callicott also suggests that ecology and physics (Quantum Theory) converge toward the same metaphysical notions and that the concepts used in both complement each other (Callicott 1985).

Philosophers and other writers articulating new trends in the new philosophy of nature in the 1960s and 1970s were indebted to the insights of both the scientific and metaphysical implications of ecology, as well as to earlier schools of thinking which suggest that humans are embedded in the "web of life."

Rachel Carson's *Silent Spring,* published in 1962, was a manifesto for the Age of Ecology and inspiration for the deep, long-range ecology movement (see Lutts 1985; Marco 1987). Carson was trained as a research scientist. She had facts to back her conclusions concerning the calamitous side effects of the use of pesticides on farm crops. She was also sensitive to the second ecology, the subversive ecology. Her emotional sensibility and her intuition fused with her scientific judgment.

Carson published several books in the 1950s, including her widely acclaimed *Sea Around Us,* which demonstrated her sensitivity to a deep ecology position. It was *Silent Spring,* however, which aroused a storm of protest from some scientific colleagues and from an army of lawyers and scientists employed by the chemical industry and in academia, but also much support from more timid colleagues who believed in her position.

She was writing about the unintended consequences of massive usage of DDT primarily to control unwanted insects (pests to farmers and foresters) feeding on monoculture crops. But her concluding statement makes a much wider indictment of our civilization. It can be read as a powerful introduction to deep ecology: "The 'control of nature' is a phrase conceived in arrogance, born of the Neanderthal age of biology and philosophy, when it was supposed that nature exists for the convenience of man" (Carson 1962).

Carson presented scientific evidence concerning the environmental effects of use of pesticides in *Silent Spring,* but in her other books she invites her readers to viable, confident experiences in nature. Categorizing nature is less important than seeing and feeling. Carson calls us to "a sense of wonder," to experiencing nature in new, unusual, astounding ways (Norwood 1987).

At the same time that Carson was writing *Silent Spring,* Secretary of Interior Stuart Udall was writing *The Quiet Crisis,* which was both an informal history of attitudes toward land in America and a call for a new environmental ethic. Udall cites Aldo Leopold's phrase, "land ethic." Udall concludes that "a land ethic for tomorrow should be as honest as Thoreau's *Walden,* and as comprehensive as the sensitive science of ecology. It should stress the oneness of our resources and the live-and-help-live logic of the great chain of life" (Udall 1963, 202).

Ten years after the publication of *Silent Spring,* Arne Naess introduced the term *deep ecology* in a lecture entitled "The Shallow and the Deep, Long-Range Ecology Movement," read at the Third World Future Research Conference in Bucharest, Hungary. Naess was participating in a movement of philosophical activism in Norway in the 1960s which saw several philosophers writing significant papers on ecophilosophy. Naess saw two contrasting approaches to environmental issues. He saw a need to prescribe a proper philosophical base for the deeper stream of environmental activism.

Reform environmentalism, as noted in the beginning of this chapter, tends to be parochial and concerned mainly with symptoms of environmental disease and dis-eases of people living in maldeveloped or overdeveloped nations. The deeper stream addresses questions which draw us to major realignment in our self and in our thinking and calls us to long-range solutions from an ecological perspective. 'Shallow ecology' is shallow because it lacks probing philosophical questioning. Naess challenged people to begin *thinking* in a dialogue process. Deep ecology *combines* the day-to-day problems of environment, including human health problems, with the global, cultural, psychological, long-range problems. Naess is convinced that people will adopt a deep ecology philosophical position if they engage in a process of reflecting on their own experiences, exploring their ecological selves, and articulating their insights as ultimate norms. Naess provided the following statements articulating his deep ecology position:

1. "Rejection of the man-in-environment image in favor of *the relational total-field image.* Organisms are knots in the biospherical net or field of intrinsic relations." There are no discrete isolated entities. From an ecological perspective all individuals or units are intrinsically made up of their relationships with other individuals or units in the ecosystem. An ecological mode of perception is articulated in terms of gestalts, wholes of different degrees of comprehensiveness. "The total-field model dissolves not only the man-in-environment concept, but every compact thing-in-milieu concept— except when talking at a superficial or preliminary level of communication."

2. *Biospherical (or ecological) egalitarianism in principle.* "The 'in principle' clause is inserted because any realistic praxis necessitates some killing, exploitation, and suppression. The ecological field-worker acquires a deep-seated respect, or even veneration, for ways and forms of life. He reaches an understanding from within . . . To the ecological field-worker, *the equal right to live and blossom* is an intuitively clear and obvious value axiom. Its restriction to humans is an anthropocentrism with detrimental effects upon the quality of humans themselves."

3. *Principles of diversity and of symbiosis.* "Diversity enhances the potentialities of survival, the chances of new modes of life, the richness of forms. And the so-called struggle of life, and survival of the fittest, should be interpreted in the sense of ability to coexist and cooperate in complex relationships, rather than ability to kill, exploit, and suppress . . . Ecologically inspired attitudes therefore favor diversity of human ways of life, of cultures, of occupations, of economies."

4. *Anti-class posture.* "Diversity of human ways of life is in part due to (intended or unintended) exploitation and suppression on the part of certain groups. The exploiter lives differently from the exploited, but both are adversely affected in their potentialities of self-realization . . . The principles of ecological egalitarianism and of symbiosis support the same anti-class posture."

5. *Fight against pollution and resource depletion.* "In this fight ecologists have found powerful supporters but sometimes to the detriment of their total stand. This happens when attention is focused on pollution and resource depletion rather than on other points, or when projects are implemented which reduce pollution but increase evils of other kinds."

6. *Complexity, not complication.* "The theory of ecosystems contains an important distinction between what is complicated without any Gestalt or unifying principles—we may think of finding our way through a chaotic city—and what is complex. . . . Organisms, ways of life, and interactions in the biosphere in general, exhibit complexity of such an astounding high level as to colour the general outlook of ecologists. Such complexity makes thinking in terms of vast systems inevitable. It also makes for a keen, steady perception of the profound *human ignorance* of biospherical relationships and therefore of the effect of disturbances. . . . It favors soft technique and 'soft future-research' . . . The implementation of ecologically responsible policies requires in this century an exponential growth of technical skills and invention—but in new directions."

7. *Local autonomy and decentralization.* "The vulnerability of a form of life is roughly proportional to the weight of influences from afar, from outside the local region in which that form has obtained an ecological equilibrium. This lends support to our efforts to strengthen local self-government and material and mental self-sufficiency. But these efforts presuppose an impetus towards decentralization."

Naess sums up his description of the emerging deep ecological movement by emphasizing the point that this is basically a movement with a broad philosophical and social basis.

The norms and tendencies of the Deep Ecology movement are not derived from ecology by logic or induction. Ecological knowledge and the life-style of the ecological field-worker have *suggested, inspired, and fortified* the perspectives of the Deep Ecology movement . . . All over the world the inspiration from ecology has shown remarkable convergencies.

It should be fully appreciated that the significant tenets of the Deep Ecology movement are clearly and forcefully *normative*. They express a value priority system only in part based on results (or lack of results) of scientific research. . . . It is clear that there is a vast number of people in all countries, and even a considerable number of people in power, who accept as valid the wider norms and values characteristic of the Deep Ecology movement.

In so far as ecology movements deserve our attention, they are *ecophilosophical* rather than ecological. Ecology is a *limited* science which makes *use* of scientific methods. Philosophy is the most general forum of debate on fundamentals, descriptive as well as prescriptive, and political philosophy is one of its subsections. By an *ecosophy* I mean a philosophy of ecological harmony or equilibrium. A philosophy as a kind of *sofia* wisdom, is openly normative, it contains *both* norms, rules, postulates, value priority announcements *and* hypotheses concerning the state of affairs in our universe. Wisdom is policy wisdom, prescription, not only scientific description and prediction. (Naess 1973, 98-99)

Naess' own articulation of ecosophy he labels Ecosophy T. His ecosophy is inspired by Spinoza's philosophy excellently developed in Spinoza's *Ethics,* and by ecology. Naess begins his philosophical statement with an "ultimate norm" which he calls universal Self-realization. He defines Self-realization in the broadest sense and contrasts it with "prevalent individualistic and utilitarian political thinking in western modern industrial states [where] the terms 'self-realization', 'self-expression', 'self-interest', are used for what is . . . called 'ego-realization' and 'self-realization'. One stresses the ultimate and extensive incompatibility of the interests of different individuals. In opposition to this trend there is another, which is based on the hypotheses of increased compatibility with increased maturity of the individuals. The compatibility is considered to have an ontological basis—that is overcoming the 'illusion' of a separable ego" (Naess, "Notes," 1977).

Images of Nature

It is also useful to consider the connotations of basic words in our dialogues. Some people prefer to use the term *environment* rather than *nature,* feeling that *nature* is loaded with romantic or sentimental connotations. *Nature,* like *spirit* in western philosophy, implies a dualism and a separation. For many people, *environment* is a neutral or scientific term, but for others it places humankind at the center and others at the periphery.

Ben Boer, Senior Lecturer in the School of Law at Macquarie University, suggests an ecocentric definition of environment: "Environment includes all aspects of the living community of earth and the natural, human-made and social surroundings of that community."

Boer says this definition "places natural communities and human communities together rather than separating them." Thus humans are "simply members of the biophysical community of the earth and the universe" (Boer 1984, 248).

Modern definitions of environment, including Boer's, are essentially surface definitions which take their meanings from science and technology. Nature is just the surroundings of human activity, the background features or stage setting where humans play their roles. Some modern theorists suggest that humans can do whatever they choose with this stage setting. If some humans want to create a green forest in the desert they can dig huge canals, create soil in the desert, plant trees, and create their own designed environment. The ultimate vision which uses the modern conception of environment as surroundings which can be molded by men, are visions of space stations with totally created environments.

In his essay on images and ethics of nature, Andrew McLaughlin says that the modern scientific, natural resource view of nature alienates us from participating in nature. In terms used by philosophers, modern science "instrumentalizes" nature. McLaughlin explains the impact this view of nature has on our minds:

> An instrumentalized nature appears as devoid of intrinsic meaning, completely desacralized, consisting of a series of discrete parts connected by causal relation. This process of taking nature as if it were only an instrument creates, in its synergistic interaction with technology, a world in which it seems true. Most of us are continually surrounded by a "nature" molded by technology. The construction of this "humanized" nature within which we dwell—particularly when it becomes one's total

experience—confirms experientially the scientific image of nature as devoid of meaning and purpose, as a plastic "stuff" capable of being molded into whatever shape happens to be desired. What is forgotten is that this image of nature is constituted by a methodological approach which, given its logic, could only yield an instrumental image of nature. Indeed, such an image is a synthetic *a priori* of modern science, one which structures experience so that nature must appear to be without intrinsic meaning. (Andrew McLaughlin 1985, 294)

Anyone who considers himself or herself an environmentalist is caught in what Neil Evernden calls "the environmentalist dilemma." Environmentalists are protesting not only the stripping of primeval redwood forests, which violates wildlife habitat and promotes unsustainable farming practices, they are also protesting "the stripping of earthly meaning." Environmentalists, including supporters of deep ecology, are acting in defense of the cosmos, not just in defense of scenery or of sustainable forestry. The contemporary definition of *environment* is part of "the nihilistic behemoth which environmentalists seek to transcend" (Evernden 1985).

In the 1980s in political debates, testimony before government committees, and in publications directed to the general public, reform environmental organizations usually take the shallow, resourcism approach to nature. Depth meanings of environment or nature are rarely brought forth in discussions over philosophy and rarely taught in schools and colleges, including colleges of natural resources. If environmentalists use a depth meaning of environment or nature they are likely to be mislabeled as romantics or sentimentalists or ignored altogether by decision-makers. But if they use resourcism as their view of nature in political debates they help to legitimate the dominant view of environment in modern societies.

Without authentic dialogue and deep understanding of nature, reform environmentalists' resource arguments are weakened because they pit resources labeled as "visual quality," "the resource of wilderness," and "recreation resources" against the monetary value of timber or minerals. When environmentalists want to defend the integrity of a mountain or a small fish (such as the famous snail darter) they are asked, "What good is it?"—meaning what good is it for some narrowly defined human purpose. Humans then become the referent for all value in the dominant worldview and anthropocentric, modes of thinking permeate our culture. Nature has no worth for itself. The dominant myth says nature is secular, materialistic, exploitable. The conventional image of nature based on science and resourcism is nihilistic.

Many contemporary philosophers have explored other approaches to nature and the implication of these images for our current crisis. These images include Eastern traditions of Taoism and Buddhism and Native American religion and cosmologies. Exploration of these and other images of nature are extremely important to the development of the deep ecology movement. As McLaughlin says, "Alternative images of nature are a sort of internal wilderness, whose cultivation may be helpful in retaining and eventually expanding external wilderness. Considering alternatives may help loosen the spell of the instrumental view, showing it as only one of many possibilities, giving a deeper vision of the world, as two eyes enable the vision of depth" (Andrew McLaughlin 1985, 305). Practicing deep ecology means, in part, experiencing both intellectually and emotionally some of these alternative approaches to nature. To me, this explains the interest (among some supporters of deep ecology) in participating in Native American rituals such as the sweat lodge and medicine wheel rituals.

Dolores LaChapelle, Director of the Way of the Mountain Center in Silverton, Colorado, wrote on Martin Heidegger's approach to nature in her book *Earth Wisdom* (1978). She explored Taoism as a pathway to deep ecology in *Sacred Lands, Sacred Sex: The Rapture of the Deep* (1988). She has also written extensively on ritual as a way to tune us into alternative realities. Tuning into natural processes such as seasonal changes and mountain places is one way to reach further into alternative images of nature and the human part of nature.

I do not intend a comprehensive review of alternative approaches to nature in this book, but I cite the summary of the classical Chinese perception of nature provided by Chung-ying Cheng as an example of the richness and depth of alternative conceptions of reality.

"In contrast with the Western externalistic point of view on environment, the Chinese tradition, as represented by both Confucianism (with the *I Ching* as its metaphysical philosophy) and Taoism (with Chuang Tzu and Lao Tzu as its content), has developed an internalistic point of view on the environment. The internalistic point of view on the environment in Chinese philosophy focuses on man as the *consummator* of nature rather than man as the conqueror of nature, as a participant in nature rather than as a predator of nature. Man as the consummator of nature expresses continuously the beauty, truth, and goodness of nature; and articulates them in

a moral or a natural cultivation of human life or human nature"
(Chung-ying Cheng 1986, 354).

In American politics, both the nihilistic and disenchanted left and
the conservative right have failed to understand the need for new
images of Nature in post-modern civilization. And both the political
left and right have failed to understand the need for a new social
contract which is concerned not only with social justice or the relations between humans, but the relations between humans and the
nonhuman world. Deep ecologists are asserting there is meaning in
an Age of Nihilism. Both reform environmentalists and supporters
of deep ecology are called to present political alternatives to a society that denies we have obligations to the nonhuman world.

Integrating the experience and philosophy of deep ecology and
a political theory which defines a new social contract between
humans and the nonhumans is one of the most challenging aspects
of the emerging deep ecology movement.

The Relation Between Reform and Deep Ecology Arguments

Having said that the deep ecology movement is a search for meaning as well as a revolt against nihilism and narrow, materialistic
approaches to nature, how can we relate reform environmental arguments to deep ecology types of arguments in public discussions?

Many people practicing deep ecology feel compelled to use
reformist-type arguments in their political lobbying efforts and in discussions with friends and neighbors. Naess argues, and I agree, that
for tactical purposes it is quite reasonable to use shallow, reformist
arguments in certain political campaigns. Furthermore, people coming from deeply held principles of ecology often support organizations which are more reformist than transformational because they
can find no organizations to support which have a deep ecology basis.
Supporters of deep ecology can be the conscience of reformist
groups. They can provide integrity, independence, and high standards for the whole environmental movement.

Supporters of deep ecology tend toward the status of radicals
when working in reformist organizations. Again, this is not a dogma
or requirement, just a tendency. They also tend to be willing to talk
with anyone, to negotiate with any representative of government,
corporations, developers, etc., but not to compromise for expedient
or narrow reasons. Supporters will not hide their innermost feelings
and deep ecology position, but neither repeat it unnecessarily often.
They diligently affirm the intrinsic worth of and well-being of the

mixed community and plants, animals, rivers in that community. They ask upsetting questions, bring out assumptions of the dominant worldview and criticize those assumptions from a biocentric perspective. They favor wild animals and protection of their habitat over more development, which impairs the habitat of other species. They ask for more information before approving any developments, public works projects, testing of new weapons of war, or building more structures for humans. They tend *not* to favor new shopping malls, freeways, military installations, or dams unless studies conclusively demonstrate there will be no habitat degradation caused by these projects. They want more complete environmental impact assessments of proposed projects than are usually provided. They listen to experts, to scientists, but respectfully assert the intrinsic worth of wild places whenever narrow human interests are asserted in negotiations. They support proposals to tear down freeways or decommission nuclear reactors. They are concerned with disposal of toxic wastes, but tend to favor reduced production of toxic wastes as more important than finding a politically expedient solution to the disposal of toxic wastes. They are willing to expose the destructive consequences of economic development projects or military projects.

However, statements which present environmental ideals far from deep ecology positions but still more deeply developed than that of mainstream thinking, are worth supporting. I support most of the statements in the World Conservation Strategy and the World Charter for Nature. However, both documents contain statements which seem solely based on narrow human well-being rather than more inclusive well-being of all living beings. Nevertheless, the recommendations and principles incorporated in these documents, if implemented by governments, communities, corporations, and individuals in their own lifestyles and as principles upon which to make decisions, would make enormous and positive changes in the way humans relate to their homeland. Similarly, if recommendations of the World Commission on Environment were heeded, beneficial changes in economic development strategies would result (Bruntland Report 1987).

I feel I can bring forth a deep ecology position as well as work on the practical, sometimes anthropocentric, strategies such as the World Conservation Strategy. One example of the kind of intellectual work which can be supported is the exposé of the activities of the World Bank by the *Ecologist* magazine in England. As the editor of the magazine said in a lead editorial, the World Bank is helping to escalate human misery, malnutrition and famine in developing nations. Development schemes funded by the World Bank are responsible for the systematic replacement in the tropics today of subsistence farming, designed to feed local communities, with large plantations and cattle raising enterprises geared to exporting food to industrial countries in order to earn foreign exchange for economic development (Goldsmith, "The World Bank," 1985).

Besides exposing the political economy of power and politics in making decisions affecting nature, I can encourage scientists, professors, or other experts, including lawyers, to speak up for the intrinsic value of nature.

For the last quarter of a century, several environmental groups have attempted to introduce the intrinsic worth of nature into international discussion.

Nearly forty years ago, the late U.S. Supreme Court justice William O. Douglas wrote a Bill of Rights for wilderness which affirmed the "rights" of wild places to exist for their own sake (Douglas 1965). Under the sponsorship of the International Union for the Conservation of Nature (IUCN) and the nation of Zaire, the World Charter for Nature was introduced into the U.N. General Assembly and approved by that body in 1982. The Charter states:

> . . . Aware that (a) Mankind is a part of nature and life depends on the uninterrupted functioning of natural systems which ensure the supply of energy and nutrients. (b) Civilization is rooted in nature, which has shaped human culture and influences all artistic and scientific achievement, and living in harmony with nature gives man his best opportunity for creativity, rest and recreation, [and] convinced that (a) Every form of life is unique, warranting respect regardless of its worth to man and to accord other organisms such recognition man must be guided by a moral code of action. (b) Man can alter nature and exhaust natural resources by his action or its consequences and therefore must fully recognize the urgency of maintaining the stability and quality of nature and of conserving natural resources.

The Charter provides some general principles which include the following. Many of these principles articulate a deeper rather than a shallow position.

1. Nature shall be respected and its essential processes shall not be disrupted.

2. The genetic viability on the earth shall not be compromised; the population levels of all life forms, wild and domesticated, must be at least sufficient for their survival, and to this end necessary habitats shall be maintained.

3. All areas, both land and sea, shall be subject to these principles of conservation; special protection shall be given to unique areas, representative samples of all ecosystems and the habitats of rare and endangered species.

4. Ecosystems and organisms, as well as land, marine and atmospheric resources which are utilized by man shall be managed to achieve and maintain optimum sustainable productivity, but not in such a way as to endanger the integrity of those other ecosystems or species with which they coexist.

5. Nature shall be secured against degradation caused by warfare or other hostile activities.

The Charter allows national and local governments to select the appropriate mix of social, political, and economic methods to achieve its goals. It states aspirations not only for all nations but all humankind (see Wood 1985, 977-996).

There is some anthropocentric terminology referring to "natural resources" rather than intrinsic worth of all aspects and species in nature in the Charter. *Natural resources,* in a deep ecology position, can be interpreted as resources for all living beings.

One initiative which attempts to put into practice some of the principles of the Charter for Nature is the UNESCO-sponsored Man and the Biosphere program (some people call it the Humankind in the Environment program). This program encourages cooperation of people of different cultures and different scientific disciplines to provide a basis for harmonious relationships between people dwelling in nature rather than exploiting natural resources. Man and the Biosphere is based on scientific information on critical habitats of different species developed through on-going research by biologists, ecologists, and other scientists, and it is based on the cooperation of host governments and the involvement of people living in or near an area to be designated a World Biosphere Reserve.

The movement to establish and protect World Biosphere Reserves, combined with growing grassroots efforts, bioregional awareness, and a shift in philosophical assumptions from "man the conqueror" to "humans the members" of a mixed community, indicate that a shift of consciousness is occurring. Deep ecology supporters can nurture this shift and support any efforts to protect biological diversity.

They can also suggest and support arguments which seem weak and excessively based on human chauvinism but are more appropriate than meaningless ones, within specific cultural contexts.

Stephen Kellert, a professor in the School of Forestry and Environmental Studies at Yale University, has conducted social surveys of the attitudes of American citizens concerning wildlife and has attempted to assess wildlife "values" in cost-benefit analyses. Many supporters of deep ecology are critical of cost-benefit analyses because economists developing such analyses reject the intrinsic worth of natural entities and attempt to value nature as resources for humans. Kellert is also critical of most cost-benefit analyses, citing inconsistent quantitative and qualitative measurement of the values considered; a bias toward assigning greater importance to values measured in quantitative terms, especially in dollars; and a lack of standardization of the values or the measurement procedures employed.

"In each case," he says, "we are confronted by the dilemma of generating prices for the priceless, of quantifying the unquantifiable, of creating commensurable units for things apparently unequatable." However, he says, in American society, in the dominant mindset or worldview of most (or at least many) of the decision-makers we tend "to be governed by a tyranny of numbers, both in custom and mandated by legal requirement. To ignore the challenge of empirical measurement is to engender, by default, decisions inherently biased toward the quantifiable. To the extent that the process is unavoidable, it seems preferable to quantify all values at risk, regardless of their presumed level of tangibility. On the other hand, the dictates of empiricism and commensurable units of evaluation do not necessitate the use of the dollar as one's yardstick. Indeed, to assess wildlife and environmental values fairly and meaningfully, it may be necessary to avoid an economic standard" (Kellert 1984).

Kellert proceeds to develop a method of valuation based on a universal value scale. The specific details of his method do not concern us here. I introduce Kellert's work at this point only to illustrate one person's approach to shallow ecology arguments which might lead to significant changes in public decisions. He effectively argues that given the dominant assumptions in our society, it is tactically better to improve the methods than to attack the assumption.

I agree, but I also agree that we should attack the assumptions of the dominant paradigm and assert slogans for the widest circulation in public discussions. Earth First! Protect Mother Earth! Save the Rain Forest! Anytime we can get more people thinking about deep ecology principles we might be able to help them begin practicing deep ecology.

Table 2 by Arne Naess summarizes some of the slogans typical of reform versus deep ecology (Tobias 1985, 257). These statements are used in discussions with politicians in college classrooms and in discussions with journalists and corporate leaders. They only faintly represent the richness of feelings and perceptions and delicate interpretations of our perceptions of being-in-the-world.

One expression frequently used by supporters of Earth First!, the radical environmental movement with strong basis in deep ecology principles, is "no compromise in defense of Mother Earth." This statement is very useful but is sometimes misinterpreted and derided by those who say that all responsible persons must be willing to compromise. Willingness to engage in realistic political compromise is the sign of a rational person, they say, while uncompromising positions are taken by fanatics. To me the phrase "no compromise" means not to compromise on deep ecology principles. In a political issue some reasonable agreement is frequently possible and desirable if it is grounded in protecting the integrity of the land.

In my work in reform environmental political campaigns, however, I have frequently been presented with environmental choices which resemble that given to a condemned prisoner: Do you want to be shot or hanged?

However, I continue working to find the best possible solutions within the constraints of specific political systems and within the constraints of specific environmental organizations. I know many environmental activists with deep ecology positions who work in many different organizations dedicated to reforms in specific government policies. Cooperation rather than confrontation seems reasonable and productive in most instances.

Many groups in California take the name "friends of . . ."— Friends of the River, Friends of the Mountain Lion, Friends of the Sea Otter, Friends of the Earth. Others take the name "network," as in Rainforest Action Network. Being a friend may not be as close as being a brother or a wife. However, friendship implies some responsibilities to care for, be concerned about, help and sustain.

TABLE 2

Shallow (Reform) Ecology	Deep Ecology
Natural diversity is a valuable resource for us.	Natural diversity has its own (intrinsic) value.
It is nonsense to talk about value except as value for mankind.	Equating value with value for humans reveals a racial prejudice.
Plant species should be saved because of their value as genetic reserves for human agriculture and medicine.	Plant species should be saved because of their intrinsic value.
Pollution should be decreased if it threatens economic growth.	Decrease of pollution has priority over economic growth.
Developing nations' population growth threatens ecological equilibrium.	World population at the present level threatens ecosystems but the population and behavior of industrial states more than any others. Human population is today excessive.
"Resource" means resource for humans.	"Resource" means resource for living beings.
People will not tolerate a broad decrease in their standard of living.	People should not tolerate a broad decrease in the quality of life but in the standard of living of overdeveloped nations.
Nature is cruel and necessarily so.	Man is cruel but not necessarily so.

Network implies interpenetration and lack of bureaucratic hierarchy. In the rapidly changing social conditions of the late twentieth century, networks tied together by various forms of communication, including computer networks, are a useful mode of organizing. Throughout this book I emphasize that deep ecology networks include exchanges between professional philosophers interested in articulating the philosophical aspects of deep ecology, as well as advocates of specific social and political changes, such as the network of activists around the Earth who are acting to preserve and protect remaining primeval rain forests.

Tasks of Deep Ecology

Practicing from deep ecology principles includes development of philosophical arguments as well as arguments within political and social contexts. It is difficult in the English language to express process and interrelationship. It is also hard to express a deep ecology approach to nature when the dominant image of nature is based on reductionist science and on nature as potential or actual commodity.

One approach to relating various forms of practicing deep ecology is presented by Australian philosopher Warwick Fox.

Fox recognizes that the territory of deep ecology is ultimately mapless, but he identifies relationships between what he calls theoretical aspects of deep ecology, practical aspects, and an ideal state of being-in-the-world. He concludes that all tasks in the deep ecology movement are themselves interrelated and interdependent (Fox 1986, 88).

In the *theoretical aspects* of deep ecology, Fox distinguishes negative and positive tasks (other writers prefer to call this Yin and Yang aspects). Negative tasks include providing critiques of the dominant and dualistic visions of reality in contemporary societies. Potent, historically based critiques include Morris Berman's *Reenchantment of the World* and Paul Shepard's *Nature and Madness.* Positive tasks include the construction of a deep ecology philosophy and visions of reality which make identification between humans and nonhumans easier. Other positive tasks include presenting new ways of thinking about human economy to be more compatible with conservation and presenting ecotopian visions or best possible solutions to environmental problems through following new cultural pathways (see Devall 1985, chapter 9).

Practical aspects of the movement include negative tasks, such as ecological resistance or self-defense against threats to the integrity of our home bioregion or to the Earth as a whole. These negative tasks are frequently the most visible part of the movement. Photos of concerned citizens marching in front of government or corporate offices demanding action to save the environment are commonly seen in newspapers and on television. Activists have demonstrated against pollution, bulldozing of wildlife habitat, and chainsawing primeval forests, for instance.

Positive practical tasks include learning to live lightly on the land. An example discussed in chapter 6 of this book is engaging in agriculture which is sustainable and based on deep ecology principles.

The basic practice of deep ecology, however, is exploring what Fox calls the "ideal state of being." This state of being-in-the-world is discussed at length in the next chapter under the subtitle *ecological self*. Other extremely abstract terms used to refer to this state of being include *ecological consciousness, Self-realization* (used by Naess as what he calls an "ultimate norm"), and *state of being that sustains the widest possible identification.*

Gary Snyder comments on the *real work,* saying that we must, paradoxically, work on all levels simultaneously. The real work of practicing deep ecology engages us thoroughly in living. We all work, whether in school, in an office, writing articles for scholarly publications, in political activism, or in our own homes and with organizations. The real work, Snyder says, is "to make the world as real as it is, and to find ourselves as real as we are within it" (Snyder 1980, 81).

The real work means working on our own lives to encourage deeper, fuller meaning and broader identification with the *land community* (a phrase from Aldo Leopold). The real work requires that we become and remain alert, attentive, attuned. It means taking the ordinary and seeing the extraordinary. Reading and commenting on the most extensive and difficult Environmental Impact Statement can be just tedious work or the real work. If we are working for the integrity and well-being of the land rather than some narrow business interest, we are engaging in the real work, which includes penetrating through the overlay of contemporary ideologies— Marxism, capitalism, socialism, fascism—and finding a creative interpenetration of being-in-the-world.

Work, in the American culture, has some undesirable connotations. We work to make ends meet. We sell part of ourselves for a weekly paycheck. We work to pay our bills. We work because we are supposed to work and those who don't lack social esteem. To be without work is to be shiftless, freeloading.

Real work is not forced action. It may be difficult work, but we choose it because we feel a vital need to engage ourselves in this life.

In articulating the intuitions of deep ecology, we can expect, and respect, regional and personal differences in the way people engage in real work. For example, there are different theoretical tendencies and cultural issues in Australia, Canada, the United States, Mexico and Europe. In the U.S.A. and Mexico deep ecology positions are frequently grounded on religious-spiritual traditions and practices. In Australia academic philosophers articulating deep ecology draw heavily on European philosophy.

Whatever intellectual traditions lead us toward a deep ecology position, on a personal level we are seeking ecosophy through our practicing. On the societal level we are seeking a paradigm shift. Paradigm, for purposes of this book, can be defined as the construct of reality which dominates our consciousness and perception. The dominant paradigm in academia and most other institutions in contemporary (as distinguished from primal) societies is that humans are the center of the historical process and all meaning comes from humans.

Warwick Fox, in describing why deep ecology is the most practical social movement for our times, says, "The idea that humans are the source or ground of all value is viewed as the arrogant conceit of those who dwell in the moral equivalent of a Ptolemic universe. Deep ecologists are concerned to move heaven and earth in this universe in order to effect a 'paradigm shift' of comparable significance to that associated with Copernicus" (Fox 1984, 194).

While it is increasingly popular to talk about the need for a paradigm shift, in reality we cannot shift paradigms just by talking about them. Even a shift in our vocabulary could be either tokenism or trendiness. Writing about the need for paradigm shift may sensitize some people to the crisis of culture, but it could also increase anxiety and lead to further denial of the crisis.

For these reasons I emphasize *practice* in this book. For purpose of illustration I use the analogy between the process of self-definition that leads one to say "I am an alcoholic" and the process of facing up to the real work in the deep ecology movement. An alcoholic person emotionally and intellectually embraces his or her condition by saying, "I'm an alcoholic and I haven't had a drink in three hours."

When we embrace our condition in so-called developed nations (some would say maldeveloped or overdeveloped), when we see excessive consumerism and shallow thinking, when we realize that we have been colonized by advertisements, especially on television, and by narrow conceptions of economic growth, then we can begin the real work. In Australia, the U.S.A., much of Western Europe, Canada, Japan, and many other developed nations, the icons of the age are based on domination and control of natural resources and a diminished sense of our real human potential.

Before changing paradigms or political ideologies or social institutions, it seems to me, we must change the way we experience life.

Notes

[1] See for example the "Religion and Nature Interfaith Ceremony," Basilica di S.
Francesco, Assisi, Italy, 29 September 1986; and *The Assisi Declarations,* messages
on man and nature from Buddhism, Christianity, Hinduism, Islam, and Judaism (World
Wildlife International, Gland, Switzerland, 1986).

The Ecological Self

F*irst you must love your body, in games
in wild places, in bodies of others,
Then you must enter the world of men and
learn all worldly ways. You must sicken.
You must return to your Mother and
notice how quiet the house is.
Then return to the world that is
not Man
that you may finally walk in the
world of Man, speaking.*
Lew Welch

In my region of North America, from northern California through
Oregon and Washington, there are many stories about and sightings
of Sasquatch—sometimes called "Bigfoot." Native American traditions include many stories of encounters with Sasquatch, and in this
century numerous expeditions have been mounted by scientists and
adventurers attempting to capture, or at least observe, Sasquatch (see
Halpin 1980).

I have never encountered Sasquatch myself, but those who have
describe him (or her) as gentle, quiet, frequently seen alone or in
a small group, perhaps a family group. Sightings frequently occur
near sunset—that time of day reserved in many cultures for meditation or contemplation.

For physical anthropologists, Sasquatch is an anomaly—a primate
living peacefully in the forests of the temperate Northern Hemisphere
without tools or shelter or fire—in a climate which features cold,
harsh winters and hot summers. All other primates known to science,

except for humans and snow monkeys in Japan, live in tropical or subtropical climates.

Some cultural anthropologists consider Sasquatch a legend which can be interpreted in terms of myth and folklore or in terms of the psychology of Native Americans. Other scientists say they won't believe in the existence of Sasquatch until they see bones or have a captured specimen.

I see another possible explanation. Perhaps Sasquatch does exist—as an ideal. Perhaps Sasquatch represents a more mature kind of human, a future primal being. Understood in this way, Sasquatch has a fully realized ecological self. While we, who are children of technocratic civilization, must bring cumbersome technology into the forest to provide shelter and to satisfy our other needs and desires, Sasquatch dwells freely in the forest unencumbered by the burden of complex and complicated technology.

While we are torn with desire for more power over other people and domination over nature, Sasquatch dwells peacefully and unobtrusively with other creatures of the forest. While we are dependent on huge bureaucracies such as schools, governments, and military agencies, Sasquatch is independent and autonomous but fully integrated with the forest. While we are natural aliens, like exotic plants surviving but not really dwelling outside of our native habitat, psychologically homeless and uprooted, Sasquatch is at home in the forests and mountains of the Pacific Northwest. Sasquatch is alert to the moment, attuned to sounds, feelings, changes in the forests, while we show our insensitivity to the moment when we ride our motorized vehicles or jog plugged into our Walkmans.

I am not saying that humans will evolve into a creature like Sasquatch, but Sasquatch shows us one possibility for a more fully developed, integrated way of dwelling on this earth.

I begin with the assumption that we all have the potential to explore our ecological self, but in contemporary societies we are not encouraged by schools, government or other institutions, or by many therapists, to do so. The purpose of this chapter is to provide some theoretical underpinning and cross-culture examples for exploring our ecological self in preparation for the practical suggestions contained in succeeding chapters.

When sociologists discuss *self* they usually are referring to the social self. When asked "who are you?", most people respond by saying: "I am a Christian" or "I am a male" or "I am a carpenter" or "a mother" or "an American." Sometimes people say "I am an environmentalist." A person expressing ecological self would say "I am a forest being."

We identify our social self with our social identity—occupation, gender, religion. And many people evaluate themselves based on perceived criteria concerning what their reference group says is important for their social identity.

While social scientists limit discussion to the social selves, many religious teachers have written about the "oceanic self," the mystical union with the One or with Wholeness or the Godhead. In the Christian tradition, the classic advice of an unknown monk in *The Cloud of Unknowing,* the writings of St. John of the Cross, and the more contemporary writings of Thomas Merton explore the process of unveiling the oceanic self through practicing prayer, contemplation and meditation. While many Christian saints encourage believers to cultivate the oceanic self, St. Francis of Assisi in the thirteenth century seemed to encourage Christians to cultivate some aspects of their ecological self, at least to the extent of asserting a kind of deep ecology position (White 1967).

Exploring our ecological self is one aspect of "all around maturity," as Naess says. Naess' conception of maturity could also be called "full maturity" or "many-sided maturity." Humans are many-faceted beings and a person might be quite sophisticated and mature in professional activities but quite immature at social relationships. Or a person could be mature as a member of a family, having broad and deep empathy with spouse, children, and other kin, but not be mature politically. A person can also be mature in social relations but have an adolescent ecological self. Such a person might be very careless or unaware or insensitive to forests or rivers or, generally speaking, to "the land."

In his Keith Roby lecture at Murdoch University in 1986, Naess said: "We may be said to be in, of, and for nature from our very beginning. Society and human relations are important, but our self is richer in its constitutive relations. These relations are not only relations we have with other humans and with the human community," they are relations we have with our home bioregion, or with plants and animals which co-inhabit our living space (Naess, "Self-realization," 1986).

The dominant view in modern society is to define what is not me as "the other." When the other is a bioregion, a forest or a redwood tree, then it is a "thing," an object which can be manipulated by and for humans for narrow purposes. But deep ecology understands the "I" in relation to the "other." The human ecologist Paul

Shepard, in a famous essay on ecology and humankind, calls the ecological self the "relatedness of self."

> Ecological thinking . . . requires a kind of vision across boundaries. The epidermis of the skin is ecologically like a pond surface or a forest soil, not a shell so much as a delicate interpenetration. It reveals the self ennobled and extended rather than threatened as part of the landscape and the ecosystem, because the beauty and complexity of nature are continuous with ourselves. (Shepard 1969, 2)

When we find our self only in our narrow ego or with certain attributes of our body which are socially desirable ("I am beautiful," "I am athletic," etc.) then we underestimate our self-potential, that is, our ability to move in a self-realizing way.

The ego has been defined in various ways by different psychologists but at the minimum it is a collection of memories, fantasies, information, and images about who we are. It is what we think we are, not what we experience as our self. A healthy ego is a sign of mental health in some theories of psychotherapy, but egotistic identity is a transitional stage from pre-egoic (early childhood) to broader existential identity of more mature persons. Clinging to rigid ego identity can be pathological and can include denial, projection, and repression (see Wilbur 1980, 1981).

The ego can be understood as the voice of the self, but when we use the ego to build a barbed wire fence around our feelings, to deny our vulnerability and deny our interconnections with watersheds, forests, and rivers, then the ego becomes a prison guard and not a voice.

From the perspective of transpersonal psychology, we are more richly alive when exploring patterns of relationships and interactions which we can call the self. Drawing upon the work of theorists such as Ken Wilbur, Frances Vaughn, a therapist and author, defines self as "an open living system in an intricate web of mutually conditioned relationships."

Vaughn continues, "This view recognizes both our biological and our psychological dependence on the environment. Although we may feel subjectively separate from nature and each other, we are actually interdependent and interconnected with the whole fabric of reality. We are conditioned by society and the environment at every stage in the evolution of self-concept. Yet we also shape the environment and co-create the social fabric that supports us. The complex web of relationships within which we exist involves a continuous flow of mutually determined interaction for which we can begin to take more responsibility as we understand our part in co-creating it" (Vaughan 1986, 33).

When a person stops defending an old ego identity—images of ourselves which do not correspond to current experiences—and disidentifies with his or her rigid social identity, growth can occur in the transpersonal self. The inner search for self-identity requires acceptance of our psyche and our physical vulnerability. It does not mean narcissistic self absorption in our problems.

Exploring ecological self is part of the transforming process required to heal ourselves in the world. Practicing means breathing the air with renewed awareness of the winds. When we drink water we trace it to its sources—a spring or mountain stream in our bioregion—and contemplate the cycles of energy as part of our body. The "living waters" and "living mountains" enter our body. We are part of the evolutionary journey and contain in our bodies connections with our Pleistocene ancestors.

Extending awareness and receptivity with other animals and mountains and rivers encourages identification and engenders respect for and solidarity with the field of identification. This does not mean there will never be conflicts between the vital material needs of different people or between some humans and some other animals in specific situations, but it does mean that a basis for "good actions" or "right livelihood" is not based alone on abstract moralism, self-denial, or sacrifice.

When exploring our ecological self openly and with acceptance, no judgment is made, nor is there a pursuit of anything. The self is not an entity or a thing, it is an opening to discovering what some call the Absolute or in Sanskrit, *atman.*

Awakening the self beyond the barbed wire fence the ego has constructed engages us in the world, in the grounding of being-in-the-world. Naess frequently talks of spontaneous joy we experience because we are part of what really is. Other aspects include compassionate understanding, wisdom, receptivity, intuitiveness, creativity, allowing to happen, connectedness, openness, and peacefulness. The expanded, deepened self is not impersonal but transpersonal.

The process of healing, in transpersonal psychology, begins with self-awareness. "We must know ourselves and accept ourselves before attempting to manipulate ourselves for the purpose of changes we think are desirable. To understand all is to forgive all, and forgiving ourselves for being just as we are is the first step to healing" (Vaughan 1986, 56).

As we discover our ecological self we will joyfully defend and interact with that with which we identify; and instead of imposing environmental ethics on people, we will naturally respect, love, honor and protect that which is of our self.

We need environmental ethics, but when people feel they unselflessly give up, even sacrifice, their interest in order to show love for nature, this is probably in the long run a treacherous basis for conservation. Through identification they may come to see their own interest served by conservation, through genuine self-love, love of a widened and deepened self. (Naess, "Self-realization," 1986)

There are many reasons to defend the integrity of a landscape from the invasion of industrial civilization. Supporters of deep ecology especially defend the integrity of native plants and animals living in their own habitat unmolested by humans. We also defend the integrity of certain places (the Grand Canyon comes to mind) because they are awesome, beautiful and unique, or because we use those areas for sport or recreation.

Another strong reason is "if we, after honest reflection, find that we feel threatened in our innermost self. If so we more convincingly defend a vital interest, not only something out there. We are engaged in self-defence and defend fundamental *human* rights of vital self-defence" (Naess, "Self-realization," 1986). No moral exhortation or dogmatic statement of environmental ethics is necessary to show care for other beings—including rivers or mountains—if our self in this broad and deep sense embraces the other being.

Naess contrasts this view of enlightened self-interest with altruism which, he says, "implies that *ego* sacrifices its interests in favour of the other, the *alter*. The motivation is primarily that of duty: it is said that we ought to love others as strongly as we love ourselves" (Naess, Self-realization," 1986). But humans have limited ability to love from mere duty or moral exhortation.

Spokespeople for the reform environmental movement, and some philosophers, offer many statements of environmental ethics and call upon people to sacrifice for future generations, for people in developing nations, etc. Now, according to Naess, "we need the immeasurable variety of sources of joy opened through increased sensitivity towards the richness and diversity of life."

We need to be reminded of our moral duties occasionally, but we change our behavior more simply with richer ends through encouragement. Deeper perception of reality and deeper and broader perception of self is what I call ecological realism. That is, in philosophical terms, however important environmental ethics are, ontology is the center of ecosophic concerns.

John Seed provides an example of the joy and sense of empowerment that occurs when exploring our ecological self. Seed is a rain forest activist living in northern New South Wales, Australia. He participated in campaigns directed at stopping logging of remaining old growth, subtropical rain forests in New South Wales in the late 1970s and early 1980s. With his growing awareness of his connection with rain forests, he organized the Rainforest Information Centre, an educational organization dedicated to preservation of rain forests around the globe. He writes about his defense of rain forests in terms of his own psyche and his extended self in an essay entitled "Rainforest and Psyche."

> I believe that contact with rainforest energies enlivens a realisation of our *actual,* our biological self. They awaken in us the realization that it was 'I' that came to life when a bolt of lightning fertilized the chemical soup of 4.5 billion years ago; that 'I' crawled out of Devonian seas and colonized the land; that, more recently, 'I' advanced and retreated before four ages of ice.
>
> . . . our psyche is itself a product of the rainforests. We evolved for hundreds of millions of years within this moist green womb before emerging a scant five million years ago, blinking, into the light.
>
> If we enter the rainforest and allow our energies to merge with the energies that we find there, then the rainforest may be a place where our roots are able to penetrate through the soft soil reaching beyond the sad 16,000-year history and into the reality of our billions-of-years-of-carbon journey through the universe. Various truths which had been heretofore merely 'scientific' become authentic, personal, and yes, spiritual. We may now penetrate to a truly deep ecology. (Seed, "Rainforest," 1985)

In his essay on anthropocentrism, Seed makes a more general statement. "When humans investigate and see through their layers of anthropocentric self-cherishing, a most profound change in consciousness begins to take place." People stop identifying exclusively with their humanness and begin a process of transforming their relationships with other beings and commitments to them. " 'I am protecting the rainforest' develops to 'I am part of the rainforest protecting myself. I am that part of the rainforest recently emerged into thinking.' " This is enlightened self-interest. Seed concludes, "There is an identification with all life" (Seed, in Devall 1985, 243).

Self-realization has no artificial boundary. Some people say they identify with Mother Earth or with the biosphere. Naess, however, prefers to use the term *ecosphere* because this term implies a broader definition of living beings.

A community with appropriate rituals, social mentors, languages, art forms and methods of education can facilitate exploration of the ecological self. When we use the phrase deep, long-range ecology movement we already have become self-conscious, and have defined a need which is not fulfilled in dominant institutions. Ecological-spiritual cultures will emerge, of necessity, as more and more people together engage the healing process of exploring ecological self.

The search for personal growth is found in the New Age movement as well as the deep ecology movement. New Age ideology, to many of its critics, remains human-centered. According to some theorists in the New Age movement, the next phase in development of human consciousness is the development of planetary consciousness. Humans will become the "eyes and ears" of Gaea—the Earth organism.

Gaea consciousness may transcend ego and even transcend narrow sectarian loyalties to ethnic group or to nationality. But such consciousness can also remain anthropocentric. The environment, in the writings of some admired New Age thinkers such as Teilhard de Chardin, is still an environment of which humans are stewards. The narrow needs of some humans are still served before the vital needs of other species of plants and animals.

This kind of New Age ideology uses some symbols of nature and uses ecology as a slogan; but this ideology continues to insist that the best civilization is a technocratic (euphemistically called high-tech) civilization, and that space programs, human domination of evolutionary processes through genetic engineering and massive computer systems, including massive computer modeling of ecosystems, is the most joyful future for humans on this earth.

Besides the emphasis on technocratic manipulation of living processes, some New Age thinkers seem to emphasize a synthetic integration of different spiritual traditions, such as Native American spirituality and various group therapy processes, into a false sense of self-awareness. This New Age spiritual consciousness is comparable to the "false consciousness" which Marxists assert arises in late capitalist societies due to the incessant propaganda of the ruling class.

Ecological self is not a forced or static ideology but rather the search for an opening to nature (Tao) in authentic ways. If a person can sincerely say after careful self-evaluation and prayer that "this earth is part of my body," then that person would naturally work for global disarmament and preservation of the atmosphere of the earth. If a person can sincerely say, "If this place is destroyed then something in me is destroyed," then that person has an intense feeling of belonging to the place.

Sometimes resignation prevails when a person feels hurt by the destruction of primeval redwood groves or by destruction of rain forests in South America. People have some desire to help the rain forest as part of their extended self but say, "I can't do anything," or "that's progress." They feel guilty or depressed.

When our joyful sense-of-place includes the whole earth we may also feel overwhelmed at the enormous task of defense, but this is a passing feeling. Gary Snyder in an article titled "Saving the Little Waterhole We Sing By" explains it thus: "We must know that we've been jumped, and fight like a raccoon in a pack of hounds, for our own and all other lives" (Snyder 1983).

Cultivating ecological self does not mean learning how to use the joy stick in "spaceship earth" but how to joyfully blend with the watershed in which we live. In other words, it encourages modesty instead of hubris.

Naess comments, however, "Modesty is of little value if it is not a natural consequence of much deeper feelings. . . . The smaller we come to feel ourselves compared to the mountain, the nearer we come to participating in its greatness. I do not know why this is so" (Naess, "Modesty," 1979).

Examples of persons who explored their ecological self include John Muir who tramped the Sierra Nevada in the nineteenth century, Aldo Leopold in the wilderness of the American Southwest in the 1930s, poet Robinson Jeffers on the Big Sur coastline of California, and Gary Snyder dwelling in the foothills of the Sierra Nevada. Jeffers carries the process of self-identification into the realm of the oceanic self when he writes of "falling in love outward." He searches for the "tower beyond tragedy"—the tragedy of human civilization destroying rain forests and Jews and homosexuals and prairies and even whole cities in the twentieth century.

Total identification with "organic wholeness," is possible only after identification with some living being more immediate and tangible. Jeffers himself describes this process in one of his poems evoking a walk in the mountains of Big Sur:

I entered the life of the brown forest,
And the great life of the ancient peaks, the patience of stone,
I felt the changes in the veins
In the throat of the mountain,
*   and, I was the stream*
Draining the mountain wood; and I the stag drinking:
*   and I was the stars,*
Boiling with light, wandering alone, each one the lord of his own
*   summit;*
*   and I was the darkness*
Outside the stars, I included them. They were a part of me.
*   I was mankind also, a moving lichen*
On the cheek of the round stone . . . they have not made words for it,
*   to go behind things, beyond hours and ages,*
And be all things in all time, in their returns and passages
*   in the motionless and timeless center,*
In the white of the fire . . . how can I express the excellence
*   I have found, that has no color but clearness;*
No honey but ecstasy; neither wrought nor remembers;
*   no undertone nor silver second murmur*
That rings in love's voice. . .
Robinson Jeffers, *Not Man Apart, Lines from Robinson Jeffers* (1965)

We identify with intermediate landscapes more readily than with remote or abstract ones. The more we know a specific place intimately—know its moods, seasons, changes, aspects, native creatures—the more we know our ecological selves.

It is characteristic of most primal (not primitive as some call these cultures in a prejorative pseudo-evolutionary mode of talking) peoples to consider spirit and matter as interwoven. The Koyukon of Alaska, for example, live in a world that watches. "The surroundings are aware, sensate, personified. They feel. They can be offended. And they must, at every movement, be treated with respect" (Nelson 1983). The central assumption of the Koyukon worldview is that the natural and supernatural world are inseparable; each is intrinsically a part of the other. Human and nonhuman entities are in constant spiritual interchange.

Contemporary ecophilosophers recall Native Americans as examples of maturity, of having broader and deeper relations with *place*.

Listen, for example, to this statement by Chief Standing Bear of the Oglala Sioux:

> Kinship with all creatures of the earth, sky and water was a real and active principle. For the animal and bird world there existed a brotherly feeling that kept the Lakota safe among them and so close did some of the Lakotas come to their feathered and furried friends that in true brotherhood they spoke a common language.
>
> The old Lakota was wise. He knew that man's heart away from nature becomes hard; he knew that lack of respect for growing, living things soon led to lack of respect for humans too. So he kept his youth close to its softening influence. (McLuhan 1971, 6)

When the Native American says: "What a man does to the earth, he does to himself," we understand that the self he is speaking about is not the minimal self but the *Great Self* (see Hughes 1983).

The Minimal Self

The great nihilistic process of modern civilization, as Max Weber succinctly put it nearly a century ago, has been "the disenchantment of the world," and the rise of bureaucratic domination, mostly in the great urban centers of modernism. When a person says "I am a New Yorker" or "I am a Californian" or when a person says "I am a bureaucrat with Z agency" (CIA, FBI, IRS, FAA, USPS, USFS) they have allowed their broad self to be diminished by a bureaucratic identity.

Under the influence of philosophical assumptions of modern science, experts on nature—biologists, zoologists, soil scientists, wildlife managers, foresters, mammalogists—treat nature only as abstracted, objectified data. They kill their positive feelings of identification in order to be detached and neutral (see Merchant 1980; Berman 1981).

At the College of Natural Resources at my own university, professors argue endlessly about various models for codifying ecosystems, forest types, soil types, etc. They develop elaborate models using the fastest computers available to describe forests and oceans. But the forests remain "out there." Students are never encouraged to find a part of some forest and learn from it through emotional as well as intellectual experience. Students are taught to be objectively neutral to the forest. To be otherwise is to be labeled a sentimentalist or, worse still, an environmentalist. Students in natural resources sciences and management, therefore, are much like the guards in Nazi death camps. Their neutrality toward forests or wildlife or fish kills any natural feelings of empathy or sympathy they might have. If emotional responses to place and spiritual awareness are killed, and if all nature is just "dead matter," then the bureaucracy can work its will on the land without having to meet the expectations of the will-of-the-land.

The Hopi have a term, *Koyannisgasti,* which can be translated roughly, "life out of balance." The Hopi, a tribe dwelling in the southwestern region of North America, worked diligently over hundreds of years to keep right relations with earth, sky, gods, and their own community of mortal humans. Hopi cosmology is a form of ecosophy and represents great ecological sensitivity and artistic expression of the embeddedness of humans in deep nature.

We contrast Hopi cosmology with modern lifestyles and the emphasis on narrow ego. When city dwellers are asked to locate their self, many point to their head or larynx. We talk much, listen very little. If we identify our self with our body, we worry about our body image and work diligently with weights or other exercises to build up our bodies to make them more appealing to other people.

The social critic Christopher Lasch calls this self-centered contemporary self obsessed with ego-gratification, social status, and the pursuit of hedonistic pleasures the "minimal self" (Lasch 1984, 16). The minimal self has contracted to a defensive core concerned primarily with psychic survival and making a good impression on certain significant people—bosses, clients, potential sexual partners. Seeing the problems of living in modern times—crime, increasing air and water pollution, terrorism, long-term economic decline, nuclear arms race, cynicism in major institutions in society—the minimal self prepares for the siege, retreats to private pleasure domes and withdraws from community service or any form of commitment to the peace movement or environmental movement.

Rootless, alienated from human community and from wild nature, from the will-of-the-land, besieged with propaganda from scientists and natural resources corporations insisting that humans can manage forests or rivers to improve productivity and that nature should be controlled by human technology, the goal of the minimal self is survival, not personal growth.

This constriction into the minimal self in many people has been linked to complex and interrelated changes in European societies during the past 2,000 years, to the rise of bureaucratic domination and to dominant Judeo-Christian traditions, especially since the Protestant reformation. The geographer Tuan, in his book *Segmented Worlds and Self,* asserts that St. Augustine in the fourth century A.D. was one of the first truly modern men because he was self-conscious, he wrote an intimate autobiography of his self-questioning, and he publicly confessed his most intimate tensions (Tuan 1982, 157).

But only with the close of the Dark Ages and the coming of the Renaissance in the fifteenth century, says Tuan, did the individual, isolated in a relatively small area or region, strive for segregation. Tuan traces the development of closed and segregated living spaces—separate rooms for toilet, sleeping, eating, holding formal parties, recreation—and suggests a correlation between segmented living spaces and segmented aspects of self-identity.

Intellectuals began to see themselves as detached observers rather than active and involved participants in all aspects of community life, and the distinction between public life and private affairs—love affairs, fantasies, dreams—became more distinct.

European intellectuals, the Catholic church, as well as economic systems, helped desacralize nature and thus opened the fields, forests and mountains to almost unlimited economic use by humans, use restrained only by technological ingenuity and limited capital for investment. Land stewardship was turned into land management for maximum crop production (see Polanyi 1944).

For Tuan, the hallmark of modern mentality is subjectivism, the discovery of intellectual perspectives or opinions. Instead of finding a basis for group consensus by a process of discussion, intellectuals, especially, found a particular opinion to defend and upon which to discourse. Reputations were made or lost on the basis of wit and intellectual banter rather than on authentic spiritual questing.

The social self became a series of presentations. Social psychologist Irving Goffman uses the imagery of the theater to express how individuals become players on a team. Presentations are staged for the benefit of an audience which evaluates the performance. Work places, restaurants, offices, and so forth are divided into front regions where the players perform, and back regions where they prepare for their presentations (Goffman 1959).

The minimal self, with its desperate defenses against any feelings of respect or love or any values other than materialism and success as measured by expensive automobiles, houses, computers, or whatever is a status symbol, is a very unhappy self. Many people who are successful in careers in their 30s and 40s become extremely unhappy. Satisfaction from material rewards diminishes with age, and without any of the traditional bonds of community and lacking a sense of extended self-identity, the minimal self is entrapped and rebellious.

If children are taught to be only "New Yorkers" or "San Franciscans" they identify primarily with a human-built environment. Biological diversity is greatly diminished in cities. When children see wild animals only in a zoo, they see imprisoned animals, not animals in their natural habitat with predator and prey dancing their dance. The "organic community" described by sociologists and historians is replaced by the "mechanical community." The ultimate of this process is the cruise through the computerized swamp at amusement parks with plastic alligators and other creatures which attack and retreat on cue.

The real, organic community is simple in material goods but rich in individuation, communalism, awareness of the way things are, in affectional and spiritual connections with a specific landscape.

Is it possible to explore our ecological self while imprisoned in the concrete streets of a modern metropolis?

Martin Kreiger suggests that the urban landscape of the future might be one of plastic trees and flowers. "Why not plastic trees?" Kreiger asks. They require less maintenance than real trees. They are always green but don't need water. They can seem like real trees (Kreiger 1973). Although not including plastic trees, some futurists suggest that we can create an ecosystem in a space station complete with plants and animals if we wish. And some visionary engineers suggest that by putting huge plastic bubbles over our cities, we can create rain forests. Such proposals are logical extensions of the dominant way of thinking in our present culture and they demonstrate that a radial shift in self-awareness is imperative.

Let there be no mistake about our situation. The enormity of human population requires that most people live in big cities, but sound ecological policies could make cities *somewhat* more livable for the all-around well-being of humans and all other living beings.

Even in the concrete depths of the largest city, a person can explore the bedrock upon which the city is built and trace the watersheds of streams and rivers channeled in concrete pipes. A person can feel the suffering of city-dominated watersheds and work for reconciliation.

We can also experience one aspect of nature which is a lesson in humility, if not modesty, in large cities. We can experience great storms which newscasters like to call natural disasters—wind storms, hurricanes, heavy snow storms, typhoons, cyclones. Humans sometimes die in these storms; travel is disrupted and property is destroyed, but frequently only because humans did not read the land appropriately and they built their houses or other structures too near an ocean or river. Building towns on barrier islands of the southwest coast of North America, for example, is an invitation to disaster for humans because these towns lie in the path of hurricanes.

When we have empathy and solidarity with beings who don't reciprocate in our own terms, we gain in richness of experience. We know when a baby reciprocates our affection or negative feelings even though we don't talk with the baby except by cooing, singing, etc. We even know when certain mammals have a relationship with us. Paul Shepard in his book *Thinking Animals,* argues that we have a need to form such relationships. Our relationships with domesticated dogs and cats are extremely important to many people, but they are pale and one-dimensional in comparison to the rich relationships our ancestors had with many kinds of animals in the wild. If we treat our domesticated animals as subservient then we only identify with them as masters, using them to give us satisfaction (see Shepard 1978).

Exploring ecological self can be partly described as discovering a sense-of-place or an ecological consciousness. Thus the more we know a place intimately, the more we can increase our identification with it. The more we know a mountain or a watershed, for example, and feel it as our *self,* the more we can feel its suffering. Some people tell me they feel the whole planet suffering during the present era. They tell me that if some of the vital organs of the planet are suffering, they want to sit with the planet just as volunteers for Hospice sit with a dying person, empathizing with that person. This is not an attempt to anthropomorphize natural entities or the planet, but an acceptance that "living beings" has a broader meaning than we usually ascribe to that term. We cannot know intimately all the suffering of a dying person and we do not know intimately all the connotations of "living being" when we use that term to describe the planet or a rain forest, for example. But without sentimentality or romanticism we can appreciate the possibility that living beings suffer and thus have empathy with them.

The positive message of deep ecology is maximal Self-realization of all beings, not just human beings and not just a narrow sense of personal growth. "Self-realization," says Naess, "in its absolute maximum is . . . the mature experience of oneness in diversity. . . . The minimum is the self-realization by more or less consistent egotism—by the narrowest experience of what constitutes one's self and a maximum of alienation. As empirical beings we dwell somewhere in between, but increased maturity involves increase of the wideness of the self" (Naess, "Identification," 1985, 261).

Eros, Gender and Ecological Self

We live to have intercourse with mountains and rivers, Henry Thoreau said over a century ago, yet how few people have such intercourse. During Thoreau's lifetime some areas of wild nature—river zones, swamps, prairies, mountains—were still in close proximity to the daily actions of many in North America. In the late twentieth century most citizens in North America, Europe, and, increasingly, in developing nations, live in huge cities. In the United States, mountains and rivers are seen through the windows of recreational vehicles, and many rivers are too polluted to risk swimming in them.

Instead of passionate communion with wild nature, many people are content to remain in their apartments or in the yards of their suburban houses. Instead of a kind of extended sexuality, many are content with passionless relationships. In contrast, in many primal cultures sexuality participated in both group bonding and in creative participation in the cosmos. Eros was understood as the creative energy of the cosmos.

In the history of western civilization, when sexuality and spiritual development were separated, especially in Judeo-Christian tradition under the influence of gnosticism, a duality of spirit versus matter was incorporated into church teachings. Spirituality was exalted and praised while sexual feelings were relegated to the night as dark, diabolical, evil, animal. Women's sexuality was especially feared. Spirit was associated with the divine, the good, the male. Nature was associated with the sexual, and especially with female sexuality.

Conflict between men and women, and contrasts between spirit and matter and between nature and human will, may spring from the same mental distortion. In his book *Nature, Man and Woman,* Alan Watts concludes "the heart of the matter begins to reveal itself when, considering nature in the Chinese sense of spontaneity *(tzu-jan),* we begin to realize that the opposition of spirit to both nature and sexuality is the opposition of the conscious will, of the ego, to that which it cannot control" (Watts 1970, 143). The sexual problem, as it is sometimes called, seems to increase rather than diminish under the impact of feminism and popular sex therapies. The battle of the sexes increases in intensity. Yet, as Watts says, the sexual problem cannot be solved just in sexual terms, "for we are trying to wrest it from subordination to the total pattern of organism-environment relationship which, in Chinese philosophy, is *li*—the ordering principle of the Tao. . . . We must see that sexual relations are religious, social, metaphysical, and artistic" (Watts 1970, 157).

Building upon and at the same time criticizing Freud's theories, several twentieth-century psychologists including Carl Jung, Wilhelm Reich, and Norman O. Brown, as well as Herbert Marcuse, sought to find the basis of neurosis so common in contemporary civilization. When psychologists focus more on human relationships than on relationships which involve us in nonhuman nature, they do not move us into wild territory. We only touch the surface of the pond if we deny the empowering energy of eros and sexuality in the web of relationships of our ecological self. Eros can be expressed through different sexual modes and different genders may express eros energy in innovative ways. Recalling eros from banishment and integrating it through our practice requires moving from our minimal self further into wild territory, listening to feelings long suppressed. In Marcuse's terms, what is required is a new radical sensibility that draws on the qualitative, elementary, preconscious world of experience. Unless this "primary experience" changes there will be no radical social change (Marcuse 1955).

This primary world of experience is probably influenced by gender. Men and women experience the world somewhat differently, according to research reports on American men and women. Jessie Bernard and Carol Gilligan, for example, provide evidence that women find rewards in establishing particular relationships, rich in texturing, meaning, and affective layering. Women and men, according to Bernard, each have their own culture. They have different vocabularies, different modes of speech, and different concerns about what is important in life. Critics of Bernard assert that men and women share a common culture but utilize different parts of it. Whichever is true, the important factor is gender (Bernard 1981). Carol Gilligan argues that ethics, for women, develop not from abstract principles but from context, attachment, and specific relationships (Gilligan 1982).

Some feminist theorists criticize any attempt to widen self-identification to the whole biotic community because they see that as too abstract (and therefore masculine) a statement. However, self-identification as defined in this book relies on in-depth relationships and experiences. In the next section of this chapter, exploration of our home place or bioregion is advocated as the appropriate context for widened and deepened self-identification.

Marti Kheel, a feminist theorist and philosopher who has written on the animal liberation movement, asserts that the preference for self-identification with the larger whole ("organic wholeness" to use Robinson Jeffers' phrase), reflects the masculine need to move from the everyday world of intimate relationships into something more abstract and enduring. Since, says Kheel, women have a different experience with nature than do men, "it is out of women's unique felt sense of connection to the natural world that an ecofeminist philosophy must be forged." Only to the extent that self-identification with bioregion or the larger Self emerges from existing connections with individual lives can deep ecology enter into feminist ecophilosophy. Many feminist theorists are suspicious of any masculine articulation of deep ecology for, as Kheel says, "identification comes from connections expressed in loving, specific actions rather than born of aggressive drives to fuse alienated self with the 'other' " (Kheel 1987).

The large literature on ecofeminism, feminist theory and women's experiences provides valuable insights into the way women experience the world and thus provides the roots for feminist deep ecology. Works by Zimmerman (1987), Cheney (1987), Merchant (1980), Cora Diamond (1978), Midgley (1984), Ortner (1974), Warren (1987), Yett (1984), French (1985), Davidson (1987), Plumwood (1986), Daly (1978), Ruether (1975), Hallen (1987) are just a few examples.

In our examination of different ways to explore ecological self, it is wise to remember the complexity of relations between gender identity, sexual roles, sexual preferences and socialization. Both women and men participate in engendering new life. Bringing forth new life is part of the creative process of sharing and discovering meaning. Humans produce or engender in a larger context, but not alone. Humans engender because they are connected, physically, emotionally, erotically, with the widening circle of energy.

Men and women have their own experiences only in context of this larger circle. Furthermore, cultural definitions of gender are more plastic than some feminist theorists concede. In English language there are three conditions on gender—masculine, feminine, and neuter. Some Native American tribes have four or more genders.

Walter Williams, in his extensive historical and sociological research on the *berdache* tradition found in many Native American tribes, asks new and important questions about gender and the relation of gender identity, social roles, and the larger context of nature. *Berdache* is a role for biological males who do not participate in some traditional male activities, such as fighting. Great variation in sexual behavior is found among the *berdache* in different tribes, but in most tribes, Williams found, such individuals are considered sacred and are given vital roles in the tribe such as shaman, seer, dancer and certain economic roles of central importance. Williams interpreted this in terms of Native American religion. The ultimate norm of these religions is basic respect for nature (the Great Mystery). "If nature makes a person different, many Indians conclude, a mere human should not undertake to counter this spiritual dictate." People who are different are not alien or abnormal or threatening. They are another reflection of spirituality (Williams 1987, 30).

There is an illustrative analogy between the treatment of non-heterosexual identity and ecological self in our society. Both are mysterious—not fully explained or explainable by scientific theory. It is possible that our culture encourages both fear of eros in all its forms and fear of exploring ecological self.

Gay and lesbian identity have been traditionally repressed by Christian religious doctrine and by social taboo. And at best there is ambivalence among many therapists toward allowing clients to explore gay and lesbian identity and ecological self.

My point in mentioning this analogy between social-sexual identities and ecological self is to further emphasize that healing ourselves is possible by simple means, but it is not easy in this society. Healing requires bringing forth that which is suppressed in our culture. Accepting the mysterious aspect of ecological self as a gift and awakening our intuition requires courage.

Many feminists conclude that women and feminine archtypes have been suppressed under the patriarchy and hierarchy of western civilization. These feminists also suggest that androcentrism (male-centeredness) is the root of our ecological crisis. Just as the patriarchy and hierarchy have dominated the feminine so have they dominated nature, especially using the methods of modern science. Feminist critiques have provided powerful insights exposing the once hidden assumptions under which modern civilization operates. I agree with feminists who argue that men have been involved in the destruction of nature more than women during the past five hundred years of western civilization and perhaps for a much longer period.

However, men and women both still, to a large degree, put nature as a backdrop to interhuman problems. Anthropocentrism remains the central concern of deep ecology. The ecological crisis has complex psycho-sexual roots. In this historical era we can continue intellectual tasks of uncovering historical causes of the crisis and at the same time move beyond divisiveness to explore ecological self.

We need to overcome, as a positive task, our dichotomy. We need each other. We need powerful ontological insights. We need to move beyond conflicts between genders to search for experience which will encourage an ethic of caring for the earth.

One of the ultimate norms based on a deep ecology insight is that diversity has worth. Gender diversity provides different, not incompatible, ways to explore aspects of *li* (life-force nature). But this exploration is in context of the larger Self, as Naess says. The phrase "all our relatives" used by Native Americans in their prayers and rituals, means not only males and females but berdache, homosexuals, bears and plants.

"Finding our power," to use another phrase from Native Americans, requires much focus, attention and at the same time spontaneity and sensitivity. Divisiveness between feminists and male philosophers or prejudice against homosexuals, non-male, or non-female individuals distracts us from the real work.

In sum, recovering eros necessitates that all energies be utilized. Our ontological crisis is so severe that we cannot wait for the perfect intellectual theory to provide us with the answers. We need earth-bonding experiences.

Beyond Borders: Experiencing Bioregion

"In a life span, a man now—as in the past—can establish profound roots only in a small corner of the world."
Tuan, *Topophilia*

Ecological self seems most accessible to us not by focusing on human-built places or on the organic whole or Gaea initially, but on our own bioregion. My own exploration of northwestern California over the past two decades illustrates some of the halting steps to understanding ecological complexity which many people experience. Raised in Kansas City and Colorado, I felt drawn to the Pacific Coast as a teenager. None in my family had ever seen the ocean. We never discussed the western shore of the continent. I do not know why I had to move. As a teenager, I felt much the same way as the author

Edward Abbey, who confesses in his book *The Journey Home,* "like so many others in this century I found myself a displaced person shortly after birth and have been looking half my life for a place to take my stand. Now that I think I've found it, I must defend it. My home is the American West. All of it" (Abbey 1977, xiii).

Place, as used in this chapter, is the homeland of ecological self. It is not just the setting for military or logging operations, nor is it described by the names given on maps by explorers or scientists. Encountering bioregional place may lead us to discover more essential names than those on any map.

Bioregion is a term combining *life* (bio) and *territory* (region or area understanding). The origin of the term is unknown, but the Canadian poet Allen Van Newkirk used the term in 1974 seeking to link the study of cultural and biotic regions. He also referred to bioregion as a point of view. Van Newkirk spoke of "bioregional strategies" for restoration of the earth's natural plant and animal diversity within a "regional framework" and of cultural adaptation to specific bioregions. Ecology, language studies, poetry, myth and cultural history are tools to be used in bioregional studies (Van Newkirk, 1975; Parsons 1985).

The central question for bioregional studies is what information do I need to know in order to live rightly and appropriately in this place?

My bioregion is not as large as Edward Abbey's. I live in Arcata, California, a university town with a population of about 15,000. The town sits between forest and ocean and during the years I have lived here public officials under pressure from environmental groups have made some attempts to repair damage done during earlier periods of logging. The town council has devoted much effort to integrating a sewage treatment plant with management of marsh areas of Humboldt Bay, a large estuary area. After closing the land fill dump which once occupied part of the site, the city restored habitat which had been denied fish and birds for over half a century.

My explorations during the years since I moved to Arcata have carried me beyond the city into the Siskiyou-Klamath region. The place I now consider home stretches from Mt. Shasta to the east in a triangle with one axis ending near the Oregon border at the mouth of the Smith River and another axis ending at the mouth of Usal Creek in Sinkyone Wilderness State Park to the south. These borders are not arbitrary political lines based on the whim of politicians. The region is best described by its watersheds—Klamath, Trinity, Smith, Redwood Creek, Van Duzen, Eel, Mattole. The back country of this region, beyond the few cities and the coastal plain around Humboldt Bay, has been described as the "Klamath Knot"—a complex storehouse of stories in geological history where urbanization, desertification and other human-caused disasters have been muted by rugged terrain combined with benign climate. Evolutionary history takes surprising twists in this knot (Wallace 1983).

My own halting explorations of the Siskiyou-Klamath region have been misguided at times in part by my own fears and partly by the bad habits I learned at school. Only after I began attending public meetings of such agencies as the California Coastal Commission and California Forestry Commission did I hear amazing stories by hydrologists, geologists, fisheries experts, foresters, wildlife scientists, and soil scientists about the plant and animal communities in this region. I read long reports on the habits of spotted owls and wolverines. I walked the ridges of the Siskiyou and Marble Mountains and explored the primeval forests of Redwood Creek. And I participated in many campaigns to save small areas from the chainsaw, the bulldozer and the dam builder. Through each year, however, I returned to the edge—the beaches, frequently covered in fog, which combine yet separate the ocean from the shore.

I have spoken some words in defense of this region, not as much as I feel I should and certainly not as much as more articulate and politically savvy activists. I do not own property in this region—no grand ranch, no redwood forest, or stretch of expensive seashore property. But I have known this territory in many of its moods—darkness and rain of winter, great storms, floods, drought, hazy long hot days of summer. I have seen the passions of some landowners as they defend their rights of private property which mean to them, the right to cut down thousand-year-old redwood trees, the right to bulldoze a road through the habitat of endangered species, or the right to build a commercial structure in a coastal wetland. My right to defend the integrity and beauty of the Siskiyou-Klamath region is based on my understanding of ecological principles and on my identification with that region which has become part of my "body."

The recent emergence of bioregional movements in North America demonstrates the ties we have to home place, even in an age of mass society. Kirkpatrick Sale calls those who defend their bioregion "dwellers in the land" (Sale 1985). The term *bioregion* is not a household word, but the love of place within which we dwell is found in the writings of many authors and poets from many countries, from America to Scandinavia. In American literature we think of Abbey in the American West *(Desert Solitaire),* Mary Austin in the deserts of California *(Land of Little Rain)*, John Muir discovering his "range of light" in the Sierra Nevada of California *(The Mountains of California)*, Sig Olsen in the lake country of northern Minnesota *(The North Woods)*, Joseph Wood Krutch in the American Southwest *(The Desert Year)*, Wendell Berry in the Kentucky Hills *(The Memory of Old Jack)*, and Aldo Leopold in the American Southwest and Wisconsin *(A Sand County Almanac)*. Extensive writings on the American Pacific Northwest attest to the vitality of the regional identity among the forests and mountains there (Robbins 1983).

Lesser known persons have written vivid accounts of experiencing place. Everett Ruess, for example, disappeared in the Escalante canyons of southern Utah in 1934 at the age of twenty-one. He traveled alone for several seasons, with little food and few comforts. During his short life, however, he wrote many letters and kept a journal through which we can see the desert as he saw it—alive. The compiler of his letters notes that Ruess "could almost resonate to the light waves that struck him from all points in the landscape." Ruess' story exemplifies the universal discovery of self as part of a greater Self, of resonating with Nature (Rusho 1983).

In her book on early childhood, Edith Cobb describes the process by which landscape, natural terrain, becomes a model for the cognitive structure of the child. From her studies of biographies of geniuses she concludes that encounters with place provides a gestalt for germinating intellectual development. The homeland of an eight-year-old child provides the reality of his life (Cobb 1977).

The main boundaries of "watershed consciousness," or bioregional identity, is that the boundaries for an individual or a group of people are not determined by obscure bureaucrats or politicians drawing lines on maps in some distant capital cities or great empires. The boundaries of self-identification are those we walk through. What area am I attuned with? What area will I defend?

While problems such as energy shortages, transportation, economic development seem overwhelmingly complex when addressed by large centralized government agencies and we seem helpless to do anything about these problems, "these problems can seem more manageable when confronted in a geographical size a person can feel comfortable with" (Garreau 1981).

Jim Dodge, a northern California rancher and writer, points to the intersection between bioregion and self-identification in a perceptive essay on bioregional theory and practice:

To understand natural systems is to begin an understanding of the self, its common and particular essences—literal self-interest in its barest terms. "As above, so below," according to the old traditional alchemists; natural systems as models of consciousness. When we destroy a river, we increase our thirst, ruin the beauty of free-flowing water, forsake the meat and spirit of the salmon, and lose a little bit of our own souls. (Dodge 1981, 7)

Bioregion is discovered by each person through physical encounters with rivers or with whole watersheds of the region, the "veins of the landscape" as some call them. Cultural history may give some clues of appropriate relationship for contemporary citizens of a bioregion. In my region of northwestern California, for example, we have ethnographic and oral traditions of several nations of Native Americans who have successfully adapted to and integrated with the Klamath, Trinity, Smith, and other rivers flowing through the complex and mountainous terrain.

Four criteria for exploring a bioregion have been suggested by Dodge. The first is based on *biotic shift,* or the percentage change in plant and animal species from one region to another. If there is a 15-25 percent change in plant and animal communities then a biotic shift has occurred. With a shift in biotic communities there is likely to be a shift in land form, climate, and soils. There is much debate among scientists over the percentage of change which constitutes a biotic shift. Personal discoveries, however, are more important in exploring our "terrain of consciousness" than definitions given by scientists.

A second possible basis for bioregion is *watershed.* Indeed, some watersheds define basic hydrological units. By following our watershed we can trace the water we drink to its source. Of course, certain very large rivers, such as the Mississippi or Amazon, may lose their bioregional character, but intradrainage distinctions can be made. In my own bioregion, Native Americans define themselves as "upper river" or "down river" people. Various segments of the Klamath-Trinity river drainage are home territory to perhaps twelve distinct nations. Also in northwestern California, some residents of small watersheds have recently banded together as Watershed Protection Associations to attempt to keep adjacent landowners (particularly large timber corporations and the U.S. Forest Service) from aerially spraying herbicides on the forests. Residents opposing aerial spraying became very conscious of the source of their domestic water supplies and such aspects of their watershed as prevailing wind direction, contamination of water sources and the bureaucracies which regulate water use in California.

A third possible criteria for bioregional consciousness is our awareness of the *spirit-of-place,* or sense-of-place.

Rediscovering sacred places in a bioregion might arise out of the common agreement within a culture, perhaps inspired by a religious leader. Although the origins of the designation of sacred place remain secret or hidden, the place is special within the human community.

> Sacred places are the sites for ceremony and ritual healing, contemplation, and rites of passage. They are honored in song and dance, through myth, symbol, and metaphor and become a catalyzing force for the celebration of nature and life itself. . . . In many cultures, such sacred places, were seen and are seen today as the very cornerstone for cultural renewal. (Swan 1983, 33)

In my bioregion, the high country of the Siskiyou Mountains in the headwaters of Blue Creek, Dillon Creek, and the south fork of the Smith River became the focus, in the 1970s, of combined efforts of environmentalists and leaders of local Native American communities, attempting to protect the integrity of the place from incursions planned by the U.S. Forest Service, the managing agency for these lands.

In traditional Native American cosmology, the high country is not owned by humans. It is not even specifically demarked with boundary markers, fences or natural features, such as rivers. It is truly a "terrain of consciousness" and a physical place. Certain high rocks on the ridges of the Siskiyou Mountains have "prayer seats" where shamans (medicine people) and others who have prepared for the journey go to engage in some of the rituals, and to meditate. Those going to the high country to make medicine bring back medicine for the whole community. Going to the high country is not a recreational backpack trip. It is part of the real work of becoming authentic and more mature.

We sometimes hear the phrase used in the American West, "this is God's country." This means that somehow the speaker feels closer to the "great silence" or the "Great Creator." "God's country" is not a place to be subdivided and sold as property.

The U.S. Forest Service is willing to grant Native Americans their high country by putting fences around the rocks containing prayer seats, but the Forest Service also wants to build paved highway through the heartland of the high country, log timber, and build recreational campgrounds in the headwaters of Blue Creek.

Environmentalists and Native Americans protested the proposed desecration, noting that the Forest Service had already impaired the integrity of the high country with logging roads and timber sales. The Chimney Rock section of the so-called Gasquet-Orleans Road was the target of protests delivered in person. Administrative appeals and plans were made to blockade the road if the Forest Service let a contract to begin construction of the road.

Lawyers for Native Americans and for the Sierra Club Legal Defense Fund filed court action. In the early 1980s both the federal district court and the federal court of appeals forbid the Forest Service from building that section of road on environmental and religious grounds. The court held that the Forest Service was violating the First Amendment rights of Native Americans. The U.S. Department of Justice appealed the ruling to the U.S. Supreme Court (Richard E. Lyng v. Northwest Indian Cemetery Protective Association, October 1986).

Even though many environmentalists do not practice rituals in the Siskiyous, they have respect for the high country as authentically sacred to traditional Native Americans and some will not do recreational backpacking there. They have agreed to go into that "terrain of consciousness" only with Native American guides.

These contrasting views by the Forest Service, traditional Native Americans and deep ecologists show the metaphysical chasm between a resource development view of landscape and deep ecology perception of the same landscape. Transpersonal psychologists tell us, however, that in many cultures the transpersonal forms the basis for discovering ecological self. The vision quests of some plains tribes of Native Americans and the walkabouts of Australian aborigines illustrate the profound interconnection between self-place-cosmos. Scientists may not be able to provide rational explanations of the effect of sacred places on our psyches, but if our association with these places stimulates our dreams, myths, stories, and songs as we connect with the place, then rediscovering sacred places in our own bioregions is one of the most important aspects of our work.

Certain environmental controversies, such as that over the high country of the Siskiyou, assume new dimensions within the intuition of deep ecology. The Forest Service, the federal resource management agency with responsibility to manage millions of acres of federal lands in the American West, likes to take a neutral position between what it calls "competing interest groups" when it comes time to plan the development of certain areas. But this neutral position is really an anthropocentric, secular, and resource-defined perspective. Forest Service manuals provide no guidelines for cultivating sense-of-place or discovering authenticity.

This is illustrated by the conflict over logging, road building and possible development of downhill ski areas on Mt. Shasta, a volcano with a summit over 14,000 feet in north-central California. For the Forest Service, the red fir forests on the slopes of Mt. Shasta and the abundant winter snows make the mountain a natural resource which could be developed with condominiums, downhill ski areas, and scenic highways. The forests could be converted into "renewable" tree farms.

But many visitors to Mt. Shasta, including John Muir and Native Americans (who lived on its lower slopes and in the valleys surrounding it before Europeans killed them in the middle of the nineteenth century) discovered a different dimension of Mt. Shasta. These people considered the mountain the source of their insights and knowledge. Some people continue to practice Buddhist forms of meditation on the mountain slopes. Some find it to be the home of "ascended masters," and each year a daylong ritual organized by "I Am" is held there. Some people under the direction of Native American medicine men conduct sweats at designated spots on the mountain for purification and healing.

I have met several people hiking in the high mountain meadows during the summer months, who were on personal quests. They came from the city, they said, in search of a message or understanding that would help them discover their own path or way out of a difficult situation or a new direction for their lives. I have met other people who were studying the plant communities on the mountain. They explained that the integrity of the alpine plant communities could not withstand the impacts of logging and downhill ski resorts planned by the U.S. Forest Service.

At the time of the publication of this book, the top of the mountain, basically the area above timberline, is Designated Wilderness, but the remainder of the mountain is open to "multiple use" as defined by the U.S. Forest Service.

A fourth criteria for bioregion is *cultural distinctiveness.* Rituals, art forms, distinctive ways of living and specialized terminology referring to land forms or weather or relationships with the landscape may indicate a biogeographical culture. The American South and the Canadian province of Quebec are noted in North America as culturally distinctive regions. In California, at the time of the coming of the Europeans, Native Americans, separated into over 500 autonomous republics, lived in relative harmony with each other and with the river valleys or bays they inhabited.

In his article "The Native American Experience in California," Jack Forbes notes that "the native Californians were not machine creating people, not monument creating people, not great city creating people, but rather they were applied philosophers, seeking not in theory but in practice to act out in their lives the beauty and harmony of the Great Mystery. The Great Mystery takes form on two levels of reality—ordinary day-to-day sense perception and on a mystical level. On the mystical level all creatures participate in life both consciously and unconsciously. On this level linear space-time relationships and physical boundaries are absent" (Forbes 1971).

Malcolm Margolin, in *The Oholone Way*, uses historical and ethnographic records to imaginatively recreate the way of one of these anarchistic nations of Native Americans who dwelled along the shores of San Francisco Bay. Although the Oholone did not have a word to refer to themselves as a nation and had no superior chiefs or political units above the village or tribelet, they shared a rich and successful, nurturing culture and shared their lifespace with bears, oak trees, and salmon (Margolin 1978). Since deep ecology encourages humans to cultivate sense-of-place, in relative balance with other creatures, the study of the life ways of bioregional native peoples might help foster the change that we deem imperative.

Discovering new aspects of our ecological self in our own bioregions is not just a matter of academic study of biogeography and anthropology of native peoples. It is a radically empirical experiment. Phenomenological geographers provide some insights to engaging in this experiment. In one of his provocative essays, the geographer David Seamon asserts that we dance in our place and that our relationships with the place are mostly taken for granted without making it the object of conscious attention.

Lawrence Durrell's essay "Landscape and Character" (Durrell 1971, 158) says, "all landscapes ask the same question in the same whisper, 'I am watching you—are you watching yourself in me?' "

We watch ourselves in the landscape if we move beyond the walls of our ordinary assumptions of space and time given to us by a clock-dominated culture (Seamon 1982).

To get inside the landscape, rather than just observe in a detached scientific way, we need to develop affective ties with "our river" or "our mountain" or "our prairies." These affective ties with a landscape include topophobia (hatred or strong dislike for a place) or topophilia (love of the region) (Tuan 1974).

Abstractions imposed on a landscape from some foreign ideology distort the authentic place. Compare, for example *The Mormon Landscape,* which recounts the way Mormon pioneers transplanted part of the midwestern U.S.A. and New England into the great southwestern desert and Vincent Scully's account of the Native American dwellers who over thousands of years discovered aspects of their place in the deserts and mountains of the Southwest. Mormons saw a desert and attempted (with some success) to make it bloom like a midwestern farm. Hopis discovered an authentic way to dry farm corn and expressed in their cosmology their relationship, with earth, sky, gods, and mountains (Scully 1975).

Human beings have rich emotional, cognitive, and body receptivity which can be used in cultivating sense-of-place. All authentic encounters with place are experiments in consciousness and body awareness—walking, breathing, seeing, touching, lying, rolling. But all encounters with place can also be perilous because our presuppositions and preconditions might be errors of perception. Even our familiar backyards can surprise us if we become aware of intimate movements. We can discover with fresh delight the same place over and over again, seeing or hearing with awe and wonder some aspect which we overlooked in previous encounters.

Although modern field ecology and the models developed by field ecologists provide some insights into the habitat needs of many species and the relationships between organism and space, many of the maps, models, and computer-generated quantification of data distract us from discovering the real, the immediate, and the mythic dimensions of space—in other words distract us from cultivating our ecological self.

The overlay maps created by hydrologists, soil scientists, biologists, meteorologists, botanists and geologists do not fully describe our emotional and bodily connections with a place. Indeed, data can be objectified, abstracted and manipulated as mere technical information. Unless planners and designers, architects and engineers are also field ecologists, cultivating their own gestalt of specific places, any master plan, development plan, city plan, regional plan will lack the quality of dwelling-in-place. Alienated intellectuals in the service of some political or economic organization—the United States Army Corps of Engineers, for example—are experts committed to destruction of free-flowing rivers for reasons which are quite logically consistent with the demands of corporations for profits and the assumption that nature is only a collection of natural resources which can be subdued by humans.

Humans, of course, like many other animals, modify their habitat. The extent and type of modification is the issue. Practicing from deep ecology principles, human communities can seek maximum co-existence with other species. Caring for our place means leaving many other creatures at peace in their own place. California condors, for example, have been brought to the edge of extinction within fifty years due to excessive human manipulation of condor habitat, especially through use of lead shot, pesticides and other chemicals. Since condors eat carrion, they accumulate in their bodies the wastes of our civilization. As David Brower said in his essay "The Condor and a Sense of Place," condors are five percent bones and feathers and 95 percent *place.* That is, condors historically developed as creatures within the complex system of mountains, air drafts, forests, and animals along the Pacific shore of California. Brower points out that "what condors need most right now is our sense of their place" (Philips 1981, 205).

As I write these lines, the last wild California condors have been captured and inducted into captive breeding programs in zoos in southern California. There is considerable difference of opinion among wildlife experts familiar with captive breeding whether it is possible to increase the flock of captive condors and whether it will be possible to reintroduce condors to wild habitat. When David Brower said his vision of southern California as a place was to restore it to condor habitat, he presented a mature awareness of maximum co-existence with other creatures and peaceful and simple dwelling with the land (Darlington 1987).

Bioregional movements are political and social expressions of our vital need to be part of, not apart from, the place wherein we dwell. The North American Bioregional Congresses brought together people from many bioregions to discuss philosophy and practical skills for making a home in their own bioregions. The following statement from the preamble to the first North American Bioregional Congress in 1984 presents statements which are consistent with the deep ecology movement as described in this book.

A growing number of people are recognizing that in order to secure the clean air, water and food that we need to healthfully survive, we have to become stewards of the places where we live. People are discovering that the best way to take care of ourselves, and to get to know our neighbors, is to protect and restore where we live.

Bioregionalism recognizes, nurtures, sustains and celebrates our local connections with: land; plants and animals; river, lakes and oceans; air; families, friends and neighbors; community; native traditions; and systems of production and trade.

It is taking the time to learn the possibilities of place.

It is a mindfulness of local environment, history and community aspirations that can lead to a future of safe and sustainable life.

It is reliance on well-understood and widely used sources of food, power and waste disposal.

It is secure employment based on supplying a rich diversity of services within the community and prudent surpluses to other regions.

Bioregionalism is working to satisfy basic needs through local control in schools, health centers, and governments.

The bioregional movement seeks to recreate a widely shared sense of regional identity founded upon a renewed critical awareness of and respect for the integrity of our natural ecological communities.

People can join with neighbors to discuss ways we can work together to 1) Learn what our special local resources *are,* 2) Plan how to best protect and use those natural and cultural resources, 3) Exchange our time and energy to best meet our daily and long-term needs, and 4) Enrich our children's local and global knowledge.

Bioregionalism begins by acting responsibly at home. Welcome home!

Frequently in the context of modern culture we encounter space in private. We spend many hours in our bedrooms or behind the closed doors of our apartments or houses. We might take care of a walled or fenced garden or a yard. Most of us spend most of our time indoors and with air conditioning in the summer and heating systems in cold weather; we don't even open the windows. In many modern structures the windows can't be opened. When outdoors we are still in a structure—a vehicle driving on a freeway, a subway, a school building, a vast shopping mall or a factory or office building. When we go for entertainment we go to a restaurant or tavern.

In the U.S.A. and Canada less than 10 percent of the population works on the land, and most of those in logging or agriculture work increasingly like factory workers, conducting their business in large barns containing cattle or chickens or sitting in the closed cab of a large piece of equipment. Thus a phenomenological approach to place versus using space only for utilitarian pursuits, is subversive to ordinary perceptions.

Summary

What will be the upshot if we embark on a voyage of discovery of ecological self? One writer asks if an active political stance is any longer appropriate with a broad ecological self. Will we come to a zenlike acceptance that we, individually, are part of nature—both in all its creative and destructive aspects? Nature survives. Why be a conservationist? Nature destroys as well as creates. It destroys more efficiently than humans with floods, fires, volcanic eruptions, meteor impacts, ice ages, and earthquakes. Humans in their nature, certainly have aggressive tendencies as well as loving, caring tendencies. If we accept ourselves in all the fullness of living and if we accept that ultimately nature is indestructible by human agents, then it no longer matters if we conserve any particular aspect of nature.

Persons with a deep ecology understanding affirm the integrity of nature in the widest sense, yet we talk incessantly about the "death of nature"—of species extinction, rain forest and wetland destruction—due to human interventions. We stress the destructive and aggressive, shortsighted tendencies of some humans. When we emphasize these tendencies in our writing, speeches, and calls for action, we might frighten many ordinary people who will engage in psychological denial as a defense of their minimal self. They literally close their eyes to toxic wastes, deforestation, and other environmental ills.

And what of those people who cling so desperately to their narrow, defensive ego they have constructed in a pathetic attempt to defend themselves from annihilation in mass society? We can carefully demonstrate that identification with the wider circle does not mean we lose our individuation. All identification is relative. We maintain a relative ontological individuation while understanding our functional unity and relationship with the place in which we dwell. When my identity is interconnected with the identity of other beings then my experience and my existence depends on theirs. Their interests are my interests.

Beings are alive, in the widest definition of aliveness, and are ruled by the principle of self-realization, that is an impulse for self-maintenance, self-preservation, and self-increase or self-perfection, to persist in its own being. Nature in the broadest sense is a self-realizing, internally interconnected cosmos. In the metaphysics of deep ecology, then, it has a will-to-live.

If I, as a part of this wider connection, also have individuation and a will-to-live, then I can act, should act, in self-defense when my broader and deeper interests are threatened. Conservation is thus self-defense. When I identify with primeval forests of redwood trees I want to defend them from logging because they are part of my sense-of-place.

However, my life is only a tiny breath in the cosmos. What does it matter if I do not conserve rain forests or redwood forests? But this begs the question of how should I live. If I express my own will-to-live then I contribute to the flourishing of aliveness in the cosmos, be it ever so small a flourishing in my own life among many lives. By expanding our will-to-live we contribute to realizing the biosphere more fully.

Since many people live only with a narrow awareness of self due to their cultural conditioning, it is most important in the deep, long-range movement, to encourage the deeper ecological self to contribute to the flourishing of self-realization in the whole biosphere.

Humans have a unique, vital place in the natural order, but that place is realized not through technological manipulation but through participation in rituals and emotions, thoughts, prayers, and what Martin Heidegger calls the "round dance of appropriation."

This is not to imply that humans are most important, or even have a central place in cosmic self-realization. Humans can enhance the cosmic will-to-live, self-realization, in a small but vital way. Nature needs us as life-affirming people. Affirmation of our own self-realizing ecological self embraces more and more of the "other" into ourself. The more open, receptive, vulnerable, adventurous we are, the more we affirm the integrity of being-in-the-world.

In order to extend our *self* from the minimal self to more mature, maximum self-realization, we need more self-conscious awareness in our daily lives.

Many of us never take the time to engage in this process of discovery. We let ourselves become colonized by mass media, by expectations in our culture. We are seduced by entertainments and promises of pleasures on city streets. We break away only by becoming self-conscious. Thus we have a paradox, in order to lose our *self* into the larger self, we must become more self-conscious in the midst of techno-scientific civilization. Without cynicism or sentimentalism, we create an opening for discovery. Outside the ordered, bordered, fenced, domesticated, patrolled, controlled areas of our region, our wild self is waiting.

An Exercise in Bioregional Studies

Ask yourself the following questions as an exercise in self awareness in your bioregion. Some questions can be answered easily while others may require a lifetime of intimate experience and mature understanding of your place.

What are the native plants of your region? What species have become extinct due to human interventions? What is the most endearing feature of the landscape for you? What do you fear the most in this region? Where are the headwaters of the river upon which you live? What is the history of human modification of the landscape in your region? Sometimes older residents of a region can tell of changes in rivers or mountains or forests and can recount the old crafts and skills of dwelling in the place.

What is the nighttime like in your region? Can you see the stars on a clear night or are they obscured by smog or city lights? How much time do you spend outdoors rather than indoors?

Have you visited all the toxic waste dumps in your city or region? Can you name all the chemical compounds which have been deposited in the dumps?

Who controls the major parcels of land? Who owns the water rights? Does the law of your region guarantee water rights for fish and wildlife, or is all the water appropriated for human use?

What was the drainage pattern of streams and rivers in your region before they were modified by the U.S. Army Corps of Engineers or other government agencies?

What native plants have edible parts at what seasons of the year?

How much fossil fuel is used and how is it distributed in your bioregion?

Climb the highest hill or mountain in your region. What do you find there?

Take a walk in your neighborhood on the stormiest night of the year. Feel the currents of the wind, rain or snow. At what point in your walk do you feel danger, fear? Can you become part of the storm without suffering discomfort? Do you enjoy the storm or hate it?

Were there massacres of native peoples in your region? If so, visit the sites, trying to visualize the killing. Try to recreate how these people lived.

Where are remnant primeval forests or native grasslands or deserts in your bioregion? Visit them in every season and mood. Discover the quality of light and shadow.

Do you always walk on pavement? Or do you seek the sand, grass, uneven terrain? Do you attempt to see undomesticated birds and animals every day? Do you listen to the noise of the city or to sounds of rain, wind, and bird calls? Do the sounds of the city—loudspeakers, motorized vehicles—calm you? Do you breathe easier when listening to these noises?

What distinctive sounds can be heard? A specific bird call, for example, can be distinguished and the answering call of a bird of the same species. Soundmarks are sounds that make a particular locality endearing, and keynotes are those sounds which occur and reoccur in a landscape created by physical geography or climate—including wind, insects or animal sounds, waterfalls, running water in streams or the coming and going of tides (see Schafer 1977). What soundmarks and keynotes identify your bioregion?

The Orphic Voice and Deep Ecology

A recording of humpback whales, made with sonar recording devices, was a commercial success in the early 1970s in North America (*Songs of the Humpback Whales* 1970). The songs of this endangered species provide an eerie contrast to the chattering trivia of living in modern cities. Recognizing that our connections with other mammals can be expressed in music, Jim Nollman and an organization called Interspecies Communication began playing music to orcas in the bays and estuaries off Vancouver Island. In a recording of these encounters, the orcas are heard responding by vocalizing in time to the music (see Nollman 1987).[1]

In our present culture, both music and poetry which celebrate, resonate with, and are inspired by the rhythms of nature are frequently ignored by music and poetry critics. But, in fact, music and poetry which express the power of nonhuman nature, as well as our own wild nature, affirm our integrity and relationship with all living beings.

Hwa Yol Jung, a philosopher and author, writes, "In the universe (uni-verse) where everything is perceived to be related to everything else in a circle or a round way, music, poetry, and ecological thinking are consonant or rounded. . . . With the power of music and poetry, we hope to make harmony a catchword for the promise of eternity and become acclimated to the way of nature as the great chain of one single biotic community. Indeed, this is the ultimate 'calling' and *principium* of ecological thinking and doing" (Hwa Yol Jung 1981, 329-340).

Many prose writers, from Thoreau to D. H. Lawrence and Susan Griffin, express deep ecology insights, but the voice of poetry is especially suited to such expression. As Gary Snyder says, poetry walks "that edge between what can be said and that which cannot be said . . . the words stop but the meaning goes on" (Snyder 1980, 21-22).

The poet finds metaphors rich in meaning while the theorist and scientists uses concepts, classifications, and reductionist labels. The poet calls us to abide in our earthly abode.

Deep ecology poetry calls us outward from our narrow self into the greater Self. Robinson Jeffers' poem "Signpost" articulates this calling outward.

Civilized, crying to be human again: this will tell you how.
Turn outward, love things, not men, turn right away
            from humanity.
Lean on the silent rock until you feel its divinity
Make your veins cold, look at the silent stars, let your eyes
Climb the great ladder out of the pit of yourself and man.
Things are so beautiful, your love will follow your eyes;
Things are the God, you will love God, and not in vain,
For what we love, we grow to it, we share its nature. At length
You will look back along the stars' rays and see that even
The poor doll humanity has a place under heaven.
Its qualities repair the mosaic around you, the chips of strength
and sickness; but now you are free, even to become human,
But born of the rock and the air, not of woman.
Robinson Jeffers, *Selected Poems*

Poetic language resonates, evokes, expresses. And I think deep ecology is best expressed, not explained. Poetic words come alive with imagery and metaphor. Metaphors, especially, allows the listener to make connections which may be difficult to express in precise, analytical words.

Earth poets are those persons who grant some degree of consciousness to nonhuman nature. They accept, with Spinoza, that "God is, all else is ideology." They accept the way things are.

In his book *News of the Universe: Poems of Twofold Consciousness*, poet and teacher Robert Bly contrasts what he calls "the old position," which accepts that human reason is superior to nature, and the "twofold consciousness," which seeks understanding, or Earth Wisdom, ecosophy. He says that some poets in modern western civilization have attempted to do what primal peoples did for a millennia—really *see. Seeing,* the ability to observe, means paying attention to something beyond one's own subjectivity and introspection (Bly 1980).

Many Native Americans knew this "second stage" of understanding. Consider a Zuni prayer, adapted by Bly (1980) from the translation by Ruth Bunzel:

This is what I want to happen: that our earth mother may be clothed in ground corn four times over; that frost flowers cover her over entirely; that the mountain pines far away over there may stand close to each other in the cold; that the weight of snow crack some branches! In order that the country may be this way I have made my prayer sticks into something alive.

Writing in the mode of deep ecology requires authentic experiencing of place. Snyder, discussing the writing of nature poetry in *The Real Work,* warns those who write poetry to experience their place deeply before writing. He is talking about the power of shamanism and our lack of understanding, in techno-scientific society, of this form of power. "So to be honest we should confess that most of us are twentieth-century waifs, rootless, and as attached to liberal white values as anyone else" (Snyder 1980, 154).

When a poet opens the door and takes a step out of the house of intellect—the house of concepts and abstractions and quantification taught in schools and demanded in environmental impact statements—he or she may spontaneously have intercourse with rivers and mountains.

Antler (Brad Burdick), a Milwaukee poet, living a simple lifestyle without a car and only few changes of sturdy clothing and working occasional odd jobs as factory worker, house painter, gas pumper, writes from the inside of life, of dwelling in society but without being colonized by it. His poem "Factory" expresses the life of a person working forty hours a week inside the techno-scientific machine. But his "wild" poems bring that unified sensibility from the darkness into light. In "The Dark Inside a Life" he writes:

To learn how to die cut down a tree,
Watch how so many years fall.
You don't need to have planted it for it to be your life.

You know countless trees have grown
and will grow where this tree falls.
Everyone alive now will be underground

and will have gone from roots, branches and leaves
    to roots, branches and leaves many times.
You've seen how the seed of a tree
    can rise from the pit of a stump.
Wherever your feet touch earth
    you know you are touching
    where something has died or been born.

Count the rings and stand on the stump and stretch your arms
    to the sky.
Think only because it was cut down could you do this.
You are standing where no one has stood
    but the dark inside a life
    that many years.
Antler, *Last Words*

While romanticism and the romantic movement are much maligned by contemporary critics and, while there is a considerable distance between romanticism as ideology and the ecological realism underlying environmentalism, the experience of some romantic poets including William Blake and William Wordsworth calls us to that opening, that silence in the clearing of our mind.

To the credit of deep ecology poets and prose writers, they are willing to subvert the conventional worldview rather than pander to cultural whims and fads or effete intellectual critics.

Smart and creative artists clearly express their vision. There is no compromise, no hesitation, no despair. Here we take our stand. The poet is an activist, as much an activist as a person carrying a placard in front of a nuclear waste dump. Indeed, the poet may do both, and write about the vitality of resistance, as Alan Ginsberg does concerning his protests at the Rocky Mountain Arsenal in Colorado.

Gary Snyder says he assumed the role of shaman in order to help living beings. "My political position," he says, "is to be a spokesman for wild nature. I take that as my primary constituency" (Snyder 1980, 49).

A bulldozer grinding and slobbering
Slideslipping and belching on top of
The skinned-up bodies of still-live bushes
In the pay of a man
From town.
Behind is a forest that goes to the Arctic

And a desert that still belongs to the Piute
And here we must draw
Our line.
Gary Snyder, from "Front Lines," *Turtle Island*

Jeff Poniewaz makes a profound statement on the ecological situation, writing that "poets and poetry readings did much to revolutionize consciousness in antiwar/pro-ecology directions during the late '60s and have the strong potential to do that again in the later '80s, but not if publishers don't give it a chance" (letter to author 1987).

One way the world
could survive in joy
is if the whole world
worshipped whales.
If ancient Egyptians
worshipped cats,
how much more we
should worship whales!
I really believe
we should worship
the whales. &
regard them as
superior (if not
actually supreme)
Intelligentsias
for they can nowise
hurt us. Unlike
most of the Gods
currently worshipped.
Their whole being
is exultation & play.
I believe we should
apprentice ourselves
to whales & dolphins
more eagerly than
to any human guru.
The whales sing &
play all day &
when they're hungry
all they do is open

their big mouths
(how can they help it
if millions of krill
happen to seep in).
Yes, the whales
sing & play all day
& don't have to mail
their songs to any
publisher whales
in order to be free
from factories & blow
geysers of ecstasy
all day long. The
whales have no factories
need no factories want
no factories & sing & play
& blow geysers of joy
all day. Their only
reason to go mad with
anguish & agony are
the lightning bolts
exploding unaccountably
into their brains,
harpoons expertly hurled
by beings made in image
of Jehovah—the explosive
harpoons of humankind.
Aikido those harpoons,
most whale-like human friends.

Jeff Poniewaz, "Whalewisdompeace Illumination,"
***Dolphin Leaping in the Milky Way* (1986)**

Lone Wolf lives on a ranch in northern New Mexico. He has published several volumes of poems, including *Full Circles.* He writes that

> deep ecology poetry must do more than ethnopoetics, must do
> more than illustrate a sense of "place." It must slap off the
> blinders that keep us running in place. It must stimulate our hearts
> into new eyeless ways of seeing. The poetics of Deep Ecology
> must drop a magic "monkeywrench" into the mind, halting the
> gears of preconception and alleged reality long enough for
> insight, for the "satori" of oneness with creation. It must inspire
> us to reach *deep* into ourselves, to feel not only the wilderness

"out there," but the wild potential within ourselves. It must be rooted in ageless pan-tribal truths, a kinetic lesson, an alchemy for our magical metamorphises. To be valid, it must excite and incite, endlessly awakening the world. (Letter to author 1987)

Music coming from the intuition of deep ecology paradoxically expresses the "great silence." Sounds resonate with earth and sky. For instance, contemporary artist Paul Winter, playing his soprano sax in "Common Ground" and "Callings: A Celebration of the Voices of the Sea," inspires our respect for wolves and sea mammals. George Winston's seasonal cycle of piano solos recalls our connection to the movement of the earth and moon.

Buffy St. Marie, Kate Wolf, Dakota Sid, Greg Keeler, Bill Oliver (Texas Oasis), Cecelia Ostrow, and John Seed have written a genre of humorous protest songs which inspire and console those who feel the wounds of the earth. Listen to Cecelia Ostrow's words:

You can remember when,
When the world, once the world was
              alive
A wilder place,
Far from the ways of men—
I can feel it again.
Cecelia Ostrow, "Cummings Creek"

Walkin' Jim Stoltz sings of magic and enchantment with an innocence unsullied by the dark destruction of life:

I walk with the old-ones,
their spirits still roam through these hills.
I can hear them again, on the desert wind,
And the songs they echo here still.
Jim Stoltz, *Spirit is Still on the Run* (1986)

Contemporary improvisation on the ancient Japanese bamboo flute—the *shakuhachi*—evokes the beautiful resonance of wind and wild beasts. Masayuki Koga's "Distinct Cry of Deer" recalls the hunter walking softly in the early morning dew, listening to the calling of deer.

The musicians and poets who find their inspiration in deep ecology are coyote figures in contemporary societies. They trick our minds, subvert our shallow perceptions, and bring us laughing into the deep waters. Jaime deAngula, linguist, anthropologist, writer, created modern coyote tales and in one of his poems expresses this sense of trickster as poet of deep ecology.

Coyote, ululating on the hill,
is it my fire that distresses you so?
Or the memories of long ago
when you were a man roaming the hills.
Jaime deAngula, *Coyote Bones* (1974)

Notes

[1] A list of recordings of music which approaches deeper feelings for nature is included in Appendix B.

Lifestyles

T o be a philosopher
is not merely
to have subtle thoughts
nor even to found a school
but so to love wisdom
as to live according to its dictates,
a life of simplicity, independence,
magnanimity, and trust.
It is to solve
some of the problems of life,
not only theoretically,
but practically.
Henry David Thoreau

When I say "the world is my body," I present a metaphor and a fact. My body draws energy from the physical processes of the earth— sun's rays into green plants and into animals. Plants and animals are eaten by me. I drink water and produce residues from my physical system. My habits, what I eat and drink, how much energy I use, especially fossil fuel, all influence my health and the quality of my life.

Many of my habits are conditioned by the built environment— the city—in which I live and the laws of the city. However, I have considerable latitude in American culture to make choices. I can choose the foods I eat. For example, I try to buy fresh vegetables which have not been sprayed with herbicides and pesticides. I can ride a bicycle, walk, or drive an automobile in my travels around town. I can save glass bottles and aluminum cans and return them to our local recycling center or I can throw them into the trash which is deposited in a landfill dump. I can use a gas furnace during the winter months with frugality or I can set the thermostat to 70 degrees. My house cannot hold a woodburning stove, but that is a choice others in my bioregion have made, as wood is abundant. I can buy more fashionable clothes at frequent intervals or wear older but still servicable clothes.

A lifestyle based on voluntary simplicity, rather than ever increasing consumption, is consistent with a deep ecology philosophical position. My lifestyle is deepened by my practice and my practice includes my lifestyle. Practicing is a deeper term than lifestyle, but lifestyle is a useful term for purposes of discussing our daily habits.

Lifestyles are more or less coherent patterns of behavior which are freely chosen by individuals or groups of persons. A lifestyle is more likely to change according to individual preference and circumstance than are basic norms or institutions of a culture. Lifestyle implies a person's central life interest which spills over into work, family, recreation and religion (see Feldman 1972). There are many different lifestyles which are congruent with deep ecology principles.

I emphasize again that deep ecology practice is evolving. The following ideas are intended to stimulate practicing, not to be taken as a code of conduct for everyone who accepts a deep ecology philosophy.

I start with the assumption that most people want a high quality of life and diversity of choice. But it is not necessary to have expensive jewelry, boats, vehicles, houses, art collections to accomplish this. Indeed, expensive artifacts are no substitute for high quality living.

Simple, elegant means can reveal rich experiences. A simple meal, created with sophistication and presented with elegance to family and friends can provide a rich experience of aroma, taste, nutrition, and can stimulate rewarding conversation, companionship, and emotional resonance among those sharing the meal.

Style is an important aspect of life in modern societies. People try to set themselves apart as distinctive based on their style. Style is sometimes confused with fashion. Many people keep fashionable with their personal grooming, clothes, home furnishings, and even the kinds of books they read, but they fail to find their own style.

We affirm our style as a person by our pattern of consumption. A lifestyle based in part on deep ecology principles can be austere but not necessarily so. It is not the self-righteousness behavior of trying to be elitist, but rather a style which states concern for quality and for the well-being of the biotic community. A person seeking to establish this type of lifestyle will be an informed and careful consumer. Such a person would reject products made from parts of endangered or threatened species. Examples include skin oil made from sea turtle oil, leopard skin coats, footstools made from elephant feet, handbags of rhinoceros skin, or any products made from sperm whales.

I try to base my own style, as much as possible, on products produced in my own bioregion. I buy milk and cheese from local dairies, salmon and other seafood in season (not frozen) caught in local waters, beer from a local brewery, house furnishings made by local craftsmen and artists. Rich experience does not have to be expensive.

Experiences can have intrinsic worth for us or we can view them as instrumental for some relatively remote goal. I can write this book either because I find it intrinsically rewarding to express my ideas or only because I want to see a book published somewhere down the line. I can attend a political rally on the theme of protecting old growth forests of my bioregion because I enjoy affirming the right of primeval forests to exist or because I want to make a good impression on my professional colleagues. If I say "I *should* do thus and so," it usually means I don't want to do it. I have no spontaneous joy in those types of activities.

I am suspicious when I'm told that I should do something for very abstract goals, such as patriotic duty. In my experience, some of the lifestyle choices consistent with a deep ecology position are deviant from average or expected behavior in the dominant culture. For example, anti-consumerism as a general principle is consistent with practicing deep ecology. Yet we are told through advertising, by many economists and politicians, to "consume more in order to keep the economy growing." Resisting appeals to buy more and more products, gadgets, and consumer artifacts just to keep the economy growing is reasonable from my deep ecology position.

Whenever possible I reduce consumption of energy—oil, gas, electricity—but try to call up the energy called in Aikido *ki-i*. I boycott restaurants known to buy beef raised on former rain forests. I don't buy clothes, vehicles, or houses just because they are new. As Naess says, it is consistent with deep ecology to have an "absence or low degree of novophili—the love of what is new merely because it is new" (Naess 1984, 58).

Rich experiences are available in activities which many people can share. Things or experiences which only a few can participate in are elitist. Many people can share enjoyment of watching a full moon cross the sky on a summer night; relatively few people enjoy large diamond necklaces or trips around the world.

A lifestyle can be complex, offering varied challenges, many stimulating and intrinsically interesting conversations, activities, and situations without being complicated, hectic, or constrained by a feeling that we must manage each time-unit (each hour, each day) for maximum productivity or payoff. Voluntary simplicity is not self-denial but a more compassionate approach to living and consideration for the vital needs of other creatures. Simple living does not mean involuntary deprivation, enforced austerity, boring or tedious daily routines, or poverty of experiences. On the contrary, voluntary simplicity is often a necessary condition for maximum richness, intensity, and deepness of experience. Simplicity in lifestyle has been practiced by members of different secular and religious communities in different eras in North America, India, and Europe. In North America, tenets of simple living are found in communities of Amish and Hutterites, some Buddhist communities, and in the writings of many prominent authors, including Henry David Thoreau.

The Simple Living Collective of San Francisco, in 1977, proposed four "consumption criteria" for simple living:

1. Does what I own or buy promote activity, self-reliance and involvement, or does it induce passivity and dependence?

2. Are my consumption patterns basically satisfying, or do I buy much that serves no real need?

3. How tied is my present job and lifestyle to installment payments, maintenance and repair costs, and the expectations of others?

4. Do I consider the impact of my consumption patterns on other people and on the Earth? (Elgin 1981, 166)

Voluntary simplicity has many parallels with the Buddhist "middle way." Buddhist teachings warn against both self-indulgence and self-denial. Ego self-indulgence is unfruitful, low, ignorant and vulgar. Self-denial is unfruitful, ignoble, painful, and increases suffering. The "middle way" is both fruitful and noble. Without finding balance in our lives we will always be driven by endless desires; we suffer deprivation because we cannot satisfy them.

A rich life does not have to be a fast-paced life. We use the phrase "life in the fast lane" or "living at ninety miles an hour" to describe lifestyles of people who want to have as many experiences as possible in the shortest period of time. They rush from activity to activity, buy tour packages to visit distant countries or fly in a helicopter to the top of a mountain so they won't have to waste time climbing the mountain to see the view from the top. They keep a scorecard on the number of experiences they have, but each activity is necessarily superficial and not necessarily intrinsically rewarding.

We can monitor and assess the impact of our lifestyles on the habitats of other creatures. Some trade-offs are necessary. In my county, for example, alder, second-growth fir trees and other species of trees grow abundantly nearby. Without excessive tree cutting, the forest can be maintained and people can have firewood. However, in some communities in southern California people import oak wood from the groves of central California because an oak fire in a fireplace is a desirable and intrinsically rewarding experience. But there are over ten million people and few oak trees per person. The oak groves are being depleted faster than they can regrow. Given the warmer climate and the abundance of electricity available from hydroelectric power, an oak fire is an expensive luxury in most southern California homes.

There are numerous situations where the impact of an individual in an activity is very small, but the collective impact of many people engaging in such an activity is very large. Thus environmentalists consistently ask for studies of "cumulative impacts" on pollution from motor vehicles, or impacts of many people walking in known bear habitat in a national park or collecting clams or some other life forms along a given seashore.

In all our work in the ecology movement we can insist on a high quality of living for all people but also make the distinction between *quality of living* and *standard of living*. It is common to equate the two. Standard of living is measured by the number of households having two cars, television sets, VCRs, or computers. Collectively, it is sometimes measured by average income or disposable income. Quality of life, individually or collectively, is measured by psychological well-being and, from a deep ecology perspective, by the well-being of the whole biotic community, not just human beings. In the narrow human-oriented definition, the quality of life in many major American cities is decreasing—poorer air quality, more traffic congestion, more crowding, less wholesome food, more noise. The old assumptions about the "good life" have been undermined and researchers are developing new bases for evaluating material and psychological quality of life for humans.

Some researchers distinguish between subsistence living, material poverty, humane living, and luxurious living. Subsistence living occurs in situations of famine, for example. But in some primal cultures there are times of lack of abundance, seasonal variations in availability of game or certain staple foods, and the group may adjust to these circumstances by sharing what food there is or by placing some members of the group at risk.

Material poverty is the condition experienced by most of the people on earth today. Living in large cities they have no direct access to agriculture or gatherable foodstuffs. They must rely on the infrastructure of techno-scientific civilization to support their lives.

Humane living means that every child has nurturing, some education, and at least minimal foodstuffs, shelter, and love.

Luxurious living is that experienced by most of the middle to upper classes in North America. Among these classes the chief interest is comfort and convenience. Microwave ovens, new cars, many adult toys—including off-road vehicles—constant indoor temperature without personal effort to get fuel, and fashionable clothes and furnishings for houses all could be part of a luxurious lifestyle.

During the past twenty years researchers at the Institute for Survey Research at the University of Michigan have conducted sample surveys on the "sense of well-being" of U.S. citizens (Campbell 1981). They discovered what they called the "paradox of well-being." When a cross section of Americans were asked in 1973, "What does the quality of life mean to you—that is, what would you say the overall quality of life depends on?," their most frequent answers were, in order 1) economic security, 2) family life, 3) personal strengths, 4) friendships, and 5) the attractiveness of their physical environments. The researchers concluded that, for the most part, people were talking about values not counted in dollars. Looking at the trends of the past twenty years, the researchers concluded that more and more people are willing to sacrifice money or a higher standard of living in order to satisfy other needs.

Commenting on these studies, one prominent researcher at the Institute for Survey Research, Angus Campbell, said, "We must recognize that people may be deprived psychologically as well as economically" (Campbell 1981).

Recent research indicates that the standard of living for the middle classes in the U.S.A. is declining and that the majority of middle class families will be unable to afford two vehicles, expensive vacations, college education for children, luxury boats, or even their own homes if the decline continues through the 1990s. The percentage of total wealth of the nation continues to become more concentrated in the top two percent of families.

This research on well-being, quality of life, and standard of living indicates that American society (and by implication other economically developed nations such as Great Britain, Canada, Australia, West Germany, etc.) has focused predominantly on a certain mode of economic development which does not well serve the vital psychological needs of humans and certainly impairs the vital needs of many other species. This nation has done poorly in providing ways for cultivating broader and deeper identification and solidarity of self in the Larger Self. The dominant worldview encourages human chauvinistic modes of thinking, encourages a separation of spirit and matter, and encourages many desires—for toys, for things—but does very little to satisfy vital human needs for companionship with other people, other animals, or wild plants.

Recent studies indicate, at least in the U.S.A., that most citizens frequently go shopping in an attempt to satisfy psychological needs rather than to acquire items to serve vital needs. One economist calls our economy a "joyless economy" and suggests that shopping is an activity which is compulsive, irrational, and distracting from other traditionally satisfying activities (such as conversation, caring for family and friends, homemaking, and creative arts). Other studies indicate that men and women, teenagers and older people, go shopping to alleviate loneliness, dispel boredom, fulfill fantasies, escape from psychological problems, relieve depression, and belong to a group, not in the sociological sense, but more a mass society sense of belongingness (Morris 1987; Scitovsky 1976; Uusitalo 1986).

Many events or elaborately staged extravaganzas distract us from the real work, from cultivating our ecological self. It seems consistent with practicing deep ecology to be underwhelmed by overrated media events, entertainment packages of the latest musical act and most political statements.

One of the most difficult choices for many of us who have a deep ecology position, is to chose a "right livelihood," a means of earning a living which is not destructive of human lives or the habitat of fellow creatures. In her famous book on Aldoph Eichmann, the Nazi condemned in an Israeli court for crimes against humanity during World War II, Hannah Arendt uses the phrase "banality of evil." She did not see Eichmann as a particularly evil person in and of himself. Although his decisions were evil, they were quite normal and acceptable within the context of the Nazi-run bureaucracy. It was a quite ordinary bureaucracy. Its goal seems bizarre to us—mass extermination of people because of their race or religion or sexual preference. Administrators of this Nazi bureaucracy dedicated to achieving their production goal—killing more people per day— sought cost-effective means. Thus they went from shooting individuals to the installation of mass gas chambers (Arendt 1963).

Similarly the goal of administrators of timber mills in my county is to produce wood products as cheaply as possible. Thus, they use the most advanced technology to, in their terms, liquidate old growth forests. I, and many people I know, feel that working in a timber mill that processes old growth logs would be inconsistent with our deep ecology principles. The same is true for working in a whale processing plant or one that processes the skins of snow leopards or grizzly bears or other endangered species.

Many people active in the peace movement find it repugnant to work in any industry or corporation connected with the development, testing, production, or deployment of nuclear weapons.

I cannot provide a catalog of the environmental impacts of all corporations in this nation, where we could see their social and environmental scorecards the way we see their financial or profit reports. But, such a catalog would be very useful for prospective employees who subscribe to a deep ecology position.

At my university, a group of students began a campaign to ask graduating students to voluntarily sign a pledge. The pledge states: "I will examine the social and environmental implications of any job for which I am applying." This is a neutral statement. The student who signs it is not promising to reject jobs which contribute to pollution, for example. The pledge merely draws attention to the impacts we have through our jobs. Many students think of a job only in terms of salary, career opportunities, and location. Thinking of livelihood from a religious perspective, for instance, involves moral choices.

Given the choice, many people (perhaps most) choose to work in less polluting industries than those that are more polluting. Some choose to work within a corporation or other large institution to reform the policies and practices of that institution. Some workers in agri-industry, for example, have exposed the illegal practices of their employers who are illegally using toxic chemicals, herbicides, or pesticides.

Scientists and other researchers working for government, business, or educational institutions can expose the illegal, dangerous, and life-threatening practices of those organizations. For every Bhopal or Chernobyl disaster there are thousands of insidious practices which reduce biological diversity, increase pollution, or impair the integrity of a forest or river system or seashore.

Even though our jobs may be benign, we might contribute indirectly to pollution or further environmental damage. Much of my salary as a college professor is involuntarily withheld for pension funds, federal and state taxes, social security and other mandatory deductions. Much of my taxes are appropriated for testing and building weapons, more freeway construction, and other uses which I find inappropriate in terms of my deep ecology principles.

Some people argue, quite convincingly, that it is better to have a lower income, so that less money will go to fund socially and environmentally destructive government projects. I try to take the middle path—to be as informed as possible to protest damaging public works projects, and to make my voice heard in public debates, speaking from a deep ecology perspective.

Some people, obviously, have more power than others in our society. Hundreds of thousands of people work as experts in this technocratic society. We call them professionals. These men and women can choose how they will handle information, how they will relate to the bureaucracies within which they work, and they have some say in establishing guidelines for professional ethics in their occupation. The next part of this chapter addresses ways of acting upon deep ecology principles within professional careers.

Experts

Experts invent the machines, repair the technocratic systems, propagate ideologies, analyze social trends, monitor the body politic, and prepare justifications for decisions made by political and economic elites.

The experts are both products of urbanism and contributors to the ideology and lifestyle of urbanism. The word *professional* includes artists, writers (including journalists), publicity directors (and what major corporation, government agency or university does not have a publicity director?), college professors, scientists, architects, city planners, economists, natural resource specialists (soil scientists, biologists, geologists, foresters, wildlife managers, fisheries experts), engineers of all sorts, theologians, lawyers, computer programmers, designers (of everything from clothes to advertising campaigns to political campaigns), and many other occupations which proliferate in the business world (financial experts and managerial experts). Professionals base their careers on abstract theories, are cosmopolitan in their attitudes and are rewarded with many privileges, including money and prestige.

In his book *Person/Planet,* Theodore Roszak points to a sociological fact that any proposal for scaling down cities or propagating the values of decentralization, bioregion or the intrinsic worth of nature must pass through the critical filter of urbanized intellectuals before it is put out for general consumption. The book you are reading, for example, will be reviewed, criticized, and either discarded as irrelevant or accepted as a legitimate contribution to intellectual discourse by some members of the organized and urbanized intelligensia.

As Roszak says, the modern city is very much the home of the bourgeoisie—the middle class who define the shape of modernity. Furthermore, Roszak continues, the intellectuals share a common class interest:

> Most class interests converge upon the wealth and power of the city, but the one interest which has buried itself so deeply in the city that it has made itself invisible to all criticism: the interest of intellectuals as the aboriginal urban class. The culture of cities is so peculiarly *theirs*—their creation, their addiction—that the drive of the city to expand and govern dissolves for them into a supposition of the conventional wisdom. Whatever other powers and privileges it may further, the empire of cities is the empire of intellectuals. [Intellectuals propagate the dominant worldview, and in that worldview] . . . the rural, the traditional, the primitive, the natural environment as a whole—all these have become the exploited proletariat of urban society. The city lives off their life's blood, in many cases confronting them not simply with oppression but with absolute extinction. (Roszak 1978, 273)

When reform environmental movements address some of the worse abuses of techno-scientific civilization, these movements must rely on what Roszak (1973, 49-50) calls a "strategy of countervailing expertise."

The rules of the game—the game of making policy and defending an argument in the mass media, in public hearings of legislative bodies, in textbooks or scholarly and professional publications, in courtroom hearings—require that experts be pitted against experts. The public, or some segment of it who feel strongly enough to act on their feelings about the degradation of nature, are left to play out their feelings in street demonstrations and letter-writing campaigns to politicians. Sometimes an organization such as Greenpeace or a movement such as Earth First! will attract media attention because of the novelty of their actions, but then the intelligentsia, through the media, question their sincerity.

Usually the politicians, judges, and political-economic elites set the questions for experts to digest. For example, experts (economists, geologists, etc.) might be asked what the most cost-effective way to develop offshore oil and gas reserves is. A less conventional question could be: How can we move from a fossil fuel based economy to reliance on renewable energy resources? Control over the questions means control over the agenda of discussion. And when experts take their questions from agencies and corporations whose values and perspectives are not deeply ecological, then they become agents for furthering the purposes of centralized, dominant (and dominating) institutions, agencies, corporations.

Of course there are many examples of experts who deserted their class interests, who were converted to a different worldview. Some Russian dissidents become heroes in the U.S.A. because they are fighting against communism. I admire the courage, concern, and integrity of writers such as Paul Goodman, Lewis Mumford, and Murray Bookchin, to name a few in the United States, who defended the organic society and the traditions of communalism and local self-sufficiency against the imperialism of modernity and urbanism.

Ecologists, including Rachel Carson, Raymond Dasmann, Marston Bates, and Paul Ehrlich, have provided excellent understanding of the unintended and unwanted consequences of continuing business as usual in techno-scientific civilization. If experts cannot solve environmental ills, they can speak out from deep ecology principles. They can expose the fallacies frequently used by experts. David Ehrenfeld provides such as exposé in *The Arrogance of Humanism*.

Sometimes only a few experts, mostly scientists, will visit and study an area of great biological diversity which is already on the drawing boards for a military installation or economic development project. The whole continent of Antarctica, for example, is known only through the descriptions of scientists and a few explorers, mostly sent there by governments, to assess natural resources and the possibilities of exploitation. But, some scientists are speaking up, *witnessing* as it were, for the continent, for the protection of Antarctica as a world wilderness preserve. Similarly, some oceanographers work through the Cousteau Society, publicizing human impacts on the earth's oceans.

The development of the atomic bomb quickly led to some perceptive scientists questioning conventional wisdom concerning nuclear weapons. *The Bulletin of Atomic Scientists* carries lively debates on government policies, the meaning of military development of atomic and hydrogen weapons and other moral, ethical, and political concerns of the nuclear arms race.

Some physicians, seeing the false assumptions of military and civilian planners, cut through the official position of government agencies and said that, in the event of nuclear holocaust, physicians would not be available to serve all the wounded and the dying. Thus was born the organization called Physicians for Social Responsibility.

A few anthropologists and other social scientists observed the treatment of Brazilian Indians by national politicians and police. In particular, they heard reports of genocide committed by government officials against tribes in the Amazon basin. They also heard reports that certain representatives of Christian missionary groups were violating the cultural integrity of some tribes. These social scientists formed an organization, Survival International, to work for protection of cultural diversity and to speak out for the rights of tribal peoples in Brazil and many other nations.

Michael Soulé, an adjunct professor in the Wildland Management Center, University of Michigan School of Natural Resources, and coauthor (with Otto H. Frankel) of *Conservation and Evolution,* is one of the biologists who speaks out for the necessity of preserving natural diversity. He encouraged biologists to form an association of conservation biology. The goal of conservation biology, says Soulé, is to provide tools for preserving natural diversity. It draws from ecology, but like the relation of surgery to physiology, conservation biology is a crisis discipline.

> Conservation biologists are being asked for advice by government agencies and private organizations on such problems as the ecological and health consequences of chemical pollution, the introduction of exotic species and artificially produced strains of existing organisms, the sites and sizes of national parks, the definition of minimum conditions for viable populations of particular target species, the frequencies and kinds of management practices in existing refuges and managed wildlands, and the ecological effects of development. For political reasons, such decisions must often be made in haste. (Soulé 1985, 727)

Conservation biologists are holistic; they do not believe that reductionism can satisfactorily explain ecosystem processes, and they are multi-disciplinary in their approach to practical problems. They are less concerned with the short-term profit of some corporation or government agency and more concerned with long-range viability of whole systems and species. They begin with a postulate based on the theory of evolution, which places plants and animals in a functional relationships to each other. Soulé (1985) says, "Many of the species that constitute natural communities are the products of coevolutionary processes. In most communities, species are a significant part of one another's environment."

According to Soulé, conservation biologists use deep ecology normative postulates in conjunction with the ecological ones. One such postulate: Diversity of organisms is good and thus the extinction of plants and animal species is bad. Biologists tend to think in terms of populations rather than the well-being of individual animals or plants but, Soulé emphasizes, "this does not in any way detract from ethical systems that provide behavioral guidance for humans on appropriate relationships with individuals from other species, especially when the callous behavior of humans causes animals to suffer unnecessarily. Conservation and animal welfare, however, are conceptually distinct, and they should remain politically separate" (Soulé 1985, 731).

Conservation biologists believe that although ecological diversity can be artificially enhanced (as in a city such as Los Angeles, where water is used to grow exotic species), this diversity is more apparent than real. Exotic species of domesticated roses, citrus fruit trees, daffodils, and begonias are found in diverse areas, from Sydney to Athens to Miami to San Diego. But original mixed communities were destroyed to make way for humans and their aesthetically pleasing plant and animal communities. "But these aesthetic benefits are costly. The price is low geographic diversity and ecological complexity. Botanical gardens, zoos, urban parks, and aquaria satisfy, to a degree, my desire to be with other species, but not my need to see wild and free creatures or my craving for solitude or for a variety of landscapes and vistas" (Soulé 1985, 731).

Soulé presents two other postulates for conservation biology: evolution is good and biotic diversity has intrinsic value.

Conservation biologists use their skills within the normative framework of deep ecology to select and design the boundaries and management strategies of parks, nature reserves, wildlands, and biosphere reserves. "Biologists can help increase the efficacy of wildland management; biologists can improve the survival odds of species in jeopardy; biologists can help mitigate technological impacts. The intellectual challenges are fascinating, the opportunities plentiful, and the results can be personally gratifying" (Soulé 1985, 733).

Norman Myers, Paul Ehrlich,and other ecologists have publicized the rising species extinction rate and presented arguments for preserving tropical rain forests and habitats of endangered and threatened species in various regions of the earth.

Australia provides us with a case study, on one hand, in the use of experts by political and economic elites and, on the other hand, the mobilization of experts into the ecology movement. Australia has less than twenty million inhabitants. But it is as industrialized, urbanized and technocratic as any nation in Western Europe or North America. National and state government policies focus on rapid development of uranium, coal, iron, timber, oil and gas, and other minerals on the continent and in its offshore areas. Genetic engineering and other high-tech enterprises are supported with government grants. Brian Martin, a tutor at Australian National University in Canberra, has compiled statements by scientists whose research, and sometimes careers, have been disrupted by superiors who felt threatened by the dissenting opinions of the experts. Martin is active in numerous environmental groups and is a sympathetic critic of some of the tactics used by the movement. He sees a symbiotic relationship between experts and deep ecology activists.

Experts of course want their jobs and they want respect from their colleagues. But many of them know that the context of their research is the specific political economy of specific nations. I have in my files records of many experts whose research was suppressed because their conclusions were at variance from what their bosses wanted. We even had a case on the campus of Australian National University where a philosophy professor was denied access to the library of the forestry school because he wrote an article critical of certain forest management policies.

I encourage experts to bring their research findings to responsible activists in the environmental movement if they feel it could help achieve our goals and if they feel they have been suppressed. Although they are not "top secret" documents, it is still very hard sometimes to get scientific reports which were commissioned by state or Commonwealth governments in Australia much less get reports commissioned for large corporations. (Interview December 1985)

In his article "The Scientific Straightjacket: The Power Structure of Science and the Suppression of Environmental Scholarship," Martin (1981) concludes:

> It would be unrealistic to expect all suppressed scientists to speak out about their cases. Those in the middle stages of a scientific career often have heavy financial or family commitments and can ill afford risking job security or promotion prospects. Those just beginning a career or with a well-established reputation often are in a better position to take risks—both in making scientific innovations and in speaking out and so inviting or challenging suppression—though sacrifices may be entailed in these cases also, for example by jeopardising job prospects or losing pension benefits. But then, power structures of any kind have seldom been reformed without risk or sacrifice.

Arne Naess joined this discussion concerning the role of experts in the deep ecology movement in a speech entitled "Experts and Deep Ecology." Naess agreed that experts frequently make indirect contributions to the movement by providing information (sometimes undercover) for environmental activists, and legal services for cases brought by environmental activists or for protection of their civil liberties in direct action.

Naess lists eight motives for the public silence of experts who in private are supporters of deep ecology:

1. Time taken away from professional work.

2. Consequent adverse effect of this on promotion and status.

3. Feeling of insufficient competence, outside "expertise."

4. Lack of training in repeating basic opinions in understandable language.

5. Lack of training in use of mass media and in facing non-academic audiences.

6. Negative attitude toward expressing "subjective" opinions, valuations, violating norms of "objectivity" and reluctance to enter into controversial issues.

7. Negative attitude of fellow-researchers, institute personnel and administrations. Decrease of status in the scientific community. Complaint of colleagues or bosses that there is a dabbling in

irrelevant, controversial fields, that going public is due to vain-glory, publicity seeking. Complaint that what is said in public is unscientific. Resulting low status in the scientific community.

8. Belief (sometimes well founded) that a public proclamation of support of deep ecology would be counterproductive: some experts with powers to modify policies in deep ecology direction would lose that power if they made clear how they feel.

In order to counteract the tendency of privately sympathetic experts remaining publicly silent on deep ecology issues, Naess suggests that we must first find the experts with scientific training, the journalists and other writers, and the lawyers. Then, listen to their concerns, their motives for remaining silent. Next, find out whether they are, in principle, willing to expose themselves and then, if they are willing, find suitable public occasions and themes on which they can present their opinions. Finally, suggest themes upon which they can write or paragraphs which can be added to books or articles they are writing which expound on deep ecology themes, and propose that they talk with colleagues about the principles of deep ecology. Presenting papers with deep ecology themes at professional meetings or seminars, for example, is one way of entering these themes into legitimate discussion.

Furthermore, principles of deep ecology can be injected into discussions of city planning, discussions over proposed development projects or urban policies. Many changes in the design of cities are affected by the attitudes of developers, members of city councils, planning commissioners, corporate leaders, banking experts, and persons working for state and federal agencies.

Environmental groups have been very active in public debates on such issues as mass transit, location of roads, zoning ordinances, location of toxic waste dumps, green belt zoning, location of large public facilities such as airports, and the size of housing subdivisions. Decision makers, however, frequently listen to experts more carefully than to other citizens. Experts who use deep ecology arguments in their testimony can encourage deeper thinking by decision makers.

There are many jobs which provide arenas for expressing a deep ecology position. In particular, fishermen, agriculturalists, gardeners, naturalists, and park rangers working for national, state or local parks, policemen (including fish and game rangers and Forest Service special rangers), and forest workers all have opportunities within the context of their work to affirm a deep ecology position.

I have a friend who has worked for many years on a trail crew in one of the designated wilderness areas of northwestern California. He rarely attends public meetings concerning planning for the national forests or other environmental issues. Yet as I have observed his work I see a person defending the integrity of several hundreds of thousands of acres. He is working with people from a wide variety of backgrounds, including teenagers from inner city California ghettos who are working on the trail crew as part of their experience in the California Conservation Corps, volunteers from the Sierra Club from urban, upper-middle class backgrounds, ranchers who bring their cattle and horses into the wilderness area, and professional employees of the U.S. Forest Service. My friend shows through his own attitude and behavior how much he loves and respects the wilderness. And many people with whom he works come to respect his approach to the wilderness and to question some of their own presuppositions in light of his example. He reminds us that most of the dedicated supporters within the deep ecology movement are not authors or academic people.

Personal Lifestyles

Besides lifestyle choices in our jobs and our consumption patterns, there are other aspects of our lives wherein we can practice from a deep ecology position or have the opportunity to explore and extend our ecological self. We can start, for example, in our own houses and neighborhoods. In response to reading my book, *Deep Ecology: Living As If Nature Mattered* (coauthored with George Sessions), a reader in Toronto wrote describing the changes she and her family made in their lifestyle based on their understanding of deep ecology. They had promoted deep ecology concepts by founding the Urban Wilderness Gardeners.

> What is most special is that people are "doing," not just "talking." Every person is a success. Every person who cuts his or her lawn once or twice or more *less* in a year is a success. Every single particle of increased awareness is a success. We are grass roots and we're effective.
>
> On the personal front we're exploring the adventure of living the concepts of deep ecology. This winter I convinced the family that Mom wasn't mean keeping the temperature of the house cool and encouraging people to use their own body heat to keep warm by wearing a warm vest, etc.—there were far fewer

complaints, more compliance. And dammit during winter this year—the one cold so far that our eldest son brought home after staying with a virusy friend for three days was thrown off in a very short time. (Letter to author 1986)

Another example of personal changes in lifestyle which shows the interplay between experience and principles is provided by Frank Fisher, who teaches environmental studies at Monash University, Melbourne, Australia. For the past fifteen years he has ridden a bicycle to work, many miles from his home. He began riding, he said, for convenience and protest, to make a statement about his environmental beliefs. But his motivation changed over time. "I still ride for the original reasons but their importance has receded and today, more important motivations are ones like enjoyment and that riding is simply a part of me."

Now those reasons do not seem based on sophisticated philosophical principles as we usually understand them in western philosophy. But the spontaneity of joy that Fisher came to experience in bicycling in the metropolis was a positive feeling, as he says,

[of] being in touch with what it takes to move oneself at speed; being in touch with the physical me whose capacity to move quickly and efficiently is so dramatically enhanced by the bicycle; being in touch with others while I move (rather than being walled off); being in touch with a knowable machine (beyond quantification, beyond automation and computer modelling) . . . . Recently I was riding to work on a cold day with fresh rain beating into my face and I was reminded of a similar morning years ago walking toward the summit of Torbreck (Victoria). The taste and feel of the rain were the same. And there it was, the missing insight: in my urban environment I'm most in touch with myself on a bike; there I feel *at one* with my world. (Fisher 1986)

A bicycle is a simple and elegant technological device. While millions of people in China and other nations ride bikes daily, in North America the bike is generally seen as a recreational vehicle. The bicycle, however, illustrates an important point on the relationship of deep ecology and technology. Fisher concludes:

Here then is a place for technology in Deep Ecology. Not so much the development of relationship between people and machines but rather the development of oneness with the earth through the technologies our lifestyles make necessary. Once this happens, the mediating technology vanishes, in a sense we are no longer aware of it; but for this to happen our technologies must be *appropriate* and few of them are appropriate or ever can be for that matter. Here then is the beginning of an answer to those wilderness lovers who have a problem with that greatest of all machines: the modern (alienated and alienating) city. Some people cultivate their gardens or community plots, others jog through misty parks, some build their own houses and some use their long distances to work to cycle. All are ways to stay in touch with one's self.

There are pointers here to where we might work on the urban environment, to improve and extend its possibilities in this direction. And there is every reason to do it. Both because the rural environment cannot tolerate massive urban inundation or excessive demands on it as a resource and because the urban millions must somehow retain access to their greater self: nature. It is after all, our interaction with nature that provides the only true mirror to ourselves; our technologies mirror us as we were or perhaps as we think we are, they do not mirror us as we *are* nor of course, as we could be. (Fisher 1986)

Changing lifestyles as discussed in this chapter does not mean sacrificing or denying oneself. Nothing is forced. There are no ration cards or policemen watching us to see how much gasoline we consume or how loudly we play our stereo tape decks. Practicing deep ecology lifestyles is a process of rediscovering what is essential, what is important and meaningful in our lives.

Lifestyles derived from deep principles make fads seem shallow and irrelevant. Recycling of bottles, cans, newspapers, and motor oil was fashionable during the 1970s in some areas of California. In the 1980s it has been fashionable to return to some of the worst excesses of throwaway consumerism. When I purchase items at some stores I am asked to take them away in a paper bag rather than in my daypack. "It's the rule of the store," I am told. I resist the rule.

Recycling cans and bottles and newspapers may seem very mundane compared to the heady debates among philosophers concerning deep ecology principles, but I think of the living rivers which have been drowned in California in the name of energy development, and I think of the demands by some economists and business leaders to consume more so we can keep the economy growing, and I know that simple actions, such as recycling, are political statements in this society.

A more severe act of resistance, and an affirmation of organic connection with my neighborhood, would be to build a compost toilet in my house. Such an act would violate numerous local laws. I see possibilities for grassroots movements for compost toilets in many neighborhoods modeled after other successful grassroots movements, such as the "no spray" movement. In my county residents of some neighborhoods and rural roads formed local watch committees to inform each other when county trucks carrying herbicides to spray along the roadways were in the area. Many people who were not politically active in other ways made handmade signs saying "NO SPRAY" and placed them along the roadways. If there was a fire danger they promised to cut grasses along the roadway, but they did not want poisons sprayed in front of their homes.

Free Air Life

"Go to the mountains and get their good tidings."
John Muir

It was a fine spring day in May, near the end of our school term. I was restless. Like many of my students I wanted to get away from books and scholarly articles, from the antiseptic college campus. I picked up my wooden bo, a staff we use in various Aikido exercises, and drove to the sand dunes between the entrance of Humboldt Bay and the mouth of Mad River. Some of my botanist friends claim these dunes are unusual; perhaps only twenty-five places in the world have coastal dune communities like these. A few hundred acres of these dunes are owned by the Nature Conservancy, a national organization dedicated to owning and managing rare or endangered ecosystems. Access to the Landsphere-Christensen Dunes, as this reserve is called, is restricted. NO TRESPASSING signs are posted on the legal boundaries of the property owned by Nature Conservancy and the property is patrolled and access monitored by volunteers.

From the public access parking lot near the Mad River, I walked up the beach side of the dunes which is open to vehicle use and to hiking. I was near the property of the Nature Conservancy practicing *bo katas,* a series of moves which teach the student to move from the center of being. I had seen many tracks of motorcycles and three-wheel vehicles as I walked up the beach and could hear the angry drone of engines in the distance, over the sound of crashing surf. But I had seen no vehicles and no other people on the beach in the past half hour. Suddenly from the corner of my eye I caught a glimpse of a moving object coming over the dunes in the Landsphere-Christensen property. I could smell the exhaust of a two-cycle engine before I saw it in full view. Two motorcycles whirled past me down the beach several hundred yards then spun around and came hurdling the opposite direction. I have read of deer and other animals who became frightened or disoriented when they encountered snowmobiles or all-terrain vehicles. I have felt the same way when motorcyclists have invaded dunes where I was quietly lying or walking.

Many motorcyclists and four-wheel drive enthusiasts use this beach and the associated dunes for joyriding. Such activity is legal as long as they stay off posted private property. Landsphere-Christensen Dunes is private and it is posted and these motorcyclists had just come from there. I was upset and getting more angry by the second. The motorcyclists were curious, or aggressive—I couldn't tell—about me. They both made donuts a hundred yards down the beach and came roaring back toward me. I held my ground. Where could I go anyway—into the ocean? The motorcyclists braked as they came parallel to me and stopped a few feet in front of me. They turned their engines to a low idle which was still loud, but I could carry on a conversation over the noise.

"What's up?"

"Just out for some riding. What's that stick for? Do you attack people with it?"

"No, just use it for *katas,* a kind of exercise."

"Yeh, is that like martial arts? My brother's in karate. He can really kick the shit out of people."

I was talking with two teenage males, having fun after school by challenging their bodies in a ride on the dune which is habitat for endangered Menzies wallflowers.

"No, we don't do that. We're just learning how to move our bodies."

"Yeh, I'd like to move like my brother. He's a great fighter."

"I thought I saw you riding in the Nature Conservancy area. I thought that was closed to ORVs."

"We ride anywhere we want. We have just as much right as anybody to ride here. We have as much right as those damn Sierra Clubbers."

The attitude of those two boys is typical of many youths, and adults, in a culture where there are thousands of advertisements for the "mean machines," for all-terrain vehicles that "get you where you want to go."

The term *outdoor recreation* in America has become synonymous with having fun. Outdoor recreation areas include specially
designated playgrounds, parks, beaches, national parks and forests,
private property (both legal and illegally used). These areas are outdoor gymnasia for a wide variety of competitive or personal recreational activities which involve taking over and dominating some
aspect of nature. Sport hunting and fishing are arts and can be central life interests of those engaging in these activities, but they can
also be done without sensitivity or respect for other life forms. I know
fisherpeople who began their career in sport fishing by attempting
to catch any fish they could, occasionally using illegal methods such
as snagging. From their own spontaneous involvement with rivers,
they came to respect the river. They changed their attitude and style
of fishing. Some of these people use only barbless hooks now.

Damage to many areas by activities of recreationists is extensively
documented. Indeed, one author reviewed the impacts of off-road
vehicles on public lands in the United States and concluded that vir-
tually every type of ecosystem in North America has been damaged
by insensitive use of off-road vehicles (Sheridan 1979).

Sociologist John Irwin says that outdoor recreation in North
America frequently is the focus of a "social scene" which he defines
as an "action set," or an open arena for social games. A social scene
involves creating a social identity with other people, playing out one's
role before an appreciative audience and risking one's reputation for
the purpose of "making it" with other people. Skiing, surfing, off-
road vehicle use in certain areas, such as the southern California desert, rock climbing in Yosemite Valley, and motorboating on many
lakes and reservoirs are played out in the context of social scenes
which have developed without regard to environmental sensitivity
or environmental ethics (Irwin 1977).

When managing agencies, such as the U.S. Forest Service or the
Bureau of Land Management, attempt to impose regulations to protect ecological values, these regulations are frequently ignored or
resented, and some recreationists will vandalize or destroy areas offi-
cially designated "ecologically sensitive."

Outdoor recreation is now a serious business in highly developed nations such as Switzerland, the United States, and Canada, and
both the facilities provided for outdoor recreation and the way participants approach their activity have larger and larger impacts on
lifespace of other species and on our own minds. For instance, massive downhill ski areas, reservoirs such as Lake Powell, and off-road

vehicle parks require building roads, bulldozing hillsides, clearing vegetation, and leveling large areas.

Because we spend so much of our lives in built-up, human-dominated environments, or in motorized vehicles, the quality of our experience during recreation (I prefer to call it *re-creation*) is especially important for cultivating ecological self. The silence and solitude of a mountain meadow or an ocean beach or a river bank is treasured and should be protected from incursions of mechanized vehicles.

John Muir, the nineteenth-century mountaineer and one of the founders of the Sierra Club, was enthusiastic when the Sierra Club started annual outings in the Sierra Nevada in 1901. He hoped those outings would provide a kind of communal, cooperative, perhaps almost tribal experience for club members and that the "good tidings" of the mountains gathered through the annual outings would flow through participants for the remainder of the year as they went about their routines in the city (Michael Cohen 1984, 311-317). National parks, to Muir, as well as to Frederick Law Olmstead and other nineteenth-century innovators, were to be places where the primal senses of men and women living in the polluted urban environments could be rediscovered. Getting away from the noise, conveniences, and vehicles common in the city means going home to primal roots.

This experience in re-creation is not escapism but is essential for the well-being and health of urban dwellers. Re-creation, to Muir and his followers, is not competitive and I'm sure that Muir would be astonished to see mountain climbing, kayaking, even hiking, turned into competitive sports (Sax 1980).

About the same time that Muir was promoting the outings program in the Sierra Club, Fridtjof Nansen, the Norwegian Arctic explorer, skier, mountaineer, and social activist, was starting a movement in Scandinavia which can be translated as "free air life." This movement was instigated to invigorate the youth of the nation by encouraging joyful, spontaneous outdoor experiences. Ski touring in these areas with long winters was especially recommended to get people outdoors during the winter months. Nansen saw that competitive sports tended to draw participants away from spontaneity into an overemphasis on training, rules, equipment, and social ranking based on points accumulated.

Free air life should never be competitive, he said. Very advanced and skilled recreationists should participate alongside beginners or children, each engaged in his or her own experience. When more powerful skiers feel the need to ski faster they can move off at their own pace and then return to the group later on (Vogt 1961).

Dolores LaChapelle, in *Earth Wisdom* (1978), writes about similar experiences as Nansen in downhill skiing. She describes how several skiers can be together as a group, aware of the movement of each other, but also autonomous at the same time, each finding his or her own track down the slope. The mountain is not a place to conquer, but a place to fall into awareness of the unity of life and death, of the interconnections of gods and humans.

The experiences which environmentalists cherish in wild places or even in very humanized landscapes such as city parks or urban seashores, contrast with experiences using motorized vehicles. Walking or horseback riding is advocated because, as John Muir said, you really can't see a landscape at forty miles an hour.

Walking restores the native logic, restores physical connection with ground. We are more alert to bird songs, to wind songs or the sound of falling waters. Walking is almost subversive in a society which has made a fetish out of traveling further, faster, with more power than any in the history of the human race. Walking has no purpose except to be in that place, at that time. The goal is not to get someplace but to be in a good place, a utopia. If we are restless or bored we can speed our steps or in mountainous terrain, take a steeper trail. We sustain our life and explore the fuller dimensions of self by following Muir's advice, stopping to make friends with flowers or trees or rocks which attract our attention.

Similarly, in climbing a mountain the goal is not to conquer the mountain, not to just reach the top, but to know the sides of the mountain which sustain us and other living beings which make the mountain their home. The summit may nevertheless have peculiar strong symbolic values, for instance, when all the lines of the sides and ridges point toward the summit. We may wish to join the lines and follow the flow upward.

When Thich Nhat Hanh, the Vietnamese Buddhist monk who teaches "engaged Buddhism" to westerners, talks of "walking meditation," he says: "Take short steps in complete relaxation; go slowly with a smile on your lips, with your heart open to an experience of peace." When we feel secure and at ease then worries drop away while walking. I call this *wandering* or *strolling*. Walking meditation encourages openness and acceptance. Engaging our minds with emptiness means openness to possibilities. By settling into a place, we discover aspects of the place which are not possible when flying over a landscape or riding through it. The experience of walking is a primal experience. We are human partly because we walk upright (Thich Nhat Hanh 1985; 1987).

Alan Drengson, the Canadian philosopher who has written extensively on the process of cultivating ecological self, considers wilderness travel as a fundamental metaphor for the deep ecology movement. I, too, have led students on mountain hikes, some lasting as long as two weeks, and find such experiences to be useful in breaking down barriers to ecological thinking. When we travel in mountains in the way discussed above, we are seeing the mountains from many perspectives and rhythms—walking, sitting, going faster, slower, up and down. Some routes are difficult, some easier. We are constantly aware of weather changes, clouds, insects, animals, ground texture, minerals, and elevation changes.

Under the right circumstances, Drengson says, wilderness travel can enhance our "realization of the sacredness of life; a growing sense of wonder and awe; a realization that the biosphere is not hostile but benign; a commitment to a life of increasing awareness and care; a respectful attitude toward life which leads to communion with other persons and other lifeforms" (Drengson 1980, 110-120).

Walking, climbing, kayaking or canoeing down a river, all involve learning some skill, but to encourage self awareness, we should consciously follow the "flow line," the streams of energy with intense connection. Such travel breaks our ordinary habits of thought to new experiences. In Aikido, the *sensei* talks of following spirals and circles to their conclusion and thereby discovering the further movement along the spiral. "No breaks. No clashes." In my own experience it requires self-discipline and a sense of giving up myself as a predefined entity to follow the flow lines.

Traveling

Many types of free air life involve travel. Since travel is a fact of life in our culture and many of us will travel far from our bioregions many times during our lifetimes, it is reasonable to ask how traveling fits into lifestyles based on deep ecology principles.

We can enrich our experiences in natural places by traveling in them. We explore our bioregions by excursions into different watersheds. I like weekend overnight hikes to revisit my favorite places in the Trinity Alps wilderness or Redwood National Park. I make an annual pilgrimage in the spring to the Lost Coast—a rugged, wooded coastline in southern Humboldt County. We can travel to demonstrate our support for protection and preservation of endangered ecosystems. For example, in my support of the Earth First! movement I have traveled out of my bioregion to attend demonstrations in Oregon and Idaho to protest policies of the U.S. Forest Service.

We can travel on pilgrimages to sacred areas in our own bioregion and to special places in other bioregions. But respect for these places and especially for the wishes of local citizens in these regions seems most appropriate.

As travelers, we should be mindful and careful of the primary and secondary impacts we have on fragile deserts, mountains, and islands. I prefer to avoid any tourist development which exploits the local environment, such as over-developed hot springs or large downhill ski areas. Tourist developments which exploit local laborers or local culture, resort hotels which are built on fragile wetlands or on habitat of grizzly bears (such as some facilities in Yellowstone National Park), are places to avoid. Simple, modest, healthy accommodations and food can serve our vital needs. Anything more than simple fare distracts our attention from the *place*. For example, some hotels in Yosemite National Park advertise gourmet meals with famous wines as part of their holiday activities. Yet we can have an elaborate meal in any large city in North America. We are distracted from our experience in Yosemite Valley if we think only of the lavish dinners we are eating in the hotel. We should focus on the best experience, not the most expensive.

Many supporters of Earth First! object to scenic helicopter and airplane flights over the Grand Canyon National Park. Their noise is not the sound of nature. Some people protested to the U.S. National Park Service about the continuation of these flights. In my estimation, such tours are not consistent with maintaining the quality of experience of the Grand Canyon.

I also object to "motorized trails." That term is a contradiction. The U.S. National Park Service has suggested that more visitors can visit and appreciate some national parks if gravel or dirt roads were built in these parks. Arguing against motorized vehicles in backcountry regions of parks, wildlife reserves, or designated wilderness areas on federal land is consistent with a deep ecology position.

There is no dogma or statement of principle which will satisfy all supporters of deep ecology, but generally we could take Edward Abbey's advise on national parks. Get out of your autos, recreation vehicles, helicopters, snowmobiles, all-terrain vehicles, buses, motorboats, and motorcycles and walk. Welcome to the freedom of beaches, mountains, and rivers (Abbey 1981, 35-59).

We should respect the integrity of areas even when we can't experience them. We can appreciate deeply their existence as we do that of friends we cannot see. Some parks are off limits to travelers except under special prearranged circumstances. Certain caves used by paleolithic peoples in southern Europe were declared off limits to tourists when it was discovered that the breath of so many visitors was damaging the famous cave paintings. Perhaps more and more large areas will have to be declared off limits because of degradation of landscapes, disturbance of animal migration and excessive crowds of tourists.

In California's Año Nuevo State Park, restrictions were placed on the movement of visitors when elephant seals began calving on the beaches. Feeding patterns of mothers and calves were disrupted by human visitors. People wanted to see the seals, which at the beginning of this century were thought to be extinct due to over hunting but have begun to reclaim their former range under protection of the Marine Mammals Protection Act. Just as tourists can disrupt calving grounds of elephant seals, they frequently disrupt local cultures. It is difficult for travelers to appreciate the manifold and frequently unstated premises of local cultures. Even travelers with the best intentions can violate local traditions and sacred places. In environmentally or culturally sensitive regions, a respectful traveler either travels with a guide or a small organized tour or does not visit areas which might not be prepared to handle tourists.

Travelers can help foster conservation measures in many third world nations. Roderick Nash, for example, describes the decision to establish large game reserves in East Africa after the governments of some nations discovered that game reserves could generate much needed foreign tourism and money. Although justifying national parks only as economic assets is a shallow argument for protection of varied and inherently worthy landscapes, it is the established, practical argument for governments in third world nations (Nash 1984).

Some tourists traveling in developing nations are taking the "soft path." Similar to travel styles of students, vagabonds, and many European travelers, soft path tourists find accommodations in hostels, farmhouses, and small bed-and-breakfast inns. In some villages, tourists are invited to be, for a short time, members of the community rather than observers. Tourists enter the villages as guests, not only as customers. Local traditions are more likely to be respected and preserved when the tourist gives something more than money to the host village. For example, a growing number of organizations provide work camp and service programs. Earthwatch, for instance, offers expeditions where participants help researchers in ecological, archeological, and anthropological studies in dozens of locales around the world.

In 1986 my own town of Arcata established a sister city relationship with a town in Nicaragua. Representatives from Arcata visited Camoapa and asked town leaders which they felt they needed most for the community. They suggested an addition to the local hospital. In 1987 a group of Arcata residents filled a bus with supplies and sent them, along with volunteers, to work on the hospital and other projects for two weeks in Camoapa. Some residents of Camoapa also visited Arcata.

In a similar way, the Environmental Program on Central America (EPOCA) organized a tour of Central American nations for environmentalists which concluded with a regional conference in Managua, Nicaragua, on environmental problems in Central America.

Having seen a rain forest in Australia or visited Antarctica as a tourist, it is more likely that we will join a support group attempting to protect the integrity of that place we have visited. We are not married to the place as we are married to our own bioregion, but we can become Friends of Antarctica, or Friends of the Rainforest, or Friends of some endangered island ecosystem, and support scientists and environmental activists who are working daily to educate the public or influence politicians to stop some unhealthy development scheme there.

In sum, through travel we can become friends with islands, ancient sacred sites, and vital ecosystems even if we don't bond with those places. We have sympathy for them, share their suffering in industrial projects or misguided tourist developments. And we can help protect them by becoming members of or even forming support groups for those areas or the native peoples there.

Silence

As I sit writing this chapter, in what many people would consider a quiet residential neighborhood in a small town, I can hear the sound of a chainsaw. One of my neighbors, a block away from my house, is cutting trees which he claims are obstructing the view from his living room. I can hear the sound of traffic on a busy street and occasionally I hear stereos blaring through open windows of pickup trucks carrying students to the nearby university campus. In comparison to the constant barrage of noise one hears on many city streets, the decibel level in my neighborhood is very low. Still I can *feel* the noises penetrating my personal space, penetrating my mind. Many mornings while I sit quietly at my desk, loud, piercing sounds cause me acute headaches. Walking through my neighborhood, I discover a neighbor blowing the leaves off his small lawn with a machine carried like a backpack. Other times I discover a neighbor using more power machinery to cut bushes that dared grow across his sidewalk.

I could muffle undesirable noises by wearing earplugs like workers on airport runways. I could fight noise with noise by playing a record or cassette on my portable cassette player. I could work on this book after midnight when it is more quiet in my neighborhood. Or I could try to dismiss the noise and continue working on my projects as if I didn't notice. But even in the middle of the night I am aware of the drone of traffic on the freeway a quarter mile from my house.

My irritation at noise in my small city could be dismissed as hypocritical, hypersensitive, or simply the quirk of an eccentric old man. Maybe I'm just not part of the "with it" generation. Maybe I don't appreciate the lifestyles of young people who are into loud punk rock music. Maybe there is a more serious problem in urban lifestyles. Perhaps living in the city drives us into weird mental space, away from the wild space, away from the great silence from which all knowledge arises.

New York City's Mayor Koch created a loud debate in the summer of 1985 when he declared certain small portions of some public beaches and parks off limits to radios and tape cassettes with loudspeakers. His proclamation of quiet spaces said that he was reclaiming a small territory in his city as a public peace zone. The fact that the mayor of one of the largest cities in the world felt compelled to establish small zones of quiet in public parks indicates to me the extent of the problem of human-generated sounds in our civilization.

Of course, not just public parks and streets in urban areas are affected. Millions and millions of acres of deserts and mountains are attacked every day in the American Southwest with the sounds of jet planes used by military forces on practice exercises. Anyone who has walked in the desert areas while jet planes are buzzing the cacti knows the dis-ease one feels when a plane crashes through the sound barrier.

In several major North American cities, persons living near major airports have gone to court attempting to get airport authorities to reduce airport noise by restricting the times of landings and take-offs and requiring muffling devices on airplanes.

Yet noise, human-created waste sound, is a byproduct of our civilization. Jackhammers, power saws, lawn mowers, trucks, autos, buses, airplanes, home appliances, and a thousand other devices sustain a level of noise never imagined in previous eras. Scientists who have studied the effects of noise on humans and some other animals say that noise—measured in decibels—can be subjectively evaluated by asking respondents how they feel concerning certain sounds from different sources. Decibels measure the pressure exerted by sound waves on the ear. Noise is annoying to us in a range of 50 to 70 decibels. Noise is painful at about 108 decibels. Even at 70 decibels, noise arouses us to action as heartbeat increases, muscles contract and adrenalin begins to flow in our system. In the 1979 report by the President's Council on Environmental Quality, a summary of scientific studies of the effects of noise concluded that "noise is one of the two leading reasons given by people who wanted to move from their neighborhoods because of undesirable conditions; the other was crime. Noise is a major environmental factor adversely affecting the quality of people's lives. More than that, noise is also a health problem" (CEQ Report 1979, 534).

The CEQ provided an extensive review of the scientific literature on the quality-of-life impact of unwanted noise and made some recommendations for standards which could regulate the noise at its source—by requiring noise suppression on all new machines, such as lawn mowers and gas-powered electric generators, chainsaws, automobiles, airplanes, and other such devices (CEQ Report 1979, 533-576).

Silence is one of those values which is not recognized in marketing technological devices. In many devices, like some motorized vehicles, often the more noise made by the vehicle the more powerful the machine is perceived to be.

Sometimes, as in jets and bulldozers, machinery operators may be unaware of the impact of the noise they are creating because they are wearing headphones.

Silence is intuitively valued. Well-being of humans and other animals is partly determined by quiet. It is not a resource or a utility. It has no existence in conventional economics except in selling soundproofing materials. We make some token concessions to silence. In my own town, there are special rooms and areas set aside in some school buildings for quiet reflection. There are several yoga centers, meditation centers and retreat houses where people practice in silence. Quiet means not only the absence of jet plane noises but quieting our chattering minds, our incessant internal monologue.

I know some people who spend many hundreds of dollars attending workshops held many miles from their homes, where the quality of meditation is enhanced by the quiet of rural surroundings. The sound mark at retreat centers may be the sound of a bell, which is used to signalize different phases of collective practicing.

Wind, the sound of waterfalls, sounds of waves crashing on the beach, rushing mountain streams, calling of birds—all these suggest an opening to nature. Chanting, use of bells and flutes and some drums in the context of ritual or daily practicing, all may be used as sound markers for our days.

The sounds of progress distract us from practicing deep ecology. Are we afraid of silence? Must we have the sounds of the city to reassure us that the machines are still supporting our decadent lifestyles? As the noise level increases, the quality of thinking decreases.

In some publications I have seen supporters of deep ecology called the "quiet people." I consider that an honorific title. In silence is the beginning of ecosophy. In silence we can begin listening and thus be more receptive to that which is.

A friend of mine in Japan suggests, somewhat misleadingly I think, that the most appropriate slogan for deep ecology is "eradicate the cities." But we could begin by eradicating the noise of the city, returning quiet to our lives, opening ourselves to joyful sounds of birdcalls, wind, rain, to our own breathing. We could extend the green lungs of the city, daily meeting a diversity of life forms on our way to work. Silence is a fullness, richness of living attentively. There is a resonant understanding in the Great Silence. For me silence is solace, relief, hope. We can express so little of deep ecological intuitions in language. My body and my mind need silence to feel my cellular relationships with my space.

Perhaps some of my neighbors and fellow citizens create so much noise because they are careless, or don't notice the noise or can't hear it. Perhaps some are actively extending their egos through the noise they make. Teenagers sometimes enjoy driving vehicles with loud exhausts and playing stereo tape decks at high volume with their windows down.

Perhaps some of my fellow citizens are afraid, as I am afraid, of the Big Bang—of an all-out nuclear war which will leave cities and forests in terrified silence, the silence of death broken only by the feeble cries of the dying.

When the *Bible* calls us to "make a joyful noise unto the Lord," I don't think it means the sound of chainsaws. We can reopen the channels of communication with wild nature—with the animals and with wild nature in ourselves if we do not fear the silence.

Being quiet in an age of noise, machine noise, political noise, mundane rhetoric, political propaganda and advertising, is an affirmation of the Tao, of belief in something more vast, greater than our noise.

The sounds of silence present us with a paradox, one of several paradoxes in deep ecology. The sounds of silence are spontaneously joyful. Yet learning silence may be one of the hardest lessons for people in our civilization. How many of us can even spend ten minutes listening to our own breath? Quiet spaces should not be a privilege of the wealthy who can afford to buy a large ranch or rural property where they can spend quiet time. Since we evolved in silence, listening to the sound of waves breaking on the shore, to running water and cries of animals appeals to us, we are alert and aroused by high-pitched noise. When we are surrounded only by human noise or by the ceaseless chatter of television game shows or so-called news shows, we lose touch, literally, with our own bodies. In sum, the level of noise generated by our machines is destructive. Unless we allow silence again into our lives we will be more hardened, less caring, less thought-filled, less alert, and less able to cope with the crises of our time.

Rituals

How we can heal our relations with the community of other living beings, not just other human beings, is a question of community therapy, not of community science nor of abstract or academic moralizing.

We know there are poorly functioning persons who damage or abuse their bodies through abuse of drugs or alcohol. Some people even take their own lives out of desperation or in a state of despair. We have somewhat elaborate institutions and programs (not always successful) in many modern, western nations to encourage people to more healthy functioning concerning their narrow ego and their relations with spouses, parents, children, employees. Ecologically oriented community rituals try to open people to new dimensions of ecological self.

Rituals and seasonal festivals may be used to connect humans with nonhumans—animals, sky, wind, earth. Many primal societies maintained, over hundreds or even thousands of years, sophisticated rituals and ceremonies which linked humans with the nonhuman cosmos. A local bioregion—valley, watershed, mountain, mouth of a stream, part of a desert—might be conceived as a living organism and all the plants, animals, soil, sky, gods might be invited to participate in community rituals relating place to the cosmos. Rituals serve to keep open connections with the net of nonhuman beings. Rituals may be complex but not complicated. And rituals can be conducted without unduly disrupting the habitat of other creatures (LaChapelle 1976; d'Aquilli 1979).

The form and purpose of rituals which are intended to affirm relations with a bioregion or Nature (life-force, *li*) are frequently misunderstood and labeled cultist or occult or devil worshipping by many Christian groups. Recognizing this common misconception, and that religious rituals have frequently been a source of divisiveness among people who share a common religious and philosophical orientation, and that ritual forms have frequently fallen into the grasp of government authority or priestly power, the Board of Directors of the Universal Pantheist Society made recommendations for sacerdotal and ceremonial policy. Of course, not all supporters of deep ecology are pantheists. Followers of the Great Goddess, Christian, Buddhist, Baha'i, Taoist, and other religious traditions draw from their own scriptures and traditions in their rituals. This statement designed for pantheists addresses the fears mentioned above and is worth considering by those participating in earth-bonding rituals outside of church traditions.

I. No special rite or ceremony is necessary for membership in the Universal Pantheist Society. Persons joining the society may undertake any ritual enactment, private or public, which they may desire to confirm their membership, or if it is their desire, none at all. . . .

II. The Universal Pantheist Society shall give to no person any priestly authority over any other member of the Universal Pantheist Society in the performance of any celebration or ritual. The Society recognizes that members may choose any person desired to officiate or witness a particular celebration or ritual.

III. The Universal Pantheist Society supports and encourages the enactment of creative demonstrations of devotion toward the Earth and the Universe. The Universal Pantheist Society supports celebratory activities which are meaningful to people as individuals, families and communities, and which may operate in legitimacy, if not always in absolute conformity, with State and global society, and the Ecosphere.

IV. The Universal Pantheist Society shall not define or fix the content of any rituals performed by members in any way, including tradition, but believes that rituals are best designed and carried out by the parties involved and their families and friends. In making this pronouncement, the Universal Pantheist Society is aware of the public and official nature of many such rituals, particularly those with civil and legal complications such as marriage and death ceremonies. Therefore, the Society avers that such ceremonies, whether held in public or private, need to be conducted in ways which are legally binding and appropriately designed for personal or social commitment and reverence, including joy or sorrow, movement or rest, seriousness or humor, and other appropriate physical, mental, emotional, and spiritual attitudes.

V. The Universal Pantheist Society encourages members who create or develop celebrations which are meaningful to them to send their ideas to the Society for sharing with other Pantheists through such publications of the Universal Pantheist Society as its newsletter, *Pantheist Vision* and "Celebrating Pantheism," a booklet produced by the Society to provide examples and ideas for celebrating Pantheist holidays, events, and ideas.

VI. Upon request of any member, the Society may assist the member in preparing a certificate or declaration to confirm, corroborate, or ratify any particular ceremony or celebration. Such certificates may contain the name of the Universal Pantheist Society where appropriate.

VII. Recognizing the validity of celebrations conducted by individuals for their own selves, the Universal Pantheist Society gives no institutional approval or endorsement of a member's celebrations or rituals unless written permission specific to that particular celebration has been given to the member by the Universal Pantheist Society at his or her request.

VIII. The Society disapproves any celebration, service, or ritual which is non-spontaneous, cultist, focused on supernatural or occult objects, or oriented toward a single leader with a dominant personality.

IX. Pantheists commonly seek out natural places, objects, phenomena, organisms, and events for celebration. These include, but are not limited to, geological, hydrological, oceanographic, meteorological, and astronomical features and events, living organisms and biogeochemical cycles, the procession of the equinoxes and solstices, and other natural phenomena. Recognizing that some cultures have conducted celebrations inimical to the welfare of the natural phenomena celebrated, the Society disapproves celebrations which cause harm to the natural phenomena celebrated.

X. In every human society critical life events such as birth, christening, puberty, betrothal, marriage, divorce, death, and other events are celebrated by a ritual enactment. Similarly, in many cultures certain rites of confirmation or commitment to friends, family, associates, institutions, and to country and the Earth are essential components of life. The Universal Pantheist Society certifies and authorizes its members to solemnize such life-events and commitments, insofar as legal authority requires such authorization, to be performed in accordance with international, national and state law, where applicable.

XI. The Society disapproves ceremonial behavior or events which are not affirming of life in the natural order of things, including, but not limited to, any form of physical or emotional violence, occult subjects, or reference to any supernatural influence or topic.

XII. Particularly in the case of marriage, because the institution conveys a special status with sweeping effects in law not limited to those of an ordinary civil contract, the Universal Pantheist Society notes that members who solemnize marriages must observe not only the form and ceremonies as regulated by the civil authority where the marriage is celebrated and the law of the country in which the parties are domiciled at the time of marriage, but must also recognize the civil, religious, and ethical responsibility required of the marital relation. Nothing in this policy implies any sort of preference for or disapproval of either a marriage relationship or the practice of "living together" with or without the benefit or a legal or contractual understanding. The Universal Pantheist Society recognizes that the marital relation is one which the Society, as a religious institution, may bless and the State make legal.

XIII. Mankind is totally a constituent part of the natural order in life and in death, because all of Nature is a unity. Each human, as well as each other living entity, is a temporary form which the eternally fluctuating universe has taken. Death is a return to the Whole which has birthed and sustained us; it may be felt to be a comfort rather than a terrifying prospect. When a human being's body ceases to function as a living entity, it is entirely appropriate that it be recycled to its basic elements in the natural world, rather than artificially and expensively delaying this return. This end can be accomplished either by cremation or by burial, as well as through organ donation. The Universal Pantheist Society supports funeral practices which recognize the fundamental unity of life and death, the value of ecological cycling, and appropriate ceremonies to consecrate and celebrate the lives of the deceased. (May 1987)

Council of All Beings

John Seed and Joanna Macy in Australia created a deep ecology ritual, seeking to combine the tendencies of many supporters of the peace movement with the supporters of deep ecology. They call their ritual a "Council of All Beings."

Seed writes the following description of this ritual:

From one point of view, the Council of All Beings is a biocentric (non human-centered) despair ritual. From another viewpoint, it is an exploration of the possibility of using the energies of the despair ritual to establish a deeply ecological consciousness.

Day 1

Vision quest. Each of us will spend some hours in the bush in search of a non-human being (animal, plant, river, mountain . . .) with whom we feel some connection and whom we will represent at the Council. We will construct a mask or other representation of this being who will help us over the following days to learn to shed our exclusively human identification.

In the afternoon we will convene for the first Council meeting. There we will learn that all we non-human beings here assembled have a most sacred responsibility: to represent at the Council of All Beings, all of the species and all of the natural features of the Earth. We are called together to consider the war being waged against us by the humans—the destruction of species life support systems and landscapes and the threats to the very existence of the biosphere, and to consider what we may do about these things.

Day 2

Using guided meditations and ritual, we learn to move in and out of our humanness, to loosen up our sense of self by feeling the dust of stars flowing through our veins, by "remembering" the evolutionary journey that "I" have followed these four and one half billion years of organic existence. Learning to let go of the culturally conditioned self and feel our interpenetration with all nature. There are in reality no boundaries. I *am* that.

In the afternoon, the Council convenes for the central despair ritual. Here the assembled beings call out to each other, and through each other to the whole Earth, everything that we have learned of the threats to the Earth and its component creatures. Expressions of sorrow, grief, despair and rage are invited.

Day 3

This day begins with preparatory exercises, rituals and guided meditations.

When the Council convenes, an invitation is issued for some of those present to don their human identity and listen, on behalf of the humans, to the voice of the other ten million species. We let the humans know how we feel about what is happening and how we feel about the whole human drama. Expressions of feelings are encouraged from all participants.

Later, we reconvene as humans and ask the earth to empower us to represent from this point on, the interests of the myriad species in our dealing with other humans ("I speak for the trees as the trees have no tongues, and I'm telling you sir, at the top of my lungs . . ." *The Lorax*).

On our last night together, the longest night of the year (on the Winter solstice) we pray for an awakening into a new, all-encompassing, sustainable consciousness.

Another workshop, facilitated by John Seed at the Meditation Centre at Terania Creek watershed near Lismore, New South Wales, was entitled "ECOBRETH." Seed describes the process of this workshop:

The two facilitators have been conducting BRETH workshops for some time (Breath, Releasing, Energy for Transformation and

Healing). BRETH is a pathway of personal growth similar to rebirthing, where connected breathing is used to put the person in touch with deeper, perhaps unconscious, levels of their being and clear through unresolved past situations that limit and condition the present life.

In a rebirthing group, people choose a partner and take it in turns being "breather" and "sitter." In a rebirthing session which may last for a couple of hours, the breather lies down and through connecting his or her breaths, often has a profound experience of insight into deep areas of his or her being. This may be accompanied by all kinds of intense visions, strong feelings and emotions, weeping, acting out, etc. A sense of problems solved or a deep sense of healing, integration, and empowerment typically follows several rebirthing sessions.

BRETH is similar, but adds a lot of emphasis on the *intention* with which the person enters the breathing session. The intention is consciously formulated, and in the group sharing following the BRETH sessions, the breather's experience in the session is often found to relate closely to this intention. That is, we can consciously choose the material to work on in the sessions.

The question addressed in approaching a BRETH workshop is how can we relate person and planet and do justice to both? As in Robinson Jeffers: "The diamond within reaches out to touch the diamond without, stretching our humanity thin between the invulnerable diamonds."

The basic idea of the ECOBRETH synthesis was to hold a workshop where the first couple of days would be BRETH, but starting day three, the intentions with which people entered the sessions would change from personal ones to planetary ones. If we see that there is no separation between person and planet, if the planet's pain is my pain, and the planet's fate my fate, then it becomes possible for me to help heal the planet directly through turning inward as well as outward. Then on day four the whole group would share one planetary intention. (Seed 1988)

Communities

Besides use of earth rituals, some supporters of deep ecology are practicing in small, intentional communities. There are many examples of communities created during the 1960s and 1970s whose members tend toward a deep ecology position.

These intentional communities focus on development of spirituality, cultivating warmer human relationships, personal growth and alternative ways of agriculture. Auroville in India, Findhorn in Scotland, Bodhi Farm in Australia, and The Farm community in Tennessee are a few of the communities which practice some form of relationship with the land that involves broad and deep identification.

What is new in many of these communities is the commitment to education through experience. Corinne McLaughlin and Gordon Davidson in *Builders of the Dawn: Community Lifestyles in a Changing World* list nine principles of experiential education as practiced in evolving alternative communities:

> 1) Drawing wisdom and information out of students rather than just pouring it in; 2) learning *how* to learn, how to ask good questions, how to draw one's own conclusions; 3) encouraging both right and left brain activity, intuitive as well as rational thinking; 4) valuing the affective domain—feelings, dreams, intuition, imagery—since building good relationships with people is as important as learning facts; 5) valuing Eastern as well as Western approaches to life—being, as well as doing; 6) the good of the whole as well as the importance of the individual; 7) encouraging planetary awareness and appreciation of other cultures; 8) seeing purpose and values as equally important as skill and knowledge; 9) and using spontaneity and flexibility to aid the learning process." (Corinne McLaughlin 1985, 49)

The human impulse to collect in communities is very strong. Alternative communities provide a social basis for practicing which is more rewarding for many people than belonging to a voluntary organization, such as an environmental group, or practicing in a solitary way. All alternative communities will change—sometimes rapidly in short periods of time. All will feel, in one form or another, the pressure from the larger society to conform to their expectations. And all alternative communities will have contradictions and will engage in actions inconsistent with their own principles. If we hold a logical philosopher's standard, all communities fail. But if we wait for philosophers to form communities, the biological diversity of earth's communities may be greatly reduced before any communities are realized or even begun. Practicing is experimental and experiential. Models of sustainable ecologically based communities are, however, available to all who seek to cultivate an intentional community. The Taoist ideal community described by Lao Tse in the sixth century B.C. and Amish communities which have existed since the seventeenth century have both been described as eco-anarchisms that work (Foster 1987). Lao Tse describes a small country where people do not seek great wealth but have simple needs and great wisdom. Since formal laws and government intervention do not improve society, Taoists advocate less government and more solidarity.

When sociologists describe communities, they mean a pattern of relationships between human beings. Relationships between humans and nonhuman beings are rarely discussed. A community based on deep ecology principles, however, includes nonhuman beings. Naess calls this a "mixed community" and Aldo Leopold refers to it as "the land community." Chapter six includes a discussion of our ethical responsibilities in a mixed community.

In this chapter I focused on lifestyles because I wanted to emphasize that we have choices—particularly choices as consumers. I also wanted to emphasize that lifestyles based on voluntary simplicity and the principle that "the world is our body" can enrich our Selves. There is much room for discussion on the meaning of voluntary simplicity and appropriate lifestyles. What is important, it seems to me, is to consume food, fuel, and as many other products as we can which are produced in our *own* bioregion, and to take responsibility for the health of the soils, water, air, animals, and plants of that bioregion.

How we live and political actions we take to defend our living place and our lifestyles are interrelated. In the next chapter, I make explicit connections between lifestyles and political activism in the deep ecology movement.

Political Activism
at the Grassroots

To say no, to set a limit, it is not necessarily to make a threat or to use power-over another. When 2,000 people say no to the licensing of the Diablo Canyon Nuclear Power Plant by blockading and going to jail, they are setting a limit. When hundreds of thousands of Europeans march in the street to protest the presence of nuclear weapons in their countries, they are setting a limit to United States foreign policy."
Starhawk, *Dreaming the Dark: Magic, Sex and Politics* (1982)

A small group of men and women kneel in front of an advancing bulldozer on a road being built by the U.S. Forest Service on Bald Mountain in the Kalmiopsis wilderness of southwestern Oregon. They have made repeated appeals to U.S. Forest Service officials to abandon their plans to build this road into a pristine forest area. They are now engaged in a nonviolent protest against the destruction of an incredibly wild and biologically diverse area.

In San Francisco, lawyers for Native American and environmental groups go to the federal courthouse to file for an injunction against the Forest Service. They are seeking to prevent the government from building a road through the sacred high country of the Siskiyou Mountains in northwestern California.

At Fishing Bridge in Yellowstone National Park, protesters dressed in bear costumes pass out leaflets to visitors. The protesters are denouncing the destruction of grizzly bear habitat by the National Park Service and calling on the agency to engage in a different kind of policy—managing visitors to the park rather than managing bears by killing ones that cause "problems."

Since 1984, many people who eat beef objected to using beef

from Latin America, raised on pasture lands which had previously been rain forests. This beef was imported to the U.S.A. and used by some fast food restaurants. Boycotts and protests at some of these restaurants by concerned environmental activists led at least one company to decide against further purchases of the beef.

These are just a few of the types of action which are labeled *political activism* in the environmental movement. As seen in previous chapters, the deep, long-range ecology movement is only partly a political movement. Political activism, however, is one way of demonstrating solidarity with our bioregion, with some other species of plants or animals, and solidarity with each other in the movement. We set limits on corporations and governments by our activism and at the same time affirm the integrity of places close to our hearts.

Grassroots activism is a basic thrust of the Green movements, bioregional movements, restoration movements, and environmental movements such as Earth First! Grassroots environmental movements are based on the principles of nonviolence and direct action. These principles are explored in the next parts of this chapter.

Power and Empowerment

"They have the power," I'm told. "What can I do that will matter? They can do anything they want."

"They"—the military, economic elites, corporations—do have a certain type of power that should be acknowledged. But we are not trapped in their type of power. The problem is this: by accepting theirs as the only legitimate source of power, we deny our own. When we say we can't do anything important we usually mean we can't see how we can achieve our goals. We get stuck on the goal and not the process.

Empowering ourselves means recognizing and acting from our own source of power. Right action includes words, acts and feelings true to our intuitions and principles.

For some people this means living our daily lives in a simple but rich and full way—saying grace at meals, growing a garden, riding a bicycle to work. Others may participate in nonviolent direct action; Greenpeace, the international environmental group, has engaged in many nonviolent campaigns. In Australia, in the late 1970s, activists protesting proposed dams on the Franklin River of Tasmania staged effective nonviolent protests over many months. Anyone contemplating this type of direct action can learn many lessons from reading the history of the Tasmanian wilderness campaign.

In California in the 1970s numerous actions were held at Norman Livermore Laboratory protesting research on nuclear weapons and at the Diablo Canyon nuclear reactor protesting nuclear-powered generating plants. Starhawk, a participant in several direct actions in California, describes in her book *Dreaming the Dark: Magic, Sex and Politics,* women's affinity groups who drew on their "power from within" rather than "power over" to say *no,* to stop the insane rush to create more and more weapons of destruction. She chronicles her own participation in direct action and provides chants and songs for building solidarity among members of affinity groups. She also suggests questions for group discussion when contemplating actions: How has violence affected my life? In what situations do I now feel powerless? When do I feel empowered? How would my life be different without the threat of nuclear war? What do I do with my anger? What feelings does this question evoke? (Starhawk 1982)

Patricia Mische, an activist and teacher, says that the question of power is central to the human challenge we face and that women can be leaders in the empowerment of both men and women through what she calls "integrative power." Instead of trying to "get a piece of the action" in some corporate or military hierarchies, instead of striving to become Boss Lady, Mische suggests that women can use their energies toward establishing viable alternatives to these masculine forms of power. There is no good reason for women to push for equal opportunity to serve in Titan missile silos or as bomber pilots or to build advanced nuclear weapons. Direct action should be focused on action derived from critically assessing political and economic structures with the goal of radically restructuring policies and organizations.

Contrasting exploitative power—which seeks to dominate and frequently humiliate the Other—with integrative power, Mische shows that when we use integrative power, we are aware of and responsive to the Other:

> Integrative power can also be called *synergic* power. As power *with* the other, it does not benefit one at the expense of the other or the community, but tends to benefit both self *and* others. It is a caring form of power. It is power aligned with love. It is the combination of both power and love that makes a good marriage or family life workable. It is this alignment of love and

power that is essential to shape a humanizing future—on a personal level and in the world. (Mische 1978, 47)

The women's movement, the peace movement and grassroots environmental movements teach us that social action is not abstract, not ideological sloganizing and posturing. Social action is personal. It is caring in the context of small groups of people seeking to witness, to affirm. Through such participation we seek to serve the well-being of the mixed community, not our own desires—not even our desires to be heroic, to engage in dramatic actions.

When a person takes a hammer to a nuclear-armed missile in its silo, that person is literally beating swords into plowshares. But it is seen in mass media as primarily a symbolic act. It is also an effective one because there is no underriding threat of violence. A terrorist would hide in the night and either threaten or use violence to dramatize the situation he is exposing. The person who takes a hammer to the nuclear-armed missile believes in the power of truth. There is no deception, no hiding in the night, no threats of violence. The activist declares: "We should end the arms race and we begin today to decommission the missiles. The politicians have had nearly fifty years to negotiate an end to the nuclear arms race. We are confronted with ever-increasing arsenals of exotic weapons. I am an ordinary person. I take the first step. I accept responsibility for ending the arms race. I invite other people to join with me in turning weapons into scrap metal." Simple. Direct. Rich in meaning.

Morel, the hero of Romain Cary's novel *The Roots of Heaven,* makes such a plea for the elephants of Africa. "I urge people, nations, to take up the burden of responsibility for my elephants." He is not handcuffed by national boundaries, by the assumptions of colonists, by nationalistic ideologies. He wants to protect elephants and motivate other people to take on the responsibility for their intrinsic worth and well-being.

It takes considerable self-respect and respect for the truth to engage in this form of direct action. There is little probability that public policy will change as a result of any specific act. But if a person has self-respect, then he or she will have patience, and will not place great hope in immediate results but will see the longer range meaning of the action.

The Way to Yes

Spontaneous acts of resistance may honestly rise from the momentum of events. But systematic programs of violence—for example, bombing offices of the U.S. Forest Service—can hardly be considered appropriate in converting employees of the government to a deep ecology perspective.

Martin Luther King, civil rights leader of the 1960s, was inspired in part by Mahatma Gandhi's philosophy of nonviolent resistance in India. King's letter from the Birmingham jail states the meaning of nonviolent direct action. I quote a part of it to connect the direct action of the deep ecology movement with the long tradition of nonviolent direct action in movements for social justice.

> You may well ask, "Why direct action? Why sit-ins, marches, and so forth? Isn't negotiation a better path?" You are quite right in calling for negotiation. Indeed, this is the very purpose of direct action. Nonviolent direct action seeks to create such a crisis and foster such a tension that a community which has constantly refused to negotiate is forced to confront the issue. It seeks to dramatize the issue that it can no longer be ignored.

> My citing the creation of tension as part of the work of the nonviolent resister may sound rather shocking. But I must confess that I am not afraid of the word "tension." I have earnestly opposed violent tension, but there is a type of constructive, nonviolent tension which is necessary for growth.

> Just as Socrates felt that it was necessary to create a tension in the mind so that individuals could rise from the bondage of myths and half-truths to the unfettered realm of creative analysis and objective appraisal, so must we see the need for nonviolent gadflies to create the kind of tension in society that will help men rise from the dark depths of prejudice and racism to the majestic heights of understanding and brotherhood. (King 1963)

Direct action in the ecology movement is one way to generate tension, to expose myths and assumptions of the dominant mindset, to create a situation in which corporations, developers and government agents are willing to negotiate. The activist is saying, "We seek negotiations. We are not interested in vandalism or terrorism. We are not seeking vengeance nor threatening the safety of citizens." Disabling a bulldozer which is posed to invade habitat of an endangered species is an act of resistance, not vandalism. Standing between seals and seal hunters is an act of resistance—creating tension—not an attack on sealers.

One aspect of the dominant mind-set is fear. Bathing in luxury unknown to former generations, living an admittedly insulated lifestyle of comfort and convenience, pursuing hedonism, materialism and the almighty career with diligence, the middle classes desire optimistic visions, not dark ones. Fear of energy shortages ("please don't turn off my air conditioner"), of other kinds of shortages, or fear for personal security (from criminals and terrorists) dominate the mind-set of the minimal self. Activists do not seek to increase the fear of the majority but to create tension in their minds and then present opportunities for growth in consciousness.

Direct action on a specific issue or site is aimed at a larger audience, and the action should always be interpreted by the activists. Smart and creative communication of the message is as important as the action itself.

The support of an affinity group is a key to surviving the consequences of direct action. In our social mechanism, people such as police, state interrogators, and some journalists may discredit, humiliate, belittle, and degrade any persons who engage in civil disobedience in defense of social justice or deep ecology.

It is important for the activist not to underestimate the ability of state agents to discredit or demean them or their actions. Physical abuse is only one of many tools available to police. Activists want to mobilize supporters, not attack state power. That should be stated over and over during demonstrations, strikes or other kinds of direct action. However, in many nations in the waning years of the twentieth century, environmental activists have had to be advocates of civil and human rights, and criticize police and internal security forces who protect destructive actions of corporations and state agencies. Government agencies become particularly aggressive against environmental activists when they perceive that state security is threatened.

Deep ecologists see many areas of nature as vulnerable. They see forests clear-cut in very short periods of time with chainsaws and bulldozers. They see habitats of endangered species destroyed with napalm. But the infrastructure of our civilization is also vulnerable. For example, in 1985 a small group of Japanese successfully shut down the Japanese National Railways, delaying hundreds of thousands of commuters in Tokyo by using firebombs to systematically sever electronic cables along the railroad tracks that direct train movements. One Japanese commentator pointed to the fact that without any great physical power or large numbers, a group can threaten—at least for a short time—the mechanism of a whole city. In California, a small storm can inconvenience millions of humans—flooded roads, shutdown of power plants, telephones and computers. These vulnerabilities suggest a need not for more security forces and back-up systems, but a reexamination of the basic assumptions of this civilization—centralization, bureaucracy, and misguided attempts to dominate natural forces rather than work with them.

The major point I want to emphasize is the need to affirm our principles. Positive suggestions, clear actions, dramatic demonstrations are always more effective than defensive attitudes.

Reform environmentalism is institutionalized in large organizations and government agencies. In many disputes concerning land use, planning, location of public facilities (such as freeways or harbors), or regulatory policies, reform environmental groups use what Theodore Roszak calls the strategy of countervailing expertise. Faced with elaborately detailed proposals by corporations or government agencies which are fleshed out with quantitative analysis of cost-benefit ratios, economic modeling and other accoutrements of intellectual one-upmanship, reformers develop their own expertise or hire experts to respond to these documents in the language and concepts of the government agencies. Liberal reform environmentalists frequently make attempts to save a unique parcel of land or an endangered species and its habitat from people who want to build an oil refinery, log the old growth trees, drive off-road vehicles across the land, or build a dam that will flood a stretch of white water or the habitat of a small fish. The reformers attempt to persuade some legislative body to create a state or federal park or to prohibit these actions. Sometimes a compromise is struck. A dam may not be built on the stretch of white water, but it is built somewhere else, and some other river is dammed and the habitat destroyed. Sometimes a state or national park is created, supposedly designed to protect the natural heritage, but it is administered to serve the needs and desires of recreationists. Even the remaining wildlife, or white water or endangered wildflowers are threatened by more proposals for roads, dams, or logging. The cycle of reform repeats itself as a new generation of environmentalists emerges to defend the river, save the redwoods or protect endangered species (see for example, Schrepfer 1983; Franklin 1983; Palmer 1982; Barlett 1985).

This strategy has been useful in a limited sort of way. Some court cases have been won by environmental law firms based on expert testimony they were able to recruit. Some harmful proposals have been revised based on input from reform environmental groups.

However, when the environmental movement becomes predominantly a refugee camp for dissident experts from corporations or academia, and when the primary emphasis in the movement is to provide expert opinion to government agencies, then reformers are helping to increase bureaucratic domination. The strategy of countervailing expertise, says Roszak (1972, 50), "leaves wholly untouched the great cultural question of our times. It does not challenge the universally presumed rightness of the urban-industrial order of life."

A basic social thrust of the deep, long-range ecology movement is transformation of the masses into a new kind of society. The aim is not to create a utopia of experts, a perfectly managed technocratic state, but to empower more and more ordinary people with their ecological self and to empower grassroots movements with solidarity and effectiveness when facing vast bureaucracies and hierarchical organizations.

The state has increasing power over the lives of ordinary citizens through computer files, innovative weapons for police and security agents, and access to mass media, providing opportunities to spread "disinformation campaigns" undreamed of by the Nazis and other propagandists before the age of television and computers. Furthermore, mesmerized by television advertisements luring us to the wonderland of comfort and convenience of VCRs, hot tubs, or vacation escapes, few people in developed nations contemplate revolutionary politics in the traditional sense of violent revolution.

As stated previously, the ecology movement is a resistance movement against domination of nature by humans. Grassroots social movements have strength because they are not dominated by experts or priests. They are flexible and less costly to maintain than bureaucratized movements. By definition they are not top heavy with administrators and hired experts. Social transformation toward an ecotopia based on deep ecological principles comes from groups of people working within their own bioregions, who combine their energies to delegitimize the dominant mechanistic worldview and present positive models for social change.

The Chipko Movement

"What does the Forest bear?
Water, soil, and pure air
Water, soil, and pure air—
These are the basis of life."
Chipko women of India

In industrialized and economically over-developed nations, activists can learn from some of the grassroots resistance movements in the third world and the fourth world—tribal peoples. One example which combines ecological themes and social development is the Chipko movement in the Himalayas.

Chipko means literally *embrace.* The Chipko movement is one of the most significant grassroots movements in India since independence in 1947. It combines ecological awareness and traditional Indian religious sense of extended community.

There are many accounts of direct action by women and children in the movement over the last twenty years to protect the native forests around their villages from clear-cutting by loggers who were granted permits by state governments. I quote one story to show the strength of this action.

On 26th March, 1974 all menfolk of Reni village had been called to Chamoli town for paying them some long overdue compensation. Suddenly a girl spotted some labourers marching towards the forest through a deserted route. Gaura Devi, a child-widow now in her fifties and accepted by village-women as their leader, was informed. Soon she had assembled 27 women and together they rushed after the labourers.

"Brother," Gaura Devi first addressed the labourers, "this forest is our maternal home. From this we satisfy so many of our needs. Do not axe it. If you do so, landslides will ruin our homes and fields." The labourers were from Himachal Pradesh, their families also lived in similar conditions in the hills. They understood the agony of these women. They agreed to return. Then the contractor and some officials, though hurling curses, also had to follow. That night the women of Reni mounted guard over all possible routes leading to the forest.

Next day the menfolk of Reni returned. People from surrounding villages had also gathered. There was no chance of the contractor and his labourers again venturing into the forest. The endangered trees of Reni had been saved. Soon after the State government appointed an official committee . . . to inquire into the validity of the demands of the Chipko movement. This committee recommended a moratorium on the commercial exploitation of Reni and several other forests of Alaknanda catchment for a decade. This recommendation was accepted by the State Government and subsequently a moratorium was imposed.(See Bandyopadhyay 1987, 26-34)

The British introduced changes in the Indian forestry practices in the 1880s. In the 1930s, residents of what is now the state of Uttar Pradish protested those practices with Gandhian tactics.

In the 1960s, Chipko continued the Gandhian Sarvodaya movement and organized around four major campaigns: the setting up of local forest small industries, the fight for forest rights, the battle against consumption of alcohol and the organization of local women.

Sunderlal Bahuguna is one of the prominent Chipko workers. He joined the Indian Independence Movement at age thirteen and speaks for Chipko with a Gandhian perspective. His outlook also reflects the views of Richard St. Barbe Baker, who wrote many books on the world forests. As a teenager Bahuguna read Peter Kropotkin's *A Word for Young Men,* as well as the writings of old sages. He traveled through India selling small books with quotes from the sages, because, he told me, "we must touch the hearts of the people."

He witnessed much tragedy, poverty, violence, and the effects of over-population and environmental destruction—especially deforestation—in India and other Himalayan nations. But he is cheerful and forthright in his presentation. He sees life beyond the sometimes shallow optimism or pessimism commonly found in the United States. And he is willing to live simply. "Social activists," he says, "must be willing and happy to make many sacrifices, or what many people would consider sacrifices."

I spoke with him in California in 1985 a few weeks after he had attended the World Forestry Conference in Mexico City. There he had spoken at length on forestry. Forestry, he said, is not just a tool for major corporations interested in creating tree plantations, but it literally means protecting the lives of local peoples in forested regions and the lives and habitat of other beings.

Many people feel that the Chipko movement is only about using trees for local purposes, such as firewood, or just about creating jobs for local villagers in the forest products industry. But Bahuguna insists that

> most people have seen only the outer form of the Chipko movement. They see the beast but not the man. The soul of the movement is the inner life which is in all creation. It is not just to save trees. The bigger thing is that it takes you higher on a special plane. You feel a part of the trees. Trees are part of your family.
>
> I say that ecology really means permanent economy. In a real economy you realize an animal is an independent being and you know it for itself not just what it can do for some human. (Interview with author 1985)

Thus the Chipko movement is not just an alternative mode of economic development. It is a movement that is richer in philosophy than many politicians like to admit.

In June 1982 at the London public meeting on The Human Environment-Action or Disaster, organized by the United Nations Environment Programme, Bahuguna spelled out the Chipko movement's ultimate demand for a harmonious relationship between forests and people:

> I was surprised to hear from so many learned speakers that it is poor people who do harm to the Environment. Let me ask you all this question: have you ever truly experienced real hunger?
>
> This is a hungry man's philosophy—before anything else can be considered he must have something to eat. We have to find out the ways and means to solve this problem; how can human beings and trees co-exist. There is only one possible answer, we must plant trees which give food for hungry people. We must plant nut trees, because nuts can be stored and they are rich in protein and fats. We must plant trees with edible seeds and oil bearing seeds. We must plant seasonal fruit trees and trees which encourage the production of honey.
>
> Our second priority in the fight against hunger must be Fodder Trees, and not just for our own domestic animals. We have become so selfish, we talk of one earth for all creatures, but we have utilised all the resources of this earth for human beings alone, we leave nothing for the beasts, the wild animals, the birds and the insects. In our Hindu philosophy we say "the whole Earth is your Family" but our family has become so small and so selfish that now we only care for mankind. So in the Chipko [movement] we stress that we must plant fodder trees for birds and beasts as well as for our domestic animals.
>
> Our third priority is to plant trees for fuel to solve the energy problem: there is always enough dead wood in a mixed forest to supply the needs of the villagers.
>
> Our fourth priority is to plant fertilizer trees which create vast amounts of rich soil nutrients every year and thus guarantee our long term soil fertility.
>
> Lastly we encourage the villagers to plant fibre trees which supply the villagers with fibre for clothes, ropes and building materials.
>
> The Chipko programme will make communities self-sufficient, in all their basic needs. It will generate a decentralized, self-renewing and permanent economic prosperity. (Bahuguna 1982, 87)

Bahuguna's own social activism is derived from a deep spirituality combined with extensive knowledge of modern ecological science. He sees the combination of science and politics in most modern nations as a prescription for destruction. However, a combination of wise science and spirituality is *sarvodaya,* which could be translated as "good for all."

The ecology movement, he says, especially needs three kinds of people: humanitarian scientists, social activists, and compassionate literary men. The humanitarian scientist has head knowledge and works for the welfare of all living beings. He or she is compassionate in dealings with other people and works to alleviate the miseries of all. The social activist provides the hands of the movement. He or she is an impatient person who wants to facilitate needed social changes. The compassionate literary person—artist, poet, journalist—works for the achievement of a noble objective. In the collective movement, but not necessarily in each person, there is the wise combination of scientific knowledge, action and devotion.

I asked Bahuguna what the Chipko movement can teach us in developed nations.

Learn the difference between real economic development and what is called development by the World Bank and by many national political leaders. Real development helps people be self-reliant in physical needs and self-realizing in spiritual development. Real development preserves a cultural integrity and nature's diversity in a specific place.

Environment is not an isolated problem but closely connected with Peace and Development. The four pillars of the present-day society are Authority, Wealth, Arms and Philosophy. The foundations of the new society will be Service, Austerity, Peace and Good Behavior. I see a close relationship between the first four. The first three always received oxygen from the philosophy. Since philosophies have been prostituted for short-term gains, they have lost the sanctity of vision, which the great men behind them had. Moreover, the present society has its selfish and limited objective to serve only the human beings and exploit other beings for this end. In a really developed society, all living beings including trees, rivers and mountains should have freedom to live and thrive in a state of peace, happiness and prosperity. The achievement of this objective is possible through Service instead of brute force, which unfortunately has become the basis of the State rather than the "will of the people."

Similarly the direction of science and technology has been to impoverish the earth for the never-ending desires of the material man. Austerity in the use of the resources to satisfy every man's need (not every man's greed) is the key to keeping Mother Earth—the source of all wealth—in a good state of health. Dreams to establish peace with the help of destructive weapons is just like adding fuel to the fire. Arms are manufactured in the factories of hatred, while peace is the manifestation of love born when we live in perfect harmony with Nature. Philosophies, though, when born have a great message but when translated into action lose their original idealism and become tools to further some vested interests. Gandhi, perhaps, could foresee this and he warned not to weave an "ism" around his ideas. On the contrary he laid stress on the unity of ideals and actions—good behavior. Ever in the service of Mother Earth. (Letter to the author 1985)

In addressing the vegetational wealth of the Himalayas, Bahuguna said that "our materialistic culture has given rise to a man-nature relationship similar to one between a butcher and an animal. The world has been made a slaughter-house for nature. He is doing the same stupid thing which a foolish maid did to a hen laying golden eggs. She slaughtered it to get all the eggs together. Man wants to massacre the earth."

Every social movement has its distractors, of course, and there are various obstacles on its way.

Chipko is facing organized antipathy and antagonism from forest contractors and industrialists. It is surprising that even the administration is giving protection to these antisocial extremists. They have attractive, immediate economic benefits as a bait and the limbs of the law as a protector. As far as ecology is concerned, it has become a fashion to discuss it and nothing more, because ours is a society of pseudo-intellectuals. Now that intellectuals have reached a conclusion that the political era has finished and has given way to a more scientifically founded system—the ecology—these pseudo-intellectuals feel proud in talking it over. The political system has failed to solve many problems of human-beings. Ecology presents a well-founded and crystal clear way of a happy and more meaningful future. Thus, ecology proposes a parallel system of life and its clash with existing establishment is imminent. In the Himalayas our small group is fighting despite all antagonistic circumstances. We request all lovers of Nature to start a mass movement in their own region against the deteriorating environment. (Bahuguna, letter to U.S. supporters 1986)

In a certain sense the deep, long-range ecology movement is moving at an angle to the dominant society. Those at the margins of society are frequently shunned, berated or degraded by the dominant culture. To activists in the movement, the fact of marginality is empowering. Persons who are marginal in their occupations or professions do not feel compelled to uphold the ideal types of the profession. They are not expected to be representatives of all teachers or all doctors. They are freer to express their heartfelt affirmation of intrinsic worth of all nature.

The movement grows as a resistance movement among marginal regions of developing and developed nations. My bioregion, for example, is frequently treated as an internal colony by large corporations and state agencies. Many people there have objected to plans by state bureaucrats and politicians from the largest cities of the state to dam the rivers of northwest California and export the water from those rivers through an elaborate series of tunnels and canals to the large cities of southern California. "We are not just a resource shed for the largest cities," people said. Similarly people object to logging primeval forests in my region just to pay off debts of multinational corporations.

Many supporters of deep ecology find common cause with and support politically oppressed peoples in many third world nations. Sometimes these are collectively called the fourth world, tribal peoples who are displaced by road building, dam building or agricultural development projects in Brazil, India or Mexico.

The Lacandon Indians of southern Mexico, for example, have resisted, until recently, modernization. Historians conclude that their fervent religious consciousness included a nature-centered cosmology. They are part of the rain forest within which they exist. Government-sponsored programs have led to clear-cutting the Lacandon's forest in the name of economic development to supply the needs of urban residents in Mexico. In the 1980s the Lacandons, whose ecological self is firmly attached to their forest, are subject to all the ills which attack fourth world peoples when exposed to inappropriate economic development and urban values—sickness, sadness, disorientation, poverty and loss of identity (Perera 1982).

In contrast to the forest-dwelling Lacandons, the Bushmen of South Africa dwell in the desert. But like the Lacandons, the Bushmen are threatened and endangered by modern civilization. Laurens van der Post, who wrote the elegy *Testament to the Bushmen* (1985), eloquently pleads for reinterpretation of the nature of human consciousness to "comprehend a scene littered with ruins." And of the Bushmen, he writes that he had "no immunities whatsoever to protect him against an infected world, sick with unschooled power and uncritical worship." The world needs the Bushmen, Van der Post concludes because they have followed "a way of the truth that would make men free."

Europeans encroached on the habitat of Bushmen and on their institutions. Modern schooling deprived children of their ancient traditions. Now the Bushmen have a culture that is in disarray.

As we can share the sadness of Bushmen, Eskimos, tribal peoples everywhere, we can also work against misguided missionary programs, misguided economic development programs (such as the road-building program instituted by the Brazilian government in Amazonia), and military adventurism by U.S. special forces in the name of internal security or stopping the drug trade.

Deep Ecology and Green Politics

Green politics or "The Greens," as they frequently call themselves, provide a channel for activism within specific countries—Germany, Australia, the United States, etc. In the late 1980s it is still unclear what form the Green movement will take in the U.S.A.—whether movement, political party or loose coalition of activists—and whether the Green movement will focus on social ecology or follow a deep ecology, biocentric philosophy, ecofeminism or some other path.

The Green movement began to gain international attention in the late 1970s after several grassroots movements in the Federal Republic of Germany joined together to form a new political party, *Die Grünen*, The Greens. Proportional representation in the West German electoral system provided the opportunity for minority parties to gain seats in federal and state parliaments. *Die Grünen* was formed out of a synthesis of ecology, alternative and social justice movements, the peace movement and other movements. The four pillars of The Greens' platform included ecology, social responsibility, grassroots democracy, and nonviolence. The German Greens say of themselves: "We are neither left nor right, we are in the front." In other words, their politics do not fall into conventional categories of liberals versus conservatives. Green movements seek not just a new government but a new way of politics—grassroots politics which empower citizens. Grassroots democracy, as envisioned by Greens in Germany and other nations, involves decentralized, autonomous regions which make wide use of referenda, rotation of office holders, and town meetings.

However, the literature by proponents of Green politics in various nations makes clear that ecology is not the only thrust of the movement and environmentalists are not the only constituency. The ecological component of Green politics in West Germany, Great Britain, and North America has not gone very deep. Most policy statements have focused on only the worst abuses to the environment—toxic wastes, acid deposition, nuclear reactors, and water pollution. These, of course, are important public issues and some theorists in various Green movements have provided sophisticated analyses of social and economic factors which contribute to problems of air and water pollution (see Porritt 1984).

The platform upon which *Die Gruen* ran in the 1983 West German federal elections included basically stewardship statements, such as the following: "Encroachment on natural habitats and the extermination of animal and plant species is destroying the balance of nature and along with it the basis of our own life. It is necessary to maintain or restore a biologically intact environment, in order to insure the humane survival of future generations" (Program of the Green Party 1986).

Any conference or meeting of Greens is one arena for introducing deep ecological arguments, as outlined in chapter one, which can draw the discussion into fundamental, deep issues. The process of developing coalitions based on Green politics can be open and conciliatory, asking "how much can we agree upon?", or it can be confrontational and militant.

Many analyses of Green parties in Europe focus on their electoral success and the continuing tensions between Marxist-leftist and post-Marxist theorists (see Weston 1986; Bahro 1982, 1984, 1986; Jean Cohen 1984; Zupan 1983; Sylvan 1986).

The debate between Murray Bookchin and Charlene Spretnak at the American Greens Conference in 1987 illustrates the tension between old paradigm anarchist-socialist and the new paradigm approach to the movement.

Bookchin, well known author of *The Ecology of Freedom* (1982), defines his position as humanistic and grounded in socialist-communalist traditions, rationalism and based on a belief in the uniqueness of human beings. He explicitly rejects a deep ecological basis for Green politics and calls for what he labels "social ecology."

Spretnak and Fritjof Capra (1984) interviewed many participants in *Die Gruen* and have written the most comprehensive book in English on the German Greens, *Green Politics: The Global Promise.* In West Germany Spretnak found an ambivalent response to linking spiritual and biocentric values with Green principles, although her informants agreed that there is a spiritual dimension to Green politics. She concluded that memories of Hitler linking fascism with a reverence for nature combined with the disdain Marxists have for religion have made the discussion of spirituality *verboten* in 1980s German politics. However, in North America many Green activists willingly discuss the spiritual dimension of their politics, and a spiritual Greens network was formed in Europe in 1987.

Spretnak asked how we can combine a sustainable religion with Green politics. She sees Green politics as possibly another expression of deep ecology. "Holistic or ecological thinking is not a retreat from reason; it is an enlargement of it to more comprehensive and hence more efficient means of analysis" (Spretnak 1986, 29). She concludes, and I agree, that finding appropriate expression for the spiritual dimension in Green politics will be difficult. "Surely no Green, whatever his or her spiritual orientation, could object to our structuring our groups according to the deep ecology principles of diversity, interdependence, openness, and adaptability—as well as the spiritual principles of cultivating wisdom and compassion. These can be our guidelines as we evolve the everchanging forms of Green politics" (Spretnak 1986, 69).

In sum, practicing from deep ecology principles may include participation in Green movements, parties, or networks. Deep ecology and Green politics can be unified in practical and specific campaigns to stop some forms of pollution or address other environmental problems. Marxist, socialist and anarchist perspectives can help deep ecologists explore and understand the political and social factors—including the role of capitalism and multinational corporations—involved in the degradation of our planet. Deep ecology can help the Green movement move beyond narrow resource definitions of nature to reach metaphysical and ontological levels and the exploration of ecological self. Discovering deeper dimensions may inspire Green alternatives more radical than anything yet proposed in Green political movements.

As Martin Heidegger said at the conclusion of his essay "The Question Concerning Technology" (1977), "Questioning is the piety of thought." It is neither gentle nor easy to question at such a level. Green political movements can be authentic and social transformatory if participants help each other to understand and move beyond the limitations of what Herbert Marcuse calls one-dimensional society.

Direct Action, Monkeywrenching and Ecotage

In November 1986 under the cover of early winter darkness, two volunteers working with the Sea Shepherd Conservation Society entered two boats used by the Icelandic whaling industry in Reykjavik Harbor. The volunteers sent the vessels to the bottom of the harbor by opening the seacocks and flooding the engine rooms. They also considered sinking a third ship but found a night watchman aboard (the Sea Shepherd Society has pledged it will not injure any person in its protest actions). During the same action, they sabotaged the whale processing plant in Reykjavik Harbor and destroyed the computer room of the Icelandic whaling industry.

Rod Coronado, the young man who planned and executed the raid on Reykjavik, is a defender of whales who agreed to follow the Sea Sheperd Society guidelines for action in the field: no explosives; no weapons; no action that has even a remote possibility of causing injury to a living being; if apprehended, do not resist arrest in a violent manner; be prepared to accept full responsibility and suffer the possible consequences of your actions.

Paul Watson, spokesperson for the Sea Sheperd Society, declared that the action "was done to strike a blow against the whaling industry." Iceland had continued to defy decisions from the International Whaling Commission concerning the number and type of whales that could be harpooned annually.

The action against the Icelandic whaling fleet was not the first by the Sea Shepherd Society against illegal whaling. In 1979 the *Sea Sheperd* rammed a "pirate" whaling vessel, the *Sierra,* off the coast of Portugal. Both vessels were towed to the Portuguese port of Leixoes and the *Sea Shepherd* was later confiscated. Paul Watson and the two other crew members who remained on board during the ramming escaped from the country. Volunteers later went back to Portugal to attach a magnetic mine to the hull of the *Sierra.* It sank quickly (*L.A. Weekly,* 11 July 1986).

The Sea Shepherd Society is not alone in taking unconventional action in defense of animals. Under the banner of animal liberation, small groups have invaded laboratories of colleges and universities to liberate primates and other animals used in experiments. In 1985 in Hawaii two dolphins were liberated from captivity.

Protests against certain logging practices have occurred in Australia, Oregon, Texas, California, and other areas. Protesters, chaining themselves to bulldozers or climbing trees, have refused to disperse when ordered by police and have been arrested. In the Solomon Islands in the South Pacific, villagers attacked and burned the logging camp and equipment owned by a multinational corporation which had been granted a timber lease to the island by the central government.

Actions such as these have been aggressively reported by the news media. Some groups, such as Greenpeace, have actively sought publicity for their nonviolent encounters with the Russian whaling fleet and with officials of the French government. In 1985, instead of stopping their nuclear weapons testing in the South Pacific, the French government tried to stop Greenpeace protests. In that instance the Greenpeace vessel *Rainbow Warrior* was being outfitted in an Auckland, New Zealand, harbor in preparation for a voyage into the French nuclear test zone in the South Pacific. On orders from officials at the top level of the French government, agents of the French intelligence agency entered New Zealand on false passports and attached a bomb to the Greenpeace vessel. The explosion sent the *Rainbow Warrior* to the bottom of Auckland Harbor and killed a crew member, Fernando Pereira, who was preparing to sail with Greenpeace into the French nuclear test zone. The *Rainbow Warrior* was refloated but could not be restored to seaworthy status. It was towed into the South Pacific and sunk.

For over a hundred years the conservation-environmental movement was remarkably resistant to use of protest demonstrations or direct action as tactics in campaigns. From the days of John Muir, environmentalists relied on letter writing campaigns, appeals to elected officials, and publicity campaigns to arouse the sympathy of the public for an endangered area. In comparison to other movements of equal vigor, such as the labor movement, the environmental movement has been remarkably free from violence and street demonstrations.

Thoreau in his famous essay "On Civil Disobedience," written after he spent the night in jail for refusing to pay a tax levied to support the War in Mexico in 1845, provided strong defense for the moral claims of civil disobedience when one is acting from deeply held convictions. Gandhi and Martin Luther King, Jr. greatly developed strategies and philosophies for civil disobedience campaigns. In the later part of the twentieth century, grassroots environmental movements have begun to use civil disobedience. To better understand these campaigns, it is necessary to define some phrases which some politicians and news media have been using disparagingly.

Direct action is action taken in defense of a forest, river, or specific species of plants or animals, in which the protester has no monetary or private property interest, but has a concern as part of his or her ecological self and makes a statement with his or her body. To paraphrase Gandhi: I serve no one but myself, but my *self* is broad and deep. A protest march in front of a U.S. Forest Service service or blocking public access to roads leading to a logging site is direct action when the protesters are attempting to call attention to the integrity of a primeval forest. Sailing a vessel into an area of ocean decreed by a government as a "prohibited zone" to protest government policies is direct action. So is sitting in a small boat between whales and whalers' harpoons.

Monkeywrenching is the purposeful dismantling or disabling of artifacts used in environmentally destructive practices at a specific site—dismantling fishing gear or logging equipment, for example.

Ecotage is disabling a technological or bureaucratic operation in defense of one's place. It is self-defense. According to the dictionary, ecotage is a combination of ecology and sabotage. Ecology comes from combining the Greek *oikos,* a household, and *logy,* to study; *saboter* means to damage machinery with wooden shoes. Ecotage, as used here, means actions which can be executed without injury to life.

Sam Lovejoy, who engaged in antinuclear ecotage in New England, wrote that ecotage is directed, targeted, and ethical action in defense of living systems. It is not action which could be considered vandalism or random attacks on technology (Lovejoy 1972, 177).

It is the opposite of ecocide. *Ecocide* is a term first used during the Vietnam War when the U.S. government authorized aerial spraying of a herbicide (Agent Orange with dioxin, a highly toxic chemical) over vast areas of forest in order to deny cover to the North Vietnamese. Ecocide means the willful destruction of habitat. Ecotage is the nonviolent defense of landscape from immoral or destructive human behavior by destroying the technology which can be used in ecocide.

Ecotage is also different from decommissioning. Ecotage is an act of resistance. It sometimes involves acts which are illegal, such as tree spiking. *Decommissioning* is a process of planned, purposeful actions intended to render harmless (or at least less harmful) some machine, factory, or structure. It involves political, bureaucratic, scientific, and citizen groups. They are cognizant of hazards and dangers of the machine or factory which is being decommissioned. After informed opinion from experts and citizen groups is heard and discussed, a board or agency undertakes to develop and implement a plan for decommissioning. In the United States debates over decommissioning nuclear reactors, nuclear submarines, and uranium processing plants provide forums where deep ecology principles can be expressed and suggestions for strategies made.

Decommissioning is technical and there is a wide range of opinion over the effectiveness of certain strategies for decommissioning complex artifacts such as nuclear reactors. Citizen groups can discuss goals and means with experts and public officials but can rarely engage in, or carry out, the actual decommissioning of a complex device. However, if agencies in a society are mobilized to decommission some technology, then environmental activists have been successful.

Direct action, monkeywrenching, and ecotage can be seen as political tactics used in a campaign to achieve some goal. They also can be seen as means for practicing deep ecology if they are based on authentic self-defense and are generally nonviolent. In this sense, the means are part of the end.

The term *nonviolence* creates problems for some supporters of deep ecology because they equate nonviolence with passivity or nonresistance. Nothing could be further from the meaning of nonviolence as used by Gandhi, Martin Luther King, Jr., and by Greenpeace. Gandhi used the term *satyagraha* to refer to his form of political action. This is an awkward term for English-speaking people and the rough translation is even more awkward and abstract—"soul-force" or "truth-force." Gandhi seems to have used the term *ahimsa* as the source of the English "nonviolence," and this usually is translated as "a way of acting that refrains from hurting others." It could also be translated as "lifestyle based on compassion for all." Other terms which have been used over the years, and mostly rejected, are nonviolent resistance, nonviolent direct action, nonviolent action, active nonviolence. Gandhian nonviolence becomes more effective with the more people involved and the more actions performed. Naess asserts that large scale, frequent ecotage would strengthen police state tendencies and fascism. However, ecotage as an emergency action may be appropriate if it gives the protesters time to block destructive actions legally, as with a court order, for example. Gandhian nonviolence can be militant, but communication is essential: Touch the brain and the heart of the opponent. State your goals clearly. Announce the intent of your actions.

People working in campaigns based on Gandhian principles are encouraged to see the implications of their actions before they are committed to following through. Nonviolent protesters have put their bodies between bulldozers and trees, but they cannot be everywhere that destruction is occurring. There are thousands more bulldozers and willing drivers than there are protesters, so each active nonviolent protest is essential not only for the endangered trees but for the deeper educational campaign.

Nonviolence can be intense. When Buddhist monks in Saigon in the 1960s made an ultimate appeal for peace by self-immolation they affirmed peace with their lives. When Brian Willson protested U.S. support for Contra rebels in Nicaragua by sitting on the railroad tracks at Concord Naval Station in California in 1987, his legs were severed below the knees by an oncoming train.

Mahatma Gandhi, acknowledged as one of the greatest practitioners of nonviolence in the twentieth century, admitted that he made "Himalayan mistakes" in some of his campaigns, but he refined and clarified political action as part of the broader and deeper movement toward Self-realization. Naess, in his systematic description of Gandhi's theory of nonviolence, discovered a number of norms and hypotheses used by Gandhi as a strategy for group struggle. The first and most general norm is "act in group struggle and act, moreover, in a way conducive to long-term, universal, maximal reduction of violence" (Naess 1974, 60).

The primary hypothesis connected with this norm, is that "the character of the means used in a group struggle determines the character of the results." In other words, there is no acceptance of the statement that the ends justify the means. The means commonly used by the dominant culture to enforce its will is not conducive to deeper social change or the cultivation of Self-realization.

In a nonviolent social movement, the Gandhian rule states: "Never resort to violence against your opponent [but rather] choose that action or attitude which most probably reduces the tendency towards violence of all parties in the struggle."

There are many ways to reduce violence by all parties. If opponents understand each others motives, they are less likely to use violence. If they see each other as people rather than as functionaries, then compassion may be encouraged. The great difficulty that many environmental activists feel working with the U.S. Forest Service, for example, is breaking through the wall of bureaucratic neutrality and indifferent action.

Mark Dubois, a young Californian in love with the Stanislaus River flowing from the Sierra Nevada into the Central Valley of California, chained himself to a boulder in the Stanislaus River canyon in May 1979, to protest the closing of the New Melones Dam and the proposed flooding of the canyon above Parrotts Ferry. Explaining to reporters why he did it, Dubois said "I came here to guarantee Parrotts Ferry for this year, so that people can stand on the bridge and look downstream to a nice reservoir and upstream to a wild river. We've compromised enough." When queried further, he said:

> Frustrations with the bureaucracies are what finally drove me to do it. We watched the Corps [of Engineers] flood the Miwok [Indian] sites of the lower canyon against the position of the State Historic Preservation Office and the Department of the Interior. We saw the chance of flooding above Parrotts Ferry, but the required mitigation hasn't been done—downstream, 4,700 acres were to be bought to replace 12,500 flooded acres upstream, and the Corps hasn't done it. We did everything else we could do. I just couldn't think of any other way to make the agencies more responsive. And I had to make a personal statement.
>
> There are no victories in the environmental movement, only delays. Maybe this will delay flooding for a year. And that can give time for longer-term protection. I never felt fear or hesitation. Something felt right inside. I didn't feel I'd drown. (Palmer 1982)

And a representative for the U.S. Army Corps of Engineers, the agency responsible for the environmental destruction to the Stanislaus, responded to the media, "Mostly, I know he's doing what he thinks is right. He just has different values."

The river was ultimately dammed and the canyon that Dubois loved was drowned (Palmer 1982, p. 178). In the long history of dam fighting in the U.S.A. this was the first time civil disobedience had been used.

Sometimes government agencies can be influenced by positive, goal-directed ecotage. After demonstrators climbed trees in the old growth forests of the central Cascades in Oregon and people spiked some of the trees, the Forest Supervisor of Willamette National Forest, Michael Kerrick, wrote a report on ecotage for civic leaders. He pleaded with activists to use legitimate channels to address their concerns the preservation of old growth forest and spotted owl habitat:

Understanding opposing viewpoints is a key to reaching resolution between conflicting parties. The Willamette National Forest is open to meaningful dialogue directed toward gaining an understanding of the concerns of all groups concerned about the way we manage the Forest. Even though resolving conflicts through legitimate channels often takes patience and perseverance, we wonder what real effects "direct action" will have, except for garnering more legal penalties and further polarization in an already polarized situation.

Anyone wishing social change must at sometime find an effective way to get the society to change of its own accord. It is unlikely that ecotage will result in the type of social change Earth First! hopes for, and hence is likely to be counterproductive. We appeal to Earth First!ers to seek a more constructive manner to address these concerns. (Willamette 1985)

This response misses the point of ecotage. Major social changes will not occur through ecotage any more than rape will forever be banished from society just because a potential victim takes a knife away from a person intent on rape. Ecotage is like working in the emergency room of a hospital. Highly skilled physicians don't expect to decrease the rate of automobile accidents by treating victims of such accidents. The physicians hope to stop blood loss, reduce trauma and ease some of the pain and suffering.

Forest activists engage in dialogue with timber corporations and other agencies determined to wound the earth, but Earth First!ers aren't convinced by the Forest Service definition of the situation, their terminology or their conceptual models.

The Gandhian rule states: engage functionaries as persons, not as representatives of the bureaucratic domination, such as the U.S. Forest Service or the Bureau of Land Management. Depersonalized, neutral, bureaucratic attitudes must be attacked by loving, personalized, and engaging actions. Without personal attention the bureaucracy will rule and death will result. Let me give an example. Many social scientists have pondered the ability of the Nazi regime to build and operate the death camps in Germany and Poland from 1939 through 1945 in which millions of humans were murdered. Using Max Weber's theory of the effectiveness of bureaucratic forms of organization, some social scientists concluded that the Nazis succeeded in their campaign for a "final solution" to the problem of inferior races and homosexuality because they understood the principles of bureaucratic domination. In an ideal bureaucracy, all feeling is eliminated. There is no love, hatred, or any other feeling. Employees are simply doing their jobs. They are indifferent to everything except the efficiency of their organization to achieve its goals. The goal of Nazi administrators was effective extermination of Jews, homosexuals, and other "inferior" people. The German people accepted the efficient programs for extermination while at the same time rejecting the random violence against Jews and homosexuals committed by bullies of the SS.

How does this relate to ecotage? Ecotage upsets, disturbs, and distresses ordinary attitudes and policies of officials of giant corporations or government agencies primarily because it is predicated on emotional responses to the situation. It springs from an individual or a small, invisible, unknown (to the bureaucracy) advocacy and affinity group (such as the Bonnie Abzug Feminist Garden Club in Oregon), rather than from a national (and bureaucratized) organization with predictable behavior, such as the Sierra Club.

Kerrick included in the Willamette National Forest report an appropriate Blade Runner cartoon in his analysis of ecotage from the Forest Service perspective. By night the hero of Blade Runner is a samurai warrior spiking trees, by day he dialogues with officials of the U.S. Forest Service.

Ecotage might involve going to the source of the danger, danger to one's homeland or to an ecosystem with which one is attached. Like monkeywrenching, it is ethical behavior when done in self-defense.

In his own nonviolent campaigns, Gandhi further distinguished between the person committing an act and the act itself. A policeman who uses a club to beat a protester at a rally is not labeled a bad person, but the action of beating the protester is a bad act. Hence the norm: "Fight antagonisms, not antagonists." And further: "Do not humiliate or provoke your opponent." This does not mean that the functionary or public agency cannot be the object of fun. Some of the most effective actions of Earth First! cut through the ponderous and cumbersome resource development rhetoric of the U.S. Forest Service to expose the Freddies. Smokey the Bear used in Forest Service campaigns, has been recruited by Earth First! and by Gary Snyder in his "Smokey the Bear Sutra." Even the slogan of the Forest Service, "Land of Many Uses," is reversed by Earth First!ers to "Land of Many Abuses."

Cartoonists poked fun at Secretary of the Interior James Watt during the early 1980s because he represented much of what environmentalists found irresponsible, destructive, and anti-environmental in the administration of President Ronald Reagan. Even with James Watt, environmentalists attempted to follow the Gandhian principle of attempting to find common ground with opponents. Finding common ground, however, does not mean that supporters of deep ecology must speak the language of the bureaucrats or the official rhetoric of the major corporations. Forest Service language, for example, is a foreign tongue in terms of deep ecology. It is the language of Resource Conservation and Development; it is anthropocentric, secular, disenchanted and scientific. When I read one of their environmental impact statements I don't hear the forest or even an ecological version of it. It lacks resonance, authenticity, and even credibility. When the Forest Service EIS on the tussock moth in the Pacific Northwest forests speaks of "pests" in the forest, for instance, I see beautiful insects. When these documents speak of "predator control" I see beautiful mountain lions, bears, and wolves. Refusing to use the language of the opponent is as much an act of resistance as spiking trees in primeval forests to protect them from logging. We protect the integrity of landscapes by speaking of them in the voice of the creative writer, poet, lover of the land. We can find the voice to speak for the forest. We don't have to rely on objectified "newspeak," as George Orwell called the destruction of the English language and its replacement by official disinformation. Finding common ground with opponents does not mean finding common ground on their terms.

In Gandhian direct actions, activists are encouraged to clearly announce their case and the well-defined goal of their campaign, thus distinguishing between non-essential demands and essential ones. Announcing the goal of an environmental campaign may include a call for a new legislative act, stopping a specific timber sale or protecting the habitat of a specific species. During Earth First! actions in Yellowstone National Park, protesters clearly announced that their goal was protection of a definite grizzly habitat. A specific goal was the closing of Fishing Bridge campgrounds, which the Park Service had promised to do in their own master plan for the park. More specific demands, of course, are easier for the general public and many protesters to grasp than general demands which would require great changes in legislation or institutional behavior.

Although ecological resistance is based on how we experience our bioregion, facts about the laws under which corporations or agencies operate are relevant. Part of a campaign may involve trying to ascertain the facts by requiring corporations or agencies to release accurate information on their plans that directly affect the environment.

Nonviolent resistance to misguided government policies has a long history in the U.S.A. (Cooney 1987). But as a political strategy within a larger political movement, the timing, target and goal of non-violent resistance by large numbers of people must be carefully considered. Civil disobedience can be overused and media and decision makers will ignore it. If it encourages discussion of the protesters' grievances and if it facilitates the changing of policies of institutions then it has the intended effect in the political campaign.

According to Gandhi (and Naess who favors the concept of non-violent conflict resolution), the activist should not deliberately harm the property of the opponent. Some ecological activists diverge at this point from Gandhian principles. It would surely be better if a man laid down a knife or a gun by himself by realizing the tragedy he could create. However, if that man is intent on committing rape and you take the knife from him, you have acted in self-defense. Gandhi even thought it acceptable to physically harm a person who attacks one of your dearest friends—provided your personal non-violent power clearly is inadequate.

Naess admits that he has strategic reasons for rejecting monkeywrenching and ecotage in Norway. Norwegians strongly dislike destroying valuable materials. Even after the Nazi occupation of their homeland, the people were against the destruction of any Norwegian factories or property that were used by the Germans to serve their needs (with one exception: a heavy water factory). On the eve of the liberation 9 May 1945, a student set fire to a chair of a professor who was hated for his collaboration with the Germans. People tolerated this "extreme" action, but probably would have turned against burning more of his furniture. When somebody was going to smash a window of another hated collaborator in the center of Oslo, a mass of people objected strongly. They pointed out the excellent quality of the glass! The few cases of ecotage in Norway (alleged or real) have been answered with the loud cry, "Terrorism!" (Letter to author 1987).

In all ecological campaigns, following Gandhian principles, participants "keep in mind and admit" their own factual errors and mistakes in their norms and look for opportunities to correct poor judgments and attitudes.

Monkeywrenching and ecotage are powerful (and personally empowering) actions which require the participant to "step outside of the system," in the words of Dave Foreman (1985), and take responsibility for defending a piece of territory to protect its integrity. "Maybe it [monkeywrenching] is not going to stop everything. Maybe it's not going to change the world, but it's going to buy that place, those creatures, some time. And maybe that's the best that can be done."

Monkeywrenching calls us to a place in our own minds that we have perhaps not visited before, a place of alertness, attention, perception to the whole situation. Foreman's book, *Ecodefense,* is concerned primarily with what he calls "strategic monkeywrenching," which he says is thoughtful, deliberate and safe for participants and other people who might be in the area. Strategic monkeywrenching is used only when attempting to protect areas which are not legally protected as wilderness but have great beauty, biological diversity, integrity of place and wildness and are threatened by some specific action such as road construction, natural resource exploration or energy developments.

According to Foreman, strategic monkeywrenching is based on the following principles:

1. It is nonviolent. "It is not directed towards harming human beings or other forms of life."

2. It is not organized by a formal group. "It is truly individual action."

3. It may be a project of a small affinity group.

4. It is targeted. The focus of activity is specific; for example, stopping or delaying destruction in a specific area as part of a larger strategy to obtain official protection.

5. It is timely. It has a proper place in the total campaign. Monkeywrenchers make a clear and accurate assessment of the political situation.

6. It is dispersed. There is no central clearing house of information on monkeywrenching. No records are kept of operations.

7. It is diverse. Many kinds of people are involved. It is non-elitist. It is *not* paramilitary action.

8. It is fun. "There is a rush of excitement." It can also be very dangerous.

9. It is *not* revolutionary. "It does not aim to overthrow any social, political or economic system. It is merely nonviolent self-defense of the wild."

10. It is simple. "Use the simplest tool and method."

11. It is deliberate and ethical, *not* vandalistic or unpremeditated. "They keep a pure heart and mind about it. They remember that they are engaged in the most moral of all actions: protecting life, defending the Earth." (Foreman 1985)

Animal rights or animal liberation advocates used strategic monkeywrenching and ecotage to rescue hundreds of laboratory animals from cruel and painful experiments. Widespread publicity concerning their actions has aroused a storm of discussion concerning ethical responsibilities of scientists and students toward these animals. Furthermore, the discussion has extended to other facilities such as zoos, fur companies, slaughterhouse operations, and cosmetic corporations using animals to test chemicals. The ripple effect has led to widespread public awareness of behavior that was considered "usual" or "ordinary." Ecotage and monkeywrenching tactics used by animal rights advocates helped unveil some of the assumptions of the dominant society and led to constructive dialogue (Weil 1986).

Specific techniques of monkeywrenching and ecotage are discussed at length in Foreman's book and in the "Ned Ludd" column of the *Earth First!* journal. Techniques should be selected after considering moral and technical factors and the competency of the persons taking part.

I see an analogy between rescuers of Jews and homosexuals in Nazi-occupied Europe and strategic monkeywrenching in the late twentieth century. As part of Dr. Samuel Oliner's academic study of helping behavior during the Holocaust, he interviewed a sample of people who had been rescued, some of the rescuers, as well as people living in the same area as rescuers who did not risk themselves to help victims. Oliner found a number of similarities among rescuers, including an openness of character, willingness to take risks, spontaneity in the desperate situation, personalizing the situation through empathy with the victims, and creativity. He collected many stories of ordinary people who, in extraordinary situations, found ways to help another person not of their own race or religion. These same traits can be applied to practitioners of deep ecology, who are, in a sense, rescuers of the environment.

In sum, nonviolence is a credo (Buddha's *do no harm*) and a way of life (selfless love for all beings). As a mode of action in political disputes, Gandhi called it "truth-force," based on four principles: feeling no ill-will in the heart toward opponent as a person; creating action over an issue that is substantial for the community; being prepared to suffer till the end and to sacrifice everything except honor; and not cooperating in anything that is humiliating.

The Oregon Earth First! movement came to a consensus on the following guidelines which are designed for mass actions involving some people who are not grounded in nonviolence as a way of life but see it as a tactic for social change. Activists might consider these points in their own discussions:

1. Our attitude will be one of openness, friendliness, and respect toward all people we encounter.

2. We will use no violence, verbal or physical, toward any person.

3. We will not damage any property.

4. We will not bring or use drugs or alcohol other than for medical purposes.

5. We will not run.

6. We will carry no weapons.

Each principle deserves considerable discussion in the specific context of a circle of people or an affinity group contemplating nonviolent action.

Dwelling in
Mixed Communities

Athing is right when it tends to preserve the integrity, stability, and beauty of the biotic community. It is wrong when it tends otherwise."
Aldo Leopold, *A Sand County Almanac* (1949)

Arne Naess introduced the term "mixed communities" in 1979 in an article entitled "Self-realization in Mixed Communities of Humans, Bears, Sheep and Wolves" (Naess 1979, 231-241). He discussed a very practical problem in the Norwegian countryside: some wolves and bears were accused of killing a few sheep owned by small farmers. The farmers wanted to shoot wolves and bears. But how many should be shot? Which ones should be shot? Could specific wolves and bears be identified who had killed specific sheep on a specific farm? If a specific killer could be identified, should it be shot or removed to another area, or should the farmer remove his sheep from the area that the predator claimed as its homeland? Environmental groups proposed a national park for wolves in the far north near the Russian border. Some people proposed allowing the wolves to roam throughout the countryside. As of this writing, the issue has not been resolved.

When we start practicing deep ecology in any particular place, we move from the intellectual and philosophical realm of theories to the practical world of individual persons, sheep, wolves, and bears. We make political decisions concerning them. We make choices with real consequences.

Naess makes explicit his concern for individuals in a mixed community. "The way in which I have talked about life-forms and life-styles suggests that it is species and other collective units, not particular living beings which realize potentialities. I do not rule out the possibility of self-realization of collectivities but prefer to think only of particular beings, particular humans, frogs, hookworms."

He continues by contrasting this concern for individuals with the concern some ecologists have for populations of species—especially endangered species.

"Many ecologists lament the preoccupation of ethics with particular specimens instead of populations. They demand a greater ethical concern with populations and animal and human societies, less preoccupation with the fate of individuals. Some add that the highest concern should be for ecosystems, not individuals, societies, or species. What is most needed is system ethics, especially strict ethical norms concerning the destruction of ecosystems. I presuppose in what follows that the arguments of these ecologists are taken seriously, but nevertheless persist in thinking of the realization of the potentials of *particular* living beings" (Naess 1979, 234).

When Naess wrote his short article "The Shallow and Deep, Long-range Ecology Movement," he was careful to state that all members of the community are equal—*in principle*—and added that "any realistic praxis necessitates some killing, exploitation, and suppression." However people with a deep ecology position acquire respect "or even veneration, for ways and forms of life." When we establish a master-slave relationship with other beings, including our domesticated livestock, we contribute to the alienation of ourselves.

Naess defines potentialities in a much broader sense than some other philosophers. At the present time, forms of achievement and lifestyles for humans are greater than those of any other life form on earth. Maximal realization of human potentials depends on a vast number of conditions, including social, environmental, economical, intellectual, physical. Potentials for other beings—such as dogs, cats and other domesticated animals—are sometimes discussed in terms of models of human potential rather than objective potential. Some natural resource managers and people with sentimental attitudes, attempt to save prey from predators—deer from mountain lion. Those who do ignore the lesson of ecology. Everything is related to everything else. Ecology also teaches us "a very brutal lesson: our vast ignorance of the interdependence of life-forms and the often tragic consequences, for the hunted and the oppressed, of the elimination of the hunters and the oppressors. Interference has to be carried out with the utmost care" (Naess 1979, 232).

Another conception of community was stated by Aldo Leopold in *Sand County Almanac*. Leopold's statement of a land ethic is based on respect for all members of the "land community. . . . a land ethic changes the role of *Homo sapiens* from conqueror of the land-community to plain member and citizen of it. It implies respect for his fellow-members and also respect for the community as such." In his definition of the community concept Leopold states that "all ethics so far evolved rest upon a single premise: that the individual is a member of a community with interdependent parts." He continues, "The land ethic simply enlarges the boundaries of the community to include soils, waters, plants, and animals, or collectively: the land" (Leopold 1949, 204).

As stated previously in this book, *living being* is more broadly defined than a species of animals or plants and may include a watershed or the associated community of plants and animals in their place.

Some critics of Leopold's land ethic note that he uses both community and organism as metaphors in his discussion. And, these critics contend, this kind of equivocation can cause problems in developing appropriate models of environmental ethics. Leopold is particularly concerned with the integrity of land communities and wrote extensively on the worth of wilderness—environments that are untrammeled by humans (see Callicott 1987).

In conceptual terms the difference between community and organism concerns the relative autonomy of individual parts. In the model of an organism, individual parts are not independent beings but are functioning units of the whole. Parts of an organism lack in inherent worth. They are not members of the organism but are units of the organic whole. In a community model, individuals have relative autonomy and relationships with other individuals. Individuals are both members and functioning units of the community (see Katz 1985).

When we use the organism model, humans can substitute parts in an ecosystem and still have a functioning ecosystem. For example, an exotic species may be substituted for a native species and fill the ecological niche. Burros introduced by miners in the nineteenth century in the area now inside in the boundaries of Grand Canyon National Park filled an ecological niche once held exclusively by native grazing animals such as bighorn sheep. However, the introduction of burros led to the decline of big horn sheep to the point the species is threatened with extinction in the park.

The integrity of the system and of many native species is violated by substitution. When native gum forests in Australia are burned and the charred remains bulldozed away to make room for vast plantations of Monterey pines (native to California), then native Australian species of birds and animals are displaced and the evolutionary processes in native forests are compromised. The mixed community has both instrumental and intrinsic value. When humans displace native forests and introduce exotic trees with the primary instrumental purpose of supporting cellulose factories, then the ecotopian ideal underlying the vision of mixed community presented in this chapter is violated.

The phrase "dwelling in mixed communities" implies consideration of instrumental functions, vital needs of individuals, the potentialities of individual beings, the community as a whole, the intrinsic worth of all members of the community, and our own sense-of-place as discussed in chapter 2.

In the following sections some practical examples of mixed communities and some of the ethical and lifestyle implications of dwelling in mixed communities are presented. Four types of situations in the biosphere are discussed—wilderness, restoration and recovery areas, sacrifice areas, and cities.

These categories are heuristic rather than scientific. They illustrate different types of situations which require application of abstract philosophical principles. In level four situations, as described in chapter 1, philosophy is embedded in social (including legal and economic) framework. Philosophy is connected to daily life through decisions made in specific situations. We are in the process of building a code for our relationships with other beings. We can expect reasonable disagreements even among the most ardent supporters of deep ecology. We cannot work out all the details of an acceptable code solely on the basis of philosophical principles. Laypersons, experts, philosophers, and educators all have necessary roles in these discussions. Practicing deep ecology within specific bioregions requires making moral, ethical decisions on a wide variety of relationships.

Human-induced Changes

From a deep ecology position, change wrought by human interference in ecosystems or species habitats is of a qualitatively different type than changes due to volcanic eruptions, hurricanes, floods, droughts, and other so-called "natural catastrophes." Especially aberrant are changes such as nuclear warfare, massive use of herbicides and pesticides, transformation of complex systems into monocultures, and manipulation of genetic material through biotechnology.

Dwelling in a mixed community means exploring our ecological self within the community, not apart from it. Environmental ethics (a misnomer, but widely used term) develop out of intimate relationships with other members of the community. Aldo Leopold states, as a basis for his version of the land ethic, that "we can be ethical only in relation to something we can see, feel, understand, love, or otherwise have faith with" (Leopold 1949, 214).

In practical experience, a real community is a mixed one. The ideal community is one of harmony with nature. This vision of mixed community inspires us and draws us away from the shallow and narrowly anthropocentric concerns of contemporary society.

We need more visions of the deep mixed community, ecotopian visions. Our visions of the ideal, however, are not based on an idealized "balance of nature." As Leopold notes, if we use the balance of nature metaphor we assume that we know more than we really do. Nature is not only more complex than we know, it may be more complex than we *can* know. This is a law of ecology, as stated by Barry Commoner in *The Closing Circle* (1971), which recalls into the modern search for ecosophy the ancient truth of Taoism: the Tao that can be named is not the Tao.

How do we formulate relevant questions concerning the most important aspects of dwelling in mixed communities? Conventional questions in human ecology begin from utilitarian perspectives. We are accustomed to asking technical, narrow questions based on conventional assumptions. For example, we ask, "How can we utilize wind to efficiently and economically produce electricity to power our factories and heat our homes?" But questions in my version of deep ecology include: how can we live with the wind? How can we think like the wind? How can we dwell in a place relating to seasonal changes in wind velocity and direction?

We are not just managers, stewards or tyrants of the mixed community. Nor do we want just to serve the narrow, egotistical desires of our minimal self. Besides having incomplete models of ecosystems, we harbor undiscovered and probably unpleasant motives for many of our actions.

Experts trained in social science, forestry, wildlife management, hydrology, agri-industry, etc., will leap into the discussion at this point and offer many definitions and theories of the habitat needs of this or that creature. All well and good. They should use their expert knowledge to help human citizens of the mixed communities to clarify the situation. But many theories of the experts are based on assumptions which form a human-centered ideology of ecosystem needs.

We can, as pointed out by Edward Goldsmith, editor of the *Ecologist*, rehabilitate ecological succession as a general framework for talking about the process of building mixed communities within which humans can begin dwelling more fully. As Goldsmith summarizes this ecological law, it states "that ecosystems develop in a series of stages which must all occur in the right order—a process referred to as 'succession' which continues until a 'climax' is reached—a situation from which there is then little change as it is the most stable one achievable in the circumstances."

There are several versions of the succession theory. What is most important, Goldsmith says, "is that the changes brought about by industrial man are, in fact, reversing ecological succession, that is why we must consider industrial development or 'progress' as an anti-evolutionary process. . . . By reversing ecological succession it is giving rise to ever greater ecological instability." And after being devastated by activities derived from principles of techno-scientific civilization, an ecosystem will then be in a state that ecologist Eugene Odum calls *disclimax* (a disturbance climax) (Goldsmith, "Ecologist," 1985, 104-112).

This is unsatisfactory. The general principle is to be moving toward climax in order to serve the well-being of the mixed community.

Another important principle is to work with the process of the ecosystem and not to put undue emphasis on the products or commodities which some humans derive from that ecosystem. Process refers to the interrelationships which at any given time have developed through evolution and geological, climactic changes to shape the landscape we know. Humans in most areas on the earth, except for oceans far from land areas, have become a major shaping influence (see Thomas 1956).

I am taking the position of what Mark Sagoff calls a "bioconservative." Bioconservatives seek less, not more, human intervention in ecosystems. They seek ways of living lightly on the land rather than forcing the land to meet the unrealistic expectations of some humans. In contrast, "biotechnologists" believe that much of nature can be improved or enhanced by humans. For example, fish production in rivers, lakes or the ocean can be increased through biotechnology by the cloning of "superior" fish or actual manipulation of DNA to produce larger species or ones suited for particular environmental conditions (see Sagoff 1986).

Natural evolution, of course, requires death and change. Some species will become extinct in the course of natural history. Humans will continue to intervene to some extent in certain regions of the Earth. Bioconservatives oppose the massive destructive interventions which are characteristic of techno-scientific civilization.

Scientists cannot fully describe the consequences of massive human intervention, but the cumulative impact is rapidly changing the state of the biosphere and ecosphere.

As extraordinary members of the mixed community, humans have great obligations to the whole, even when other members of the community do not reciprocate as moral agents. This is consistent with biocentric egalitarianism properly defined.

The great task of this and future generations of humans (for this is surely a long-term process) is the reconstruction of the mixed community. Our central convictions are in disorder, and both metaphysical reconstruction and practical reconstruction and restoration where possible are necessary for the health and maximization of potentials of individuals and the community as a whole.

Ironically, the future of relations between humans and other members of the mixed community may be decided in a potato patch in a remote area of California or in the rain forests of Amazonia before supporters of deep ecology can effectively stabilize relationships. The future of the community is problematic, as contrasts between the vision of mixed community presented here and the techno-scientific, "new age" vision of human domination of the whole biotic community illustrates. In order to dramatize the condition within which supporters of deep ecology must work, I want to describe an incident which occurred in 1987.

Experimenting with Evolution

In May 1987 researchers working for the University of California released a genetically altered bacteria (*Peudomonas syringae*) onto a potato patch near Tule Lake, California. This "ice nucleation minus" research field test was the first time in which scientists had legally released organisms altered through biotechnology into California land. The environmental impact statement written on this experiment did not discuss the historic situation in which the experiment was conceived and executed (Ice Nucleation Minus Research Field Test, Draft Environmental Impact Statement 1986).

While scientists were developing ice minus to prevent freezing of some crops, other scientists estimated that one species a day, somewhere on this earth, became extinct as a result of human actions, mostly as a result of conventional, everyday activities including road building, farming, burning forests, logging, dam building and grazing domesticated livestock (Myers 1984; Ehrlich 1981; Wolf 1987; Michael Fox 1987).

Purposeful genetic tampering is yet another way humans can change species. Release of genetically altered organisms into the environment is regulated in the United States. Once such an altered organism is released into the environment it could spread and be impossible to eradicate. While the whole enterprise of genetic engineering has been criticized by Jeremy Rifkin *(Algeny)* and others, who conclude that our pell mell rush into the age of genetic engineering shows dangerous hubris and a will to have power over nature, some scientists have deliberately introduced altered organisms into the environment without prior approval from the Environmental Protection Agency.

The fast developing biotechnology industry and the rising species extinction rate are two aspects of a rapidly changing biosphere. Ever since humans began using fire, the human species has been an important factor in the evolution of local areas. In the late twentieth century, however, the human species has become more and more important in the earth's system, in the biosphere.

When V. I. Vernadsky, a Russian mineralogist, published his book *The Biosphere* in 1929, he defined the biosphere as that portion of earth within which life exists, including the litosphere (a layer of earth approximately three kilometers deep), the hydrosphere (oceans), and the troposphere (lower atmosphere). All living matter is the organic product of the biosphere (Vernadsky 1945, 4).

Walter Truett Anderson, a political scientist and author of *To Govern Evolution* (1987), says we are in the midst of a turbulent era during which humans have become conscious of their impact on the biosphere and have begun to develop a global system of governance of the biosphere. Furthermore, the chief actors in the world polis, including corporations, national government agencies, environmental groups, and scientists, have begun to gather and publish enormous amounts of information about the biosphere, to develop models and theories of human impact, and to negotiate treaties, laws, agreements, and contracts which drastically change the life situation of many species of plants and animals.

Humans are also intentionally altering the evolution of their own species through genetic transfer, surrogate motherhood, artificial insemination, and other procedures.

We affect the conditions of whole ecosystems as seen with the changes induced by acid rain in areas of North American and Europe.

We are rapidly altering the biomass of the earth through transfer of genetic material from one continent to another, human-induced extinctions, intentional alteration of many types of ecosystems, genetic erosion resulting from habitat loss, mutations and biotechnology (Anderson 1987; Elkington 1985).

Biologists, writing on the domestication of evolution, conclude that it is not just human folly or stupidity—such as over-hunting, polluting, dumping toxic wastes—that is increasing the rate of species extinction. The most important agent of extinction is the biological success of humans and their domesticated plants and animals. The increase in numbers of human and domestic species, is inversely proportional to the number of wild species that can share a limited environment and supply of energy.

Coppinger and Smith predict that "as human population may double in a little less than 40 years and cattle in a little over 40 years, before the year 2020 we and domestic beasts may make up approximately two-fifths of the world's territorial animal biomass. . . . By the middle of the next century, then, we can expect, at the very least, that about three-fifths of all terrestrial animal biomass and about one-fourth of all plant life will be composed of humans and a few domesticated species."

These authors suggest that "the perhaps-too-successful symbiosis among humans, livestock, pets, and plants, is a natural phenomenon—indeed, an adaptive strategy of evolutionary origin and significance." In a protected community, as for example between Monterey pines and humans on forest plantations, commercial orange groves and humans, or between dogs and humans, the domesticated species is spread more widely and develops greater biomass than any wild populations of the same species.

Specialized species which adapt to specific ecological niches are outreproduced by interdependent, less specialized forms. "The fittest still survive, but despecialized inter-dependencies among species is a newly important strategy in nature and is redefining the concept of 'fit.' " They conclude that we may be entering an age of interdependent forms marked by a massive rate of human-induced extinction of specialized forms and increasing biomass of species exhibiting neotenic (juvenile) forms. Humans intentionally select tamer genotypes in domestication of animals and thus select more youthful behavior (Coppinger and Smith 1983, 283-291).

While Coppinger and Smith's conclusion is not universally accepted by evolutionary biologists and ecologists, it illustrates the turbulent situation of the biosphere within which environmentalists and supporters of deep ecology must act.

What should supporters of deep ecology do when they participate in global political movements? What does it mean to dwell ecologically in a mixed community of humans and genetically changed beings?

The deep, long-range ecology movement as stated earlier is only partly political. It is primarily a spiritual-religious movement. Tendencies toward a deep ecology position are found in many reform environmental groups, feminist movements, peace movements, and bioregional movements. Each of these has spokespeople who express various opinions on the global commons and the emerging system of governance of the biosphere.

Some new age theorists and biologists suggest that humans are becoming the "business managers of evolution." This position has been criticized as anthropocentric and dangerous because it emphasizes power without humility, knowledge without wisdom, and technology rather than ontology. It is evident, however, that only clear policies and commitment will slow the mass extinction currently underway.

I make no predictions concerning the long-term outcome of the human experiment on this earth. However, given the deep ecology assertion that humans can have a full rich life without unduly destroying other life forms, it is natural that supporters of deep ecology engage in intricate politics of biosphere management.

Even with a sudden transformation by hundreds of millions of people to ecological consciousness, the changes already underway which are human-caused will drastically alter the biosphere, and policies may continue to be unecological, even if the majority sympathize with the deep ecology position.

Wilderness

As I write these lines, the U.S. Secretary of the Interior is attempting to open the Arctic Wildlife Refuge on the north slope of Alaska to oil and gas exploration and leasing. Since Earthday 1970, humans have continued killing endangered whales to the most remote ocean areas of the Earth, even though it is economically inefficient to continue whaling. According to Day, only subsidies from the Japanese government keep the whaling fleets of several nations on the ocean (Day 1987). Tropical rain forests have been clear-cut at a rate equal to the size of the state of West Virginia each year, even though it is well documented that many development projects in those areas are not sustainable economically or socially (see Myers 1985; Rich 1985; Caufield 1985).

Since the activities of government agencies and huge corporations are worldwide, the environmental movement has become a worldwide network of movements and organizations using their own sophisticated tactics and strategies to resist the plundering of the last wild areas on Earth.

Supporters of deep ecology from all religious, philosophical, and political positions combine to defend wilderness for, as Henry Thoreau proclaimed over a hundred years ago, "in wilderness is the preservation of the world."

Vast areas of the Earth, whole continents—including Antarctica—should be declared "off limits" to massive invasions of military, scientific and corporate raiders who seek to extract minerals, oil and gas or other resources from the Earth's last wild places. Preservation is the highest priority of political activism from a deep ecology viewpoint.

Wild plants and animals, mountains, rivers, coastal and freshwater wetlands, deserts, islands all change and evolve in their own ways irrespective of the monetary or aesthetic value any human puts on them. Ecological communities coevolve in wilderness. New species develop to fill ecological niches. In the words of Nancy Newhall, "wilderness holds answers to questions men have not yet begun to ask." Some of these questions are scientific or ecological, some of them spiritual.

Designated Wilderness is a social institution. There are several forms of it, including national parks, nature reserves, biosphere reserves. In the U.S.A., federally controlled land or water areas have been assigned wilderness status by the U.S. Congress since 1964 when the federal Wilderness Act was passed (see Allin 1982).

Designated and de facto (usually defined as roadless areas in the U.S.A.) Wilderness areas have been called islands of hope, ecological sanctuaries, sacred places, and areas of land health. Some ecologists collect data in Designated Wilderness to compare with data collected in the Damaged Lands to see the effects human have on landscapes.

For advocates of Designated Wilderness, the attempts to use this institution to preserve wilderness is one side of a two-sided movement. Ultimately contemporary nations could be transformed into a graceful civilization based on a new ecological paradigm. In the interim we can work to designate vast areas of the earth as Wilderness to protect them. In particular, wilderness advocates seek to protect all types of ecosystems from Arctic to tropical rain forest and to maintain the centers of Earth's ecological diversity.

Big Wilderness is defined in several ways, but a minimum size, according to Dave Foreman of Earth First!, is 100,000 acres. A more important criteria, in my estimation, is that entire watersheds, mountain ranges, river estuaries, continents, islands and the surrounding ocean, be designated as Wilderness.

The international wilderness movement is campaigning with agencies of the United Nations and various national governments to designate all of the Antarctic continent and adjacent ocean as a World Wilderness—off limits to oil and natural gas or mineral development, nuclear waste deposits, harvesting of marine mammals or krill, and permanent human habitation.

Many organizations are working to protect remaining rain forest areas as ecological reserves. It is estimated that one-half of all species on earth currently are found in tropical and subtropical rain forests. Yet at current rates of deforestation, very little rain forest will remain within fifty years.

Many proposals to develop, or humanize, de facto wilderness are predicated on our greed, ignorance, lust for power, military objectives, or wrong assumptions about the ability of natural resources found in de facto wilderness to solve pressing problems of poverty, military security, or population.

Like many other institutions in our civilization, Designated Wilderness poses some dilemmas. It is subject to bureaucratic control, inadequate enforcement of regulations, and political conflicts based on issues which are not central to wilderness preservation. But this institution is a tool for protecting the integrity of wild places and for teaching ecophilosophy and deep ecology. Designated Wilderness is a sanctuary for wild beings and for confused humans seeking to cultivate ecological consciousness. Defending wilderness is an affirmation of our connections with wild nature, both metaphysically and ecologically. Defending wildlife in their habitat affirms the inherent worth of other species.

Attitudes, policies and behavior of sports enthusiasts and government agencies towards wildlife and its habitat is crucial to its survival. Furthermore, attitudes toward wildlife show whether a person has a biocentric rather than anthropocentric position.

In the 1980s under the policies of the Reagan administration, many federal agencies embarked on pro-development programs and minimized protection of habitat for threatened, rare or endangered species. Experts arguing over what is a "minimal viable population" of spotted owls, California condors or grizzly bears, were under political pressure to reduce estimates of some species' habitat needs to allow some areas to be developed to serve narrow human purposes such as building vacation homes in grizzly habitat or clear-cutting old growth forests and replanting those areas with monoculture tree plantations.

Establishing Designated Wilderness where large-scale development projects are prohibited is the major land use policy issue facing the global community during the next twenty years. There is considerable scientific evidence that large-scale human intervention into remaining tropical rain forests and natural resource development in Arctic regions are disrupting ecological communities and will not serve the needs of masses of urban dwellers for more than a few decades (until the oil is depleted in the Alaskan north slope or until soil depletion and erosion occurs in Amazonia.) Native peoples (the fourth world) and biological diversity will be severely depleted unless strong legal, political, and military protection of wilderness is provided during the next two decades.

I am using the term *wilderness* here to mean relatively unstressed, untrammeled, and undisturbed habitat for wild species of plants and animals, that has been protected and preserved. Interactions among different species give ecosystems integrity and only ecosystem-based wilderness protection can preserve these complex interactions. Fragmentation of natural habitats can lead to "living dead" species— species which remain for some years in human-modified habitats but have no viable population for reproduction to sustain the species or viable interactions in the ecosystem so that evolutionary processes can continue.

Many initiatives already proposed and programs already in existence can provide a foundation for national and international strategies to avert mass extinction of species and destruction of habitat areas. One of the greatest cultural achievements of our civilization will be the marshaling of financial, political, and social resources to develop and implement effective policies to protect biological diversity. This will require concerted effort by professional biologists, ecologists, wildlife scientists, and other researchers in academia to educate policy makers and the lay public on the need for protection of biological diversity as the highest priority for conservation in the 1990s. This work has already begun through such organizations as the Association for Conservation Biology and the national conference on biodiversity held in Washington, D.C., in 1986 (see Wilson 1988).

New initiatives are required in the law and in management of wildlands. Policies based on ecosystem models rather than only on individual species protection, as in the U.S. Endangered Species Act, may shift thinking of managers away from specific species to models of human interactions with ecosystems.

Financial resources are needed to implement existing programs and to fund proposed land acquisition and conservation easement proposals. As a point of discussion, in California, which is projected to have thirty million human inhabitants by the year 2000, I suggest that a dollar of public funds (through sale of bonds or direct appropriations of the legislature) be spent on habitat acquisition and conservation easements on rare, threatened, and endangered ecosystems for every dollar spent on building new prisons or highways for the next decade. This proposal would yield several billion dollars a year for the next ten years. Private organizations, such as the Nature Conservancy, are only able to raise and spend several million dollars a year in a program of acquiring lands for preservation.

Norman Myers, the biologist and author of *The Sinking Ark* and *The Primary Source,* in his Horace M. Albright Lecture at the University of California-Berkeley (1986) calls the protection of ecosystems and species from mass extinction "a great creative challenge. . . . No generation in the past has faced the prospect of mass extinction before. No generation in the future will ever face a similar challenge: if this present generation fails to get to grips with the task, the damage will have been done and there will be no second try."

Although programs and laws can provide a foundation in society for embarking on a path away from mass extinctions, radical departures in our way of thinking about nature and in established land use policies and management priorities in well-established public land managing organizations such as the U.S. Forest Service, are required.

An example of this kind of radical departure is found in the "modest proposal" by Dave Foreman and Earth First! activists for an American Wilderness Preserve System (Foreman 1985). The first priority of this system is protection of intact ecosystems. General guidelines for preserves include:

• No permanent human habitation except, in some cases, indigenous people living traditional (pre-1500 A.D.) lifestyles.
• No use of mechanized equipment or vehicles.

- No roads.
- No logging, mining, water diversion, industrial activity, agriculture, or grazing of domestic livestock.
- No use of artificial chemical substances.
- No control of wildfires (except during a transition period if needed to return to a natural fire regime).
- Reintroduction of extirpated species.
- Removal of exotic species where possible.
- Dismantling, removal, or destruction of dams, roads, power lines, buildings, structures, toxic substances, etc., where feasible, or allowing them to deteriorate otherwise (over time).
- No overflights by aircraft.
- Elimination of outside adverse influences such as acid rain.
- Priority given to preservation of the ecosystem and native species over the safety and convenience of the human visitor.
- Limited corridors may be designated in some preserves for necessary pre-existing transportation, utility, and communications systems.

Foreman says that the Earth First! draft for a Wilderness Preserve System "allows meaningful wildness to coexist with human civilization on the North American continent. Of course it is ambitious, even visionary. But it is impractical and outrageous only in the context of the bizarre utilitarian philosophy which separates one specie (Homo sapiens) from its place in the biosphere and from its relationship with the land community and life cycles of the entire planet." (Draft available from Earth First! P.O. Box 5871, Tucson, AZ 85703.)

Damaged Lands

The second land use situation involves those lands which could provide vital needs (food, timber, water) for a small human population using appropriate technology.

Damaged Lands (Restoration and Recovery Areas) include much of the land and water and some of the air space used by industry and government. Damage comes in the form of degradation, erosion, or pollution. I have seen no convincing evidence indicating that preservation of wilderness, and thus the world, and further imperialistic expansion of our civilization are compatible. The integrity of most wilderness is jeopardized by our continued economic and population expansion. A noninclusive list of negative impacts includes bulldozing roads, acid rain from sources in cities hundreds of miles distant from wilderness areas, oil and gas development, mineral extraction, building of power lines, dam building, geothermal development, hydroelectric development on streams, recreational use of off-road vehicles on delicate wetlands, deserts, etc., residues of toxic chemicals, grazing by domesticated animals, and radiation from atmospheric testing of nuclear weapons. The probable destruction of many, if not most, of the mammals in the U.S.A. as a result of unlimited nuclear war has been projected in several recent studies.

Within the context of their own bioregion, people can ask the following questions: how can we dwell with our machines in a sustainable way while serving the vital needs of the mixed community? What principles can we use for fishing, agriculture, forestry, grazing practices, and mining as well as energy production? Appropriate strategies can be developed in each bioregion.

Destructive human impacts on fragile areas—islands, estuaries, forests, high mountain regions, deserts, prairie pothole regions, riparian habitats—are well documented. In North America, logging corporations and agriculturalists, in the name of increasing production or bringing more land into production, have within a short period of time reduced wildlife and native plant habitat by 90 percent or more in some bioregions.[1]

For some areas of the earth information has been collected on the habitat requirements of some species of wildlife and plants, although the data is incomplete. This information is useful in determining vital needs and should be utilized any time significant human impact on a region is proposed.[2]

A third situation includes those areas which could be returned to land health and used primarily for human habitation and to supply vital human needs. In protecting land health, Leopold emphasized the importance of native plants—those inhabitating a region especially before European colonization began in the sixteenth century. "The native plants and animals kept the energy circuit open; others may or may not." He then asks: "Can the land adjust itself to the new orders? Can the desired alterations be accomplished with less violence?" (Leopold 1949, 218)

Harold Koopowitz describes in *Plant Extinction* the impact of the introduction of goats on islands in the Atlantic by European sailors after 1500. Goats pillaged, despoiled and ravaged continental land masses and islands. They defoliated all plants within reach and climbed into bushes and scrambled up trees to reach the green parts. After 1500 A.D., they were introduced onto almost all islands as they were discovered by Europeans. They were considered fresh meat on the hoof and could fend for themselves, reproduce easily and grow in numbers in the absence of large predators.

The island of St. Helena located in the south Atlantic Ocean is an example of the impact of goats. They were introduced to the island in 1513 by the Portuguese. Originally covered by forests, by 1800 only the central ridge of the island contained remnant forest. A nineteenth-century botanist, J. D. Hooker, estimated there were one hundred endemic species on the island before the introduction of goats. After the goats were wiped out in the 1950s, thirty-three endemic species were identified of which eighteen were classified as endangered (Koopowitz 1983, 93).

What guidelines can we use to determine when to leave exotic species, or attempt to eradicate them? Generally, our ecosystem models are developed without reference to historic uses of a region by humans. Given the extreme impacts on many regions by European settlement and introduction of domesticated animals and a few varieties of plants for crops, forage, etc., a guideline I find appropriate is to try to determine species diversity at the time of European contact and consider that as possibly a near climax community. Of course Native Americans or Aborigines in Australia over the course of 35,000 years had drastic impacts. These impacts are difficult to determine with accuracy. The time of European contact provides a baseline for data. Programs to remove exotics which have become an integral part of the landscape are difficult, but possible. These procedures are recommended and necessary in order to restore the bioregion to a stable condition.

However, in an extreme, near disclimax circumstance, such as the Sahel region of Africa, which is becoming a desert due to overgrazing, drought, increasing human population, and diversion of water sources by humans, some experts recommend introducing exotic species which include rapidly growing trees, nitrogen-fixing plants, and drought resistant plants. These would rapidly increase the biomass and possibly stabilize eroding areas and provide forage for livestock. A drastic human-caused destruction in a landscape requires drastic, sometimes experimental measures.

Permaculture is one agricultural approach which emphasizes humans living within constraints of natural systems. Australian Bill Mollison coined this term to emphasize human participation in a design process with nature. The practice excludes hard path agricultural technologies, (massive use of herbicides, for instance) but encourages soft path principles, such as companion planting and use of perennials, fruit trees and year-round gardening. One description of permaculture principles is presented by Dan Hemenway, the editor of the *International Permaculture Seed Yearbook,* an ongoing exploration of sustainable agricultural practices. Hemenway emphasizes humility and respect for the natural way in which things happen. Nothing is forced, nothing is rushed. When in doubt, the best guideline seems to be, wait a while (Hemenway 1985).

Dan Hemenway's Principles of Design

1. *Do only what is necessary.* Have respect for the natural way in which things happen.

2. *Multiply purposes.* Never do anything for only one reason.

3. *Be redundant.* There is always a variety of pathways by which an ecosystem can proceed about its business.

4. *Check your scale.* Design and act within an appropriate size frame.

5. *Work with edges.* Straight lines have far less edge than waves.

6. *Encourage diversity.* Diversity design allows both stacking and repeating of function.

7. *Look both ways before crossing.* Death of individual cells is necessary for the life of other cells.

8. *The gift must always move.* To survive and be well and joyous, we must transform and give away all gifts which come to us.

The general rule: develop mixed communities based on experiencing our place, rather than imposing on the place. Recently some exponents of permaculture have begun exploring the ramifications of native plant permaculture. Rather than relying on use of exotic species, these proponents use native species to increase biomass. There are many issues involved in using native plants, not the least of which is the definition of *native.* In some regions plants and animals may be acclimated to a small territory. Some species introduced by humans to a region might hybridize with native plants. This is one of the dilemmas faced by land managers which must be resolved in their own bioregion based on their own wisdom.

For example, European settlers to Australia after 1788 carried with them a vision of an English pastoral landscape, a humanized nineteenth-century landscape where wild nature was reduced to small sections of remote mountains and native species reduced to living in hedgerows planted by farmers. In Australia, Europeans introduced deer, rabbits, pigs, sheep, and cattle. Only in the late twentieth century did some Australians begin to more fully understand and experience native wildlife and forests on that continent (Mosley 1977).

In New Zealand in the nineteenth century only a few naturalists studied the natural diversity of the island's flora and fauna. But during the past half century biologists, laypeople and some foresters have formed associations to defend native species and their habitat, and to urge government action to retain the remaining native forests for their own sake as well as the values that humans derive from them (see Crosby 1986; Wilson 1982).

Aldo Leopold spent some of his life in the sand counties of central Wisconsin, where he bought a farm which had been abused by several generations of farmers. These farmers, practicing a kind of land exploitation common in the nineteenth century, increased the rate of soil erosion, disrupted natural succession cycles, and replaced complex native ecosystems with a disclimax of a few cereal grain crops for their animals. Leopold considered his experience on this farm an experiment. He studied the needs of the land in hopes of finding ways to restore what he called "land health." He realized that practicing management of human-damaged ecosystems engages a person in an ironic dilemma. The human manager makes adjustments in natural systems, hoping to restore them to become self-regulating so that adjustments by humans, at some future time will be unnecessary. The land restoration movement consists of healers, rather than stewards of the land. Stewards seek to optimize profits for themselves or their bosses. Healers seek to restore their own integrity as part of, not a part from, the integrity of the land. An active restoration movement has been developing in North America, Australia, and New Zealand as well as some other nations, where many people are working on the land, mindful that long, diligent practice will be required to understand the wounds. One aim of combining restoration with deep ecology principles is largely to assist the healers in feeling a part of a land community, and not so alone. The restoration movement is partly based on our experience, partly on intuition, partly on the insights of scientific ecology and biology, and partly on the commitment of scientists to engage the task of creating a conservation biology, which provides healers with scientific models of helping the land move toward a climax situation.

As emphasized throughout this book, supporters of deep ecology are in the service of their place—their bioregion or Earth as a whole. The broad, deep self-in-Self includes identification with the Damaged Lands as well as the pristine wilderness.

John Berger defines restoration as "a process in which a damaged resource or region is renewed. Biologically. Structurally. Functionally." He says that restoration is not traditional environmentalism or preservation. Restoration means not only stopping pollution but replacing missing components of the ecosystem. In particular, native plants are sown and soil is rebuilt with fungi and mosses. Endangered species are returned to their habitat, and the resulting resource is not only aesthetically pleasing but sustains new jobs for humans (Berger 1985, 5).

Such a vision is admirable and Berger tells many inspiring stories of people working on a specific river or land form, often times working alone or with a small group of comrades, with a passionate commitment to heal the Damaged Lands. *Restoration Notes,* a magazine providing technical and theoretical discussions of damaged ecosystem recovery, carries many stories about experiments which engaged people in their own bioregion. Restoration workers seldom receive monetary reward for their work and very little public recognition. But they tend to have a deep sense-of-place and commitment to their work.

One strategy for planning restoration and recovery of damaged areas would be to hold local and regional assemblies of ecologically aware citizens. Assessing the needs of the mixed community would not be left to experts or bureaucratic agencies. In order to mitigate impacts on the human community, economic studies could be undertaken to devise projects of employment and resource use.

A model restoration worker is found in Steve Sorensen. Sorensen worked for ten years building roads and bridges and fighting fires in the Sierra Nevada backcountry of California. But after employment in national parks, domesticating the landscape, he concluded: "I began to realize that we had already built too many things in these mountains. How do you reverse the process? How do you go from being a builder of things, to an unbuilder? . . . There is no such thing as building a wilderness. There isn't even such a thing as rehabilitating a damaged wilderness. It's just patchwork cosmetics. The best we can hope for is to destroy man's patterns in the wilderness. Then the real work will be done by nature, in due time" (Sorensen 1985, 28-32).

The restoration movement in North America supports many approaches. David Kaplow, director of Design Associates Working with Nature in Berkeley, California, shows the uses of appealing to various constituencies on their own terms, rather than on our terms as supporters of deep ecology.

Kaplow says that while in graduate school he thought there would be many firms where he could find work. "To my surprise, I found there are very few organizations in California doing this work at all. As a result, much of the basic restoration research has not been done, and the information that has been developed is badly in need of being organized and presented in a coherent form."

"Meeting the expectations of the land" is a phrase used by Wes Jackson and Wendell Berry (1985) in a collection of essays on agriculture. Jackson is a farmer who founded the Land Institute on the Kansas prairie. He has developed a practice of introducing perennial grasses as a possible food crop for humans. Wendell Berry is a farmer, essayist, poet who lives in Kentucky.

"Meeting the expectations of the land" could be a principle for a deep ecology approach to Damaged Lands. Robert Brothers (Bobcat) suggests another principle: "meeting the survival needs of the community of indigenous species of the land."

In discussing the sustainable agricultural systems of North America which serve vital human needs with minimal disruption of the well-being of other beings, Alan Drengson suggests the term "ecoagriculture" (Drengson 1985, 18). Instead of thinking of productivity, mechanization, management of labor, input and output for a market of some agricultural commodity, ecoagriculturalists think of soil fertility, needs of the mixed community, land health, sustainable human relationships with a specific place, and the real work. Ecoagriculturalists take their commitment as a way of life, not as just a job.

Many terms have been used to refer to ecologically sound agriculture and to dwelling as an agriculturalist in the land community—organic gardening, sustainable agriculture, natural farming, agroecology, and regenerative agriculture are only some. While differing in specific methods and practice and while some are more anthropocentric in orientation than others, all these systems "reflect the underlying philosophy that nature knows best, that all things are interconnected, that every benefit has some cost, that everything has to go some place, that we have to understand holistically in terms of process. Also, that there is a proper time and place for things" (Drengson 1985, 19).

Activities of humans in mixed communities—humans engaged in recreation, farming, ranching, fishing, forestry, natural resource exploitation—fit into larger patterns and cycles. Some of these cycles we can infer through observations with our scientific instruments. Thus we might fit into the dynamic cycles of climate—drought, wetness, ice ages, etc. Some of these cycles are cosmic.

An example of working within cycles, of meeting the expectations of the land, is given by Bobcat, who lives in a Pacific Northwest forest region. He argues that the agriculture model is not appropriate for managing lowland temperate forests of the Pacific Northwest.

In a community near Galice, Oregon, Bobcat lives near other people who at one time were members of the counterculture of the 1960s. He says:

> It does not surprise me that some people involved in the counterculture movement of the '60s on the west coast migrated to woodland areas of the Pacific Northwest. The forests themselves became our teachers. The forest, even second growth douglas fir forest, is awesome. We began to ask—what can we take that the forest itself can replenish rather than how can we maximize a profit off this land? People began making shelters out of standing trees.
>
> We see the forest as a teacher. The healthy forest ecosystem is a self-reliant community which does not need to depend upon other regions for the joys and necessities of life.
>
> The healthy forest ecosystem and the practice of sustainable forestry can provide an appropriate model for the interaction of basically self-reliant bioregions with each other—in a world where human society parallels the patterns of Nature. . . . If we can learn to practice with each other the kind of all-species gardening which nature practices so well in the forest, then we will be at peace with the diversity in our society. [Bobcat prefers the phrase "all-species gardening" to sustainable agriculture because it allows the full recognition of the inherent worth of all beings.]
>
> Those of us who care need to make clear that as food producers, our concern is not only for our crops, but for all species native to each place. This means that before choosing a piece of ground to nurture for our sustenance, we must first look at the full context in which our intervention will take place.
>
> Meeting the expectations of the land must begin with the bottom line of all-species survival. In fact, the present ecological crisis may provide the only justification for any form of agriculture. So much land has been scarred, deforested,

desertified, and poisoned, that only the ancient processes of evolution operating on the scale of geologic time can hope to heal the wounds—unless some humble, respectful people intervene now to patch the wounds and contain the toxins.

Where I live . . . food production is mainly dependent on irrigation throughout the dry, rainless summer months. Unfortunately, this practice is untenable for the fish such as salmon and steelhead. Water withdrawals for irrigation lower the summer stream flows and raise the stream temperatures above tolerable limits. Out of respect for all species, food crops need to be grown in the mild winters, when rain is abundant, and the fields be dry-farmed or left fallow in the summer drought. As far as I know such a proposal has yet to be made by anyone in the Pacific Northwest. (Interview with author 1986)

Wendell Berry's phrase to describe the intermingled, co-habitation of humans and other beings dwelling in mixed communities is "in continuous harmony." In his essay "People, Land and Community," Berry states two major assumptions which inhibit the cultivation of land communities: "The assumption that knowledge (information) can be 'sufficient,' and the assumption that time and work are short" (Jackson et al. 1985, 64).

It takes time to learn the specific conditions in a local watershed. I am convinced that "right livelihood" and deep ecological practice is most effective in small areas. Practical knowledge is based on collective experience in a local community. It is recounted in stories passed down through generations. This knowledge includes specific information about a hillside erosion created by improper farming in the past, about where nesting pairs of birds have returned season after season and favored resting places of resident herds of deer or other large, undomesticated mammals. Sarah Ebenreck, a feminist philosopher, proposes a partnership farmland ethic from an ecofeminist perspective, and concludes that working with the land implies three principles: 1) respect for the fundamental nature of the land, 2) use that does not destroy that nature, and 3) returning something of value in exchange for that use (Ebenreck 1983, 42).

Wendell Berry uses two principles to summarize his approach to dwelling as a farmer—Correct Discipline and Enough Time. I would add Deep Practice and Keep Practicing. Deep Practice can be based on Taoistic, Buddhist, Native American or other compatible principles which manifest the intuition and central understanding of deep ecology. Keep Practicing means we are informed by our practice if we listen carefully and care for the place wherein we dwell.

Authentic dwelling-in-place means stripping our minds of expectations given us by style leaders, by the mass media, by fads in the culture. Authentic dwelling-in-place is developed through a place ballet. Dancing with the place is both discovery of our totem animals in that place and letting the place penetrate our bones and our consciousness.

Dwelling with the Wounds

The rapid accumulation of highly toxic byproducts of industrial production—from nuclear power generating plants, the nuclear weapons industry, pesticides, herbicides, and thousands of other chemicals—has reached crisis proportions. Many technical studies of the chemical effects on the environment have been completed by government agencies and corporations. Proposed sites for disposal of nuclear and chemical wastes have been debated by politicians, scientists, environmental activists, and citizen groups in the communities which are expected to receive the wastes.

We can state the principle that when men reveal some aspect of nature never before revealed to humans, they are required to assume responsibility for their discovery. Thus taking care of nuclear and toxic wastes of all sorts will be a responsibility for humans for many generations in the future, even if we were to stop mining and refining uranium immediately. This may mean "sitting with" toxic chemicals. Sitting with attentiveness, not passively, is a type of caring practiced by Buddhists in some of their forms of meditation.

Given the history of corruption in government, bureaucratic ineptness, the willingness of many corporate executives to dump their wastes in violation of existing federal, state, and local laws, and our failure to clearly understand many of the long-term consequences of chemicals in existing waste repositories, what possible approach could we propose for living in mixed communities of humans and wastes?

I propose a community where humans are part of a "priesthood" of nuclear and toxic waste guardians. This priesthood would use scientific knowledge and would be dedicated to guarding and living among the wastes. This priesthood would recognize and respect the power of these wastes and treat that power with honor. They would be in service to the waste as other people would be in service to the wilderness.

Many scientific, technical rituals would be required at such waste sites. Continuous monitoring of air and water and soil quality would be mandatory, as would containment of leaking storage vessels to protect the integrity of surrounding land forms and human populations.

There would be many hazards to this priesthood including explosions, poisoning from the wastes, possible terrorist attacks, warfare which might endanger the community. Given the historical record, including the persistence of Christian and Buddhist monastic orders and priesthoods even in the face of severe repression, war, and social disruptions of all sorts, a priesthood seems the most viable sociological model for a mixed community of humans and toxic wastes.

The specific rituals of such a priesthood and its charter, sexual composition, methods of recruitment of new members, and modes of behavior are subject to continuing discussion. There may be many different orders of priests taking care of different kinds of nuclear and chemical wastes.

It is important to move the discussion of nuclear and toxic chemicals away from political rhetoric or regulatory politics and into deeper discussion of our responsibilities to the well-being of the mixed community. Without such a shift in the focus of discussion, decisions concerning nuclear depositories and toxic waste dumps will be made on the basis of short term political expediency and manipulation by powerful interest groups including corporations which do not want to bear the responsibility and liability of storing their own wastes.

Situations of Conflict

Even people who wholeheartedly support the principle of biocentrism ask what humans are to do in situations of conflict. Are there any guidelines from a biocentric position for resolving conflicts between humans and other life forms? I want to turn that question around and ask if there are principles upon which to resolve conflicts when humans interfere with vital needs of other life forms both as individuals and as communities?

First we can attempt to establish if there is a genuine situation of conflict. For example, some humans have paranoid fears about snakes or other types of animals. Some people have phobias of forests. Persons carrying such unreasonable fears might consider counseling. Once we resolve that there is a situation of real conflict based on vital needs, or nonbasic needs, then some principles can be applied at either the macro or micro level. A conflict between a national policy and a whole forest ecosystem is a macro level conflict. The decision by the Brazilian government to build roads into Amazonia and encourage settlers to clear-cut and burn the forests is a macro level decision. Encounters between individual snakes and individual settlers in Amazonia are on the micro level.

Both on the macro and micro level, biocentrism teaches that conflicts are ideally resolved with species impartiality. Fairness in resolution of real conflicts can only occur when humans are not given any special privileges because they are humans.

Philosopher Paul W. Taylor, arguing from a biocentric position, suggests five principles for fair resolution of conflicting claims: self-defense; proportionality; minimum wrong; distributive justice; and restitutive justice. Taylor concludes that these principles cover all possible situations but will not yield a neat solution to each and every possible conflict. We cannot deduce conclusions from them, but they serve as rough guides to reaching decisions (Taylor 1986). We may also make mistakes in our judgment.

In seeking to resolve real conflicts between living beings, objective and empirical information is needed in addition to principles governing behavior. In particular, decision makers need objective data on the vital needs of organisms and ecosystems, a detailed history of human intervention and alteration to the landscape, and a full account of the current situation within which the conflict occurs. Objective, empirical information is of little use unless decision makers appeal to the ecotopian ideal underlying a deep ecology, biocentric position—an ideal which embodies harmony between nature and human civilization and is based on a principle of species impartiality. While many actions humans take are reasonable, acceptable, and morally defensible from an anthropocentric position, they are not reasonable from a biocentric position.

Taking each of Taylor's principles in turn, we will explore how these principles have been used appropriately and inappropriately in conflict resolution between humans and other living beings. Many of these examples are from my own bioregion in California. I hope you will find other examples from your own bioregion.

The principle of self-defense states that in a situation of real conflict it is permissible for an organism to defend itself if attacked by another organism and, if necessary, to destroy the attacking organism in order to protect its own life. When humans use this principle, however, there are many qualifications. The claim to self-defense can be misused and abused in relations between humans. Careful consideration must be given to the charge that a human was attacked. Paranoia is rampant in American society. People have shot another person to death and claimed self-defense—"I thought he was reaching for a gun in his pocket"—when in fact the victim was reaching for his wallet.

The defender may have put him or herself in a position which arouses fear and defensive reaction in another organism. Walking between a female bear and her cubs could arouse maternal instincts in the sow who might then charge the human. In such a situation the human has made an unwise decision and might fight the bear. Aikido teaches to keep proper distance from potential attackers, and training humans in such tactics might reduce the probability of conflicts between bears and humans (Herrero 1985).

Some situations are not clearly self-defense. I have a friend who has been bitten twice on different occasions by rattlesnakes. A few years after these incidents, he lived for several months in a house on the north coast of California with his wife and child. They raised a garden during the summer and a rattlesnake took up residence under the house. The snake was seen hunting in the garden in the morning hours. My friend was both apprehensive of all rattlesnakes and fearful that, perhaps inadvertently, his child would encounter the snake. The man found it impossible, in his fearful situation, to live in close proximity to the rattlesnake. Even though he holds a biocentric position and could have taken other options (such as moving from the house to another location), he decided to shoot the snake. I urged him to make peace with the rattlesnake the way St. Francis made peace between a wolf and villagers in northern Italy in the famous thirteenth-century story. In the end, his fears ruled his action.

The principle of least harm is tied to the principle of self-defense. Aikido was called by its founder "the loving protection of all beings." Attacks, in Aikido practice, are considered neutral flows of energy. The victim, of course, does not wish to be harmed but neither does the victim want to do unnecessary damage to the attacker. The Aikidoist takes responsibility for restoring harmony in the relationship with minimum effort and minimum damage to any party. Killing another organism in self-defense is done only if it is absolutely necessary to protect the integrity of the person attacked.

Economic self-defense is not a valid principle under the general principle of self-defense. For example, many ranchers in the American West claim (with scant objective, scientific justification in some cases) that lambs or calves were killed by eagles, coyotes, and bears, and that their own economic well-being is threatened. Coyotes, of course, are killing to fulfill a vital need—food. Sometimes ranchers put out poisoned pellets in their fields which are eaten by coyotes or bears, or domesticated dogs. This is indiscriminate killing. The rancher does not know if the coyote which ate the poison is the one which killed the lambs.

The rancher's life is not threatened by an eagle or coyote or bear. Most usually ranchers kill these predators in order to use the range for their own slave animals—sheep and cattle. Furthermore, there are other ways to live in harmony with coyotes and bears. The ranchers can keep sheep or cattle in a barn or enclosure close to their house during calving or lambing season and thus protect them during this vulnerable period.

The principle of proportionality applies in those situations in which nonvital human desires conflict with the inherent and vital needs of other organisms. When humans treat other organisms or whole ecosystems as mere instruments serving some human purpose, they deny the inherent worth of the nonhuman organism. There are many situations in which humans can have rich, full experiences without harming other organisms. For example, rhinoceroses in Africa are endangered as a species, and individual rhinoceroses are threatened primarily because some wealthy persons desire their horns as decoration on dagger handles. This is purely a cosmetic use of the horn. Dagger handles can be made from many other substances and can be equally beautiful to those made with rhinoceros horn. Other examples, from my own bioregion, include killing bears to obtain their gall bladders as a specialty food and their claws to make necklaces, and digging rare plants for private collections.

The principle of proportionality applies in those situations in which one organism (or community of organisms) is not threatening another. Greater weight is given to vital needs of an organism than to the nonvital needs of another. Of course, in relations between humans and other organisms or whole ecosystems, the nonhuman organisms cannot reciprocate. Humans by their special abilities (cognition, biosocial characteristics, and developed moral sensibility) have ethical obligations to other organisms.

Many actions by humans, such as building a shopping center, are not in themselves incompatible with respecting inherent worth of the living beings, but the consequences of those actions are. Building a shopping center on an historic wetland has negative consequences for many other nonhuman organisms. In California it is estimated by some experts that 95 percent of the historic wetlands, since

1850, have been filled or otherwise altered for human uses—parking lots, shopping centers, office buildings, schools, military installations, etc. So much of this type of ecosystem has been used by humans that the principle of proportionality suggests no further development of wetlands should be allowed.

This type of situation is sometimes part of a land use decision. Reform environmental groups frequently engage in the process of making such decisions, or at least are one of the players in the process. Often these reformists are placed in untenable situations when they use anthropocentric arguments. Environmentalists must find a better *human use* for the area when they argue that some proposed facility *not* be built there. In my town several years ago, the local Sierra Club argued before the State Coastal Commission that the commission should deny a permit for a baseball park on a parcel of land which was historic wetland. The club used the principle of proportionality, to a limited extent, citing the reduction of amount of wetlands in Humboldt Bay during the past century. Inherent worth of wetlands was not mentioned however. Instead the club argued that the Little League could find another site for their ballfield and made several suggestions for alternatives (all of which were considered too expensive or had already been designated for other commercial uses). The Sierra Club was heavily criticized in local newspapers, by some community organizations and educators. The issue was polarized into a division between the need for healthy recreation for children versus the Sierra Club defense of wetlands.

After hearing testimony favoring the permit for the ballpark, the Coastal Commission approved the permit and thus went against their own planning guidelines. From a biocentric position the decision was fundamentally wrong.

If such a decision is made to favor humans over other organisms, the principle of minimum wrong asserts that the least damage possible be inflicted based on the best factual information.

Environmental pollution from industrial production, for example, impacts human health and the health of whole ecosystems but is considered necessary because of human desires for certain products. Establishing thresholds of pollution where real effects are felt by humans is extremely difficult. It is even more difficult to establish thresholds for damage to nonhuman organisms. The issue of acid deposition is an example. Many scientists conclude that the integrity, stability and beauty of many lake and forest areas in the northeastern U.S.A. and portions of Canada have been threatened by acid emitted from industrial production operations. Under the principle of minimum wrong, reduction of industrial wastes to a minimum level is required. This level is based on extremely complex negotiations concerning objective information, available technology and equality among all those who must bear the cost of installing pollution control equipment.

A biocentric-individualistic position, some critics contend, cannot describe an ethical approach for the Earth as a whole. Yet more and more scientific evidence indicates human impacts on the life support system of Earth during the past forty years are cumulative and detrimental to humans and other organisms. The recent revelation of the dramatic decrease in the ozone layer over Antarctica and findings indicating a similar pattern over several large cities in North America, as well as the increase of the greenhouse effect due to the release of CO_2 during industrial production indicates that industrial civilization could cause the literal death of nature to a large extent. If we see the Earth as part of ourself, then we seek to minimize harmful human impacts on it.

The principle of minimum wrong applies to many other situations where humans seek to satisfy nonessential needs. In designing recreational facilities such as resorts, marinas, golf courses, and ballfields, humans can reduce their impact on essential habitat of native plants and animals. In my town, for example, the Bureau of Land Management designed a park for off-road vehicle use in sand dunes which also served as habitat for endangered Menzies wallflowers. An attempt was made to fence off some dunes so the vehicles would not destroy the flowers. While some environmentalists argued that the species were so threatened that the whole area of the proposed park should be zoned for use only by wallflowers, the decision to build the park was made on the basis of compelling human need for recreational facilities. Given the already degraded condition of the site, the protection of some of the site through fencing was considered by the BLM to be the best resolution of conflict between vital habitat needs of Menzies wallflowers and nonbasic recreational needs of some humans.

Habitat destruction is cited as the chief reason for declining populations of many species. Humans can reduce their impact on habitat of wild species by withdrawing their activities from wildlands. They can designate huge areas as "off limits" to future roads, dams, grazing, logging and mining. They can recycle areas which have already been polluted by human activities—such as large industrial areas in major cities—for other purposes. If some destruction of habitat is unavoidable, it can still be done with minimum impact.

Killing of plants and animals to collect specimens for educational collections or for display in natural history museums can be done with minimum harm to the individual organisms and to their whole populations. For example, it seems wrong from both the proportionality and minimum harm principles to kill individual organisms from endangered species just to collect examples for a museum, to exhibit them as "endangered species." Photographs and drawings could easily substitute for actual specimens.

Killing individual grizzly bears accused of attacking hikers in a national park is another example where these principles apply. Humans may have a vital need for recreation, but they can walk in millions of acres of public lands in North America which are not known grizzly habitat. Encounters between humans and grizzly bears can be reduced by restricting humans. When the National Park Service orders the execution of grizzlies accused of attacks in Glacier and Yellowstone national parks, it violates all three principles thus far discussed. Hikers who feel they must enter grizzly habitat should be informed of the risks, take precautions (such as ringing bells) to warn grizzlies of their presence, contain food which might attract grizzlies, avoid actions which might arouse the bears, and be alert to the habits of bears during the different periods of the day and different seasons.

In recent years another issue concerning black bears has arisen in northern California and parts of Washington and Oregon. Some large timber corporations have declared black bears to be industrial pests. In Humboldt County in 1987, one corporation alone obtained forty-five depredation permits to have bears killed. The corporation claimed a loss of property of over $500,000 for one year from bears who chewed the cambian layer—the green layer just below the bark—of some young trees. The fact is, only some bears engage in this behavior and only for two months out of the year when they come out of hibernation. Researchers have not determined the reason for this activity. Since the timber corporations have cut most of the primeval trees, some of them over two thousand years old, there are many young evergreen trees.

Is this really a serious problem? Can't the corporations let the bears do what they have probably always done? Doesn't the history of human interference in these bear habitats require some concessions? One solution, based on the principle of minimum harm, is to identify problem bears and feed them sugar-coated wood fiber pellets during May and June. Another solution is to trap bears and remove them to primeval forests. Another is to let bears continue to chew and sometimes kill some of the young trees, and increase the rotation cycle of cutting so that there will be fewer young trees and more older trees on the company property.

In practicing from deep ecology principles, bears should be able to use their own historic habitat. If we cause further harm to bears after humans have altered, disrupted and reduced their habitat for the last hundred years, we exacerbate the inharmonious relationships between bears and humans.

In some situations wild animals have been conditioned to do circus tricks for the amusement of humans. It seems morally wrong to deprive bears, lions, and elephants of their freedom for such shallow purposes. In a few cases animals have been trained for use in military operations. In 1987 the U.S. Navy admitted it deployed trained dolphins in the Persian Gulf with the mission to detect and report the location of mines. The navy refused to release detailed information on the use of dolphins, but a spokesman stated that dolphins were not used to detonate the mines. When dolphins are used in military operations they are given the same consideration for life as human military personnel by the navy.

By contrast, John Lilly and his associates proposed a kind of ecotopian community of wild dolphins and humans. A small group of humans would live in a seaside home in warm waters, which would be designed to provide access for dolphins to come and go freely. Those dolphins who wanted to play with humans would come into the facility and signal. Humans could enter the water and swim freely into the open ocean if the dolphins permitted the humans' presence. Dolphins would be under no restrictions and no attempt would be made to train or condition them. Such a community maximizes possibilities of interaction and respects the living space of all. In a human-dolphin mixed community, humans might learn some of the ancient wisdom of dolphins.

There are many perceived conflict situations in which nonhuman beings are not harming humans. Thus the principle of self-defense does not apply. When both humans and nonhumans have vital needs, the principles of proportionality and minimum harm do not apply. Neither humans nor other beings have more important claims (impartiality rule). Distributive justice will not guarantee perfect allocation and treatment by itself in some situations, therefore it is combined with restitutive justice.

Take for example the necessity of killing wild animals, including whales, wild goats and pigs, when other food is not available to a population of humans. Killing is morally permissible because, as Naess said, in practice some exploitation is necessary to serve the vital needs of humans. However, killing must be done without unnecessary pain to the animal and with regard to the population of animals. Native species must be given special consideration and protection where humans have historically abused the habitat or killed more of the percentage of a species than will allow it a good chance of reproduction, or where environmental stress has occurred, such as after a hard winter.

Preservation of wilderness is one method of fulfilling the principle of distributive justice. Many of these areas are in so-called developing nations such as Brazil or China. These nations can engage in programs to encourage birth control for humans and redistribution of wealth from developed nations rather than entering wilderness areas of their own countries with the intent to build large dams which impair the riparian habitat of some other species or burn rain forests which are the home to hundreds of thousands of endemic species.

Humans can conserve resources and share those resources with other species. For example, some California environmental groups urge a practice of "in river flow," meaning that an amount of water is *not* appropriated for human uses. In stream flow provides for native fish, birds and animals which use the stream to sustain their lives.

Planning which integrates a facility used by humans with habitat requirements of other species is another approach to distributive justice. Ian McHarg in his book *Planning with Nature,* provides guidelines for minimizing disruption to plants and animals due to developments. This principle is not appropriate if human developments interfere with vital needs of endangered species, if some species in the area of the proposed development cannot tolerate the presence of humans, or if humans will not tolerate the presence of another species. Building a residential development in known grizzly habitat, for example, is unlikely to fulfill the vital needs of grizzlies.

Distributive justice is frequently combined with restitutive justice because it is not possible to give justice to one party in the conflict without taking from the other party. That is, in many situations, because of decisions made in the past, we are playing a zero sum game. A population of humans living in a certain watershed cannot cut the remaining primeval forest in the watershed (assuming that a large portion of the forest was cut sometime in the past and has not regenerated enough to cut during the lifetime of the present generation of humans) and still preserve the primeval forest as a habitat for a residual population of spotted owls. Since spotted owls are dependent on primeval forests and humans can obtain a livelihood from other means besides cutting the primeval forest, and since very little habitat for spotted owls remains because of past logging in many other watersheds, the principle of restitutive justice suggests preserving the remaining primeval forest in the watershed as special compensation to the spotted owls. Because of abuses in the past, people in this generation may gain less wealth from exploiting natural resources and may devote themselves to restoring damaged watersheds by replanting and caring for trees.

Nor can the fact that some humans have greater satisfaction of their vital needs than other humans be used to justify entering primeval forests. People in developing nations with rapidly expanding human population, who have already degraded large portions of their nations and who have scarce capital for improvements in services to humans, do not have any claim under the principles outlined here to enter remaining tropical rain forests, for example, for the purpose of clear-cutting and converting the area into farms. Developed nations have great wealth in part because of exploitation of nonhuman beings in the past. Redistribution of wealth from developed to undeveloped nations is a possibility to satisfy the principle of distributive justice among humans. It is chauvinistic anthropocentrism, however, for citizens of developing nations to violate tropical rain forests to satisfy their nonbasic needs based on the model of "standard of living" in the U.S.A. or some other developed nation.

In providing examples of conflicts between humans and other life forms, I have focused on animals and especially mammals. Can we consider each insect an individual organism? How do we dwell in mixed communities with insects and microbes? It is absurd to carry the individual organism argument to an extreme. A mixed community frequently includes, however, close contact with myriads of insects and microorganisms. By and large these are in symbiotic or neutral relationship with humans.

Dwelling in mixed communities means having respect, even reverence, for that which is unseen as well as seen. The primary importance of developing mindfulness of the broader sense of community is that it elicits a generalized respect for all Earth's inhabitants. Biologists tell us that life begins with the unseen (to the naked eye) world of microbes. Without the unceasing activity of soil bacteria, algae, mycrolzal fungi and other microscopic soil organisms, terrestrial plant life, and therefore animal life, would not be possible. The microorganisms create conditions in the soil allowing plants to flourish. As we walk upon the ground we know that there are countless beings whose activities are certainly more important to life on Earth than those of humans.

Use of chemical insecticides frequently violates the principle of minimum harm. Rachel Carson's famous book, *Silent Spring,* showed the unintended and harmful consequences of DDT used as an insecticide.

What about our relationships with domesticated plants and animals and with our own creations—creatures of biotechnology? Paul Taylor calls for institutions and practices which provide the ethical basis for relations between humans and domesticated and biotechnological creatures a society's *bioculture.* The bioculture includes zoos, the pet trade, sports using animals (horse and dog racing and rodeos), the breeding and training of animals, forest plantations, many forms of agriculture, scientific experiments using animals, some wildlife management and commercial endeavors (such as fish hatcheries, game bird farms and game ranching), and exhibitions of animals like Sea World.

In all these examples, plants and animals are used for human ends. In applying the principle of minimum harm, some activists in the animal liberation movement have protested unnecessary cruelty to animals in laboratory experiments, use of electric prods and other stimulation devices in rodeos, and the treatment of animals in slaughterhouses. They also protest such practices as force feeding animals to enlarge their meaty portions for human consumption, keeping animals in confined places, artificial manipulation of the environment (lights in hen houses, for instance, to regulate egg production) and castrations. Killing to feed humans should not include cruel treatment of animals.

Ethical relations with our creatures which we manufacture through biotechnology has emerged as an important issue. Unless scientists stop experimentation and enforce restrictions on genetically altered organisms, within a short time we will have novel organisms, including crosses between species. The development of the bioengineering industry involves fundamental questions concerning the cosmology of modern science. Deep ecology calls us to examine these questions thoroughly before irreversible policy decisions are made.

Many supporters of the deep, long-range ecology movement are strongly opposed to rapid development of biotechnology and see it as the most perverse outcome of the dominant mind-set in our civilization. Unless more compelling arguments are presented by supporters of biotechnology than those presented to date, I suspect we will see more protesters uprooting genetically altered plants and killing genetically altered animals which are released from laboratories into wildlife habitat.

As a conclusion to this section, I will describe the historic situation of the southern sea otter along the coast of California, because it illustrates how deeply ingrained the anthropocentric and greedy attitudes are of some humans, and that only by changing those attitudes can a fundamental change be expected in our society.

During the eighteenth and nineteenth centuries, fur trappers traveled from Russia to the coast of California to hunt otters. By the end of the 1800s, it was thought that the southern sea otter was extinct. However, a few hundred otters were discovered along the central California coastline in the 1930s after a paved road was built along the coast. By 1948 biologists estimated that there were 300 members of the sea otter colony, and they were protected from hunting. By 1978 the population had increased to an estimated 1800 otters. The official refuge of the sea otters had filled to its capacity. Otters, who require large amounts of marine life daily (such as clams, sea cucumbers, scallops, crabs, and abalone) to support them in the cold waters of the northern Pacific, began returning to their ancient homelands north and south of Monterey. With few natural predators, the otters moved with impunity until they reached the Pismo Beach area of southern California, and a situation developed which Jane Bailey, in her book on the sea otter, called the "Waterloo" of sea otters.

As the otters, numbering less than a hundred, traveled south from their sanctuary along the Big Sur coast,they encountered the range of the Pismo clam. These clams were also highly prized by an increasing horde of recreationists. A combination of low tides, long vacation weekends, beach buggies and clear weather brought between 150,000 and 200,000 pleasure-seekers to the Pismo dunes each summer.

Besides clam diggers, commercial fishermen who sell high-priced abalone to seafood restaurants also converged on the beach. These people were infuriated at the invasion of otters. Both sport and commercial fishermen are able to make a powerful political lobby which influences game management. Despite attempts by the Fish and Game Commission to protect sea otters, including the threat of a $1,000 fine and one year in jail for killing an otter, otter corpses were found containing gunshot wounds and an increasing number of corpses were found with wounds only a diver's gun would make (Bailey 1979).

To add to the other problems of otters, some experts suggested that in the event of a massive oil spill from off-shore rigs or passing tankers, most if not all of the otters would die because their specialized fur could not be cleaned of the oil.

The U.S. Fish and Wildlife Service sought another home for the small colony of otters and picked as one possible site the coastline off southern Humboldt County. There are many issues involved in capturing and transporting otters, but the wildlife managers favored establishing a colony of otters in an area away from possible oil spills.

Upon hearing that their county was being considered as a possible otter sanctuary, the Humboldt County Board of Supervisors voted unanimously against the sanctuary after some fishermen claimed that otters would destroy abalone fishing, even though abalone and other sea life eaten by otters are not basic foods for humans.

Otters present no physical threat to any humans. They do not serve as host for any microorganisms which are harmful to humans. They dwell in cold waters where humans cannot live. Thus they can never life in close proximity to humans. Humans invade otter habitat only with extremely specialized equipment such as scuba gear and specialized ships.

Given the history of human exploitation of otters during the past several centuries and the life chances of both individual otters and the whole species, it seemed reasonable to grant sanctuary to otters off the coastline of Humboldt County, a coastline which is not heavily populated or used extensively by recreationists. Denial of sanctuary violated the principles of proportionality, distributive justice, and restitutive justice. No issue of self-defense was involved. Supporters of deep ecology principles became friends of the sea otter and lobbied on their behalf before state and federal agencies and commissions.

The end result was that a small colony of otters was transported to waters off Nicholas Island, the most remote of the channel islands off southern California. Whether this colony will grow in population is unknown at this time.

In sum, underlying this discussion of resolving conflicts is a vision of harmony and freedom. Humans are freed from narrow, anthropocentric conceptions of nature. Harmony involves humans in the process of dwelling lightly on the land while richly developing their special talents. Based on this vision, conflicts can be resolved using empirical data concerning vital needs of life forms and information concerning the consequences of proposed human actions.

Humans need many different ecotopian visions based on biocentric equality and Self-realization to inspire them in this great process of dwelling in mixed communities. Practicing deep ecology means,

in part, articulating these ideals and proposing resolutions to conflicts based on ecotopian-biocentric ideals and empirical facts.

Deep Ecology and Megalopolis

The modern city is a necropolis—a vast city of the dead. Landscapes
are remade into concrete. Many rivers in urban areas are channeled
into concrete-lined ditches. Communities of plants and animals are
killed, bulldozed, burned, and buried under human-created artifacts.
Most plants and animals living in cities are those domesticated by
humans. When wild animals, especially naturally occurring predators such as mountain lions or coyotes, attempt to reenter their habitat, as in the suburbs of Los Angeles, they are hunted, poisoned,
exterminated. Only a few species, such as rats and some insects, seem
to thrive in close company with humans but are not domesticated.
They have learned to be invisible. Coyotes are mostly invisible, but
they are noisy. They are opportunistic hunters who will sometimes
prey on dogs and cats in suburban yards. A practice recommended
by many wildlife specialists is to keep domestic animals (and small
children) indoors after dark.

Megalopolis is a term used by geographers to describe vast urban
aggregations spreading across county, state and even national boundaries. A megalopolis may, in the twenty-first century, have twenty
or thirty million human residents. Mexico City is approaching eighteen million population in the late 1980s. These huge urban areas create their own environment, and influence local weather patterns by
spreading pollution from factories and vehicles.

Megalopolis must draw on a vast hinterland for food, water, fuel,
and other natural resources to sustain its human inhabitants. In some
nations whole regions consisting of millions of acres are declared
"national sacrifice areas" to provide fuel and water to support a
megalopolis.

Megalopolis is a center of economic and political power. Corporations headquartered in New York City, Los Angeles, Tokyo,
Mexico City, and London send agents around the world as modern
hunters and gatherers, collecting forests, oil and gas leases, mineral
leases, and other commodities (see Catton 1980).

Megalopolis is also home of the cult of individualism. There the
minimal self is played out to a critical but receptive audience while
deeper and broader aspects of self are ignored. The domesticated
ego is all important and the wild self is only glimpsed through the
windows of high-rise office buildings in the most convoluted

perspective. Only wild dreams may still attach the urban dwellers to primal aspects of themselves.

Many social movements, including Earth First! and Green movements, condemn the rate of pollution in large cities and seek ways to reduce toxic waste dumping. Such movements also encourage birth control programs. Although there are disagreements about the effectiveness of different forms of birth control, there is general agreement among environmental organizations that wealthy nations should help fund family planning programs and distribution of contraceptives in third world nations, just as wealthy nations fund development projects and give food to them.

Per capita consumption is, of course, highest in Western Europe, Australia, and North America, and the rate of consumption in large cities in those regions requires exploitation of wilderness in other regions of the world. But population is beginning to stabilize in Western Europe and North America, except for in-migration. Explosive rates of growth are still occurring in cities of third world nations from Cairo to Lagos and from Mexico City to Calcutta.

Misplaced humanism is used to justify large-scale in-migration to Western Europe and North America from Latin America and Africa. And as human ecologist William Catton, Jr. has effectively argued, increasing technology will reduce carrying capacity for humans in a finite world. Humans have begun to compete with their machines for fuel (Catton 1987, 413-419).

Some critics of cities suggest the principle "eradicate the cities." However, cities can be places of celebration, cultural richness and exchange. A realistic principle is "contain the cities." Contain the population of cities so they do not disturb the habitat of threatened and endangered species. Contain the pollution generated by megalopolises. Contain the power of urban elites and intellectuals. Contain the materialist ideology and nihilism associated with the secular city.

Encourage the wild in the cities—wild self, wild animals. Encourage higher quality of life of people living in cities and intensify policies of population control.

We lack compassion and seem misanthropic if we turn our backs on hundreds of millions of humans who reside in megalopolises. However, when a choice must be made, it seems consistent with deep ecology principles to fight on the side of endangered plants and animals. As I write this chapter in 1987, California newspapers report that the last wild California condor, a seven-year-old male named AC-9, has been arrested and transported to the Los Angeles Zoo.

20 April 1987 should be recorded in history as a sad Earth Day. For tens of thousands of years condors have soared over the mountains and valleys of California. Human impacts on their habitat and outright murder reduced their numbers. In the name of helping the condors, all live condors were captured and placed in a "captive breeding" program. The goal of the program, according to authorities, is to someday return condors to the wild. There may be no wild areas to return to, however, if development is permitted to expand in condor habitat. It is an ecotopian ideal to return the megalopolis of Los Angeles to a situation which allows condors to use it as habitat. This may mean limiting the number of people living within the Los Angeles basin.

Environmental groups have been very active in public debates on such issues as mass transit, location of roads, zoning ordinances, greenbelt zoning, location of large public facilities like airports, and size of housing subdivisions; but we need more urban planners who are dedicated to the principles of deep ecology. There literally is no place in many contemporary cities for the kind of mixed communities discussed in this book. And only visionary city planners such as Ebenezer Howard with his "garden city" concept at the turn of the twentieth century and the concepts of Paul Goodman, Lewis Mumford, and Ian McHarg, provide the space for such a mixed community to develop. However, I cannot point to any model city which has developed on deep ecology principles.

Roy Rappaport, in a visionary essay entitled "Restructuring The Ecology of Cities," suggests the goal of restructuring cities is to focus on creating a social organization which can continually respond and adapt to changing circumstances. He defines adaptation as the ability of living organisms to face short-term fluctuations and long-term changes in their environment.

Control hierarchies in contemporary metropolises are pathological because they elevate their own purposes above the needs of the more inclusive system. For cities to develop into good places, both private organizations and public agencies need a vision of dwelling fully and deeply with the wounds created by urban-industrial civilization (Rappaport 1986).

As a spiritual-religious movement deep ecology calls us beyond the physical and psychological pathologies and borders of megalopolis into a consciousness which allows ecotopian ideals and ecosophy to emerge.

Thinking Like a Mountain

In one of his poems, Gary Snyder concludes, "The USA slowly lost its mandate in the middle and latter twentieth century because it never gave the mountains and trees a vote" (Snyder 1974, 77). Citizens of modern western nations pride themselves on their progressive social movements that touched the consciences of men in political power, moving them to free the slaves, give the vote to women, establish strong commitments to redressing centuries of injustice—including homophobia, racism, and sexism. However, these leaders have great difficulty discovering the broader and deeper community of trees, rivers, mountains, and animals. "Giving the animals the vote," of course, is a metaphor used by the poet to call our attention to the boundaries of community.

In order to realize the fuller implications of dwelling in mixed communities as more mature persons with more realized ecological self, we may need to practice a kind of mental gymnastics that will open us to a different way of being-in-the-world. We may, in the words of Aldo Leopold, begin this practice by "thinking like a mountain." Of course, says the rational mind, mountains don't think. Only humans think. We must be careful not to presume that we can actually think like a mountain. Leopold, introduced this phrase in an essay on hunting wolves in the American Southwest. "Only the mountain has lived long enough to listen objectively to the howl of a wolf" (Leopold 1949, 129).

The deeper meaning, known only to the mountain itself, tells human beings that we cannot fully know. We have a separation from the bear and wolves which may not be healed in our lifetime. We have an arrogant and inflated belief that we know enough about ecosystems to really manage them. What we need is respect for what we don't know yet and what we can't know.

People working a Buddhist tradition find a master to help them jump beyond the constraints of dualistic thinking into the broader and deeper stream of Self. By becoming empty, fully empty, Buddhist teachers say, we become full of possibilities. Without sharply defining "either-or," "this and that," "living and non-living," the limits of conventional thinking can be transcended.

The heroic mind-set, frequently found in modern western society, is "when in doubt, act and let others take the consequences." When people jump from the heroic mode to the intrinsic mode of being-in-the-world, they know that when in doubt, do nothing.

We actualize the oneness of the community by respecting and responding to the needs of others. We simply find a place to live, put down our roots and look for our friends—mountains, rivers, trees, birds. One instant we are the mountain contemplating the wolf, then the wolf howling at the moon, then a human going hunting, then a human hearing the mountain laugh at the human comedy (Naess 1985).

Naess, in his keynote address to the Second International Conference on Conservation Biology describes a philosophy taken from a standard handbook from the 1930s on how to treat our domestic animals. The author was talking of caressing pigs. "Those who have experienced the satisfaction of pigs stroked this way, cannot but do it." The scientist in us may answer, "I cannot experience the satisfaction in the consciousness of the pig, but I can obviously refrain from stroking the pig. I have free will, don't I?" But what if we accept the joyful impulse to stroke the a pig? What textbook today on scientific agriculture talks of techniques for stroking pigs for their own sake and the joy this brings to the stroker?

Encourage stroking pigs, thinking like mountains, and respecting wild animals. Each of these contributes to dwelling in mixed communities.

Problems in our Mind-set

There are many different aspects of our common worldview which inhibit us from fully dwelling in mixed communities. I will review only a few of these here. We begin to change our behavior when we become mindful of conventional assumptions that we have complacently accepted.

First, in the dominant worldview, we project our narrow perception of human needs and our desires into the mixed community. Rather than taking responsibility to fully serve the mixed community, we cling to our "right" to suit narrow, short-term desires. Attempts to protect the integrity of riparian habitat, to protect endangered species or the configuration of a land form from human-induced drastic changes are likely to be challenged based on "property rights of landowners," or "my rights as an individual to maximize my income," or "my right to do whatever I want with my property."

Second, we tend to see our decisions in terms of a short time frame. For some people, land is only another asset, an opportunity to make a profit limited only by the constraints of finances, market conditions, and labor and capital costs. The long-term well-being of the mixed community is usually forfeited for the sake of maximizing the short-term profit. Some philosophers posit that short-term maximizing of profit always is at the expense of the sustainable community. Profits are privitized while costs are communalized.

Third, we tend to have boundless faith in the ability of technology and technologists. If soil is losing its fertility we solve the problem by searching for new discoveries, including new chemical compounds to enhance productivity of crops. The 1980s have witnessed attempts to apply genetic engineering to manipulation of plant and animal DNA to enhance productivity.

Fourth, we confuse our personal preference for types of landscape with the intrinsic needs of the land community. Some theory of aesthetics might require certain symmetry or artistic relationship of areas of land, water, trees, and plants. The much admired grand gardens of aristocratic estates in Europe, for example, are the basis of lawn design in millions of suburban lots around the world regardless of the communities of native plants and animals which existed there before conversion to housing developments.

Fifth, we allow the workings of the political economy to rule our actions. Large corporations base their plans for development of mineral deposits on their perceptions of the market, on government incentives or disincentives, on their desire to enhance their market power. For example, studies of the forest products industry in British Columbia indicate that large corporations, attempting to maximize profits, created a situation of unstable human communities and forest communities, Damaged Lands characterized by erosion, inadequate reforestation and destruction of wildlife habitat (Mackay 1985).

Sixth, inadequate knowledge, both intuitive and scientific, relative immaturity, and immaturity of our ecological self inhibit our attention to the vital needs of other members of mixed communities. Instead of restraining our actions in the face of ignorance, the dominant mind-set encourages maximizing profits and economizing natural resources (M'Gonigle 1986).

Seventh, even those who want to do something for whales or bears fall into the narrow version of wanting to be heroic. But in wanting to appear to be heroic, we may act in inappropriate ways, in ways not mindful of the vital needs of the long-term community. We want to see results of our efforts—now. Sometimes people rationalize their actions by saying they are serving the needs of the people. Foresters who order whole forests to be clear-cut will say they are serving the needs of people for timber and wood products. Some of these foresters believe in their ability to turn forests into factories—tree farms—which produce trees as a crop. But these tree farms may diminish species diversity and inhibit the spiritual growth of humans as part of a mixed community. Humans remain the dominating, controlling agents of evolution and control the forest based on their narrow self-interest.

Finally, we all utilize the psychological defense mechanism of denial. Psychologist Ernest Becker in his book *Denial of Death,* demonstrated some of the consequences of the near universal denial of our own mortality. The "it can't happen to me" syndrome leads us to bury thoughts which then work on our psyches in unconscious ways.

There are other forms of denial. Even though there is extensive documentation that environmental quality deteriorated during the 1980s in the U.S.A., the mood of the nation, fostered by the Pollyanna-like statements of President Ronald Reagan, has been denial. The most impactful denial has been the denial that the human species has a dominant influence on evolution and on many of the critical factors in ecosystems and the biosphere as a whole.

As a political movement, deep ecology cannot afford to deny the human impact on evolution and the biosphere. Earth First! makes some clear statements concerning wilderness. The Green movements in Western Europe and the U.S.A., as of this writing, have yet to mobilize their political resources for preservation of wildlife habitat and species diversity. Both Green and bioregional movements have yet to integrate a wilderness protection program into their platforms and statements.

This chapter does not provide complete answers to any of these issues, but it does address some questions and helps to clarify the dilemmas deep ecology supporters face and some possible responses.

Conclusion

In a mixed community, human members are respectful and demonstrate their respect through the modesty of their actions, through rituals, and through the grace of their behavior with individuals and populations.

Neither an individual tree nor a species has to prove its evolutionary function or value, nor do human defenders of old growth forests have to prove the value of such to a human economy in order to justify their protection.

We are in service to a place. We serve the needs of the land community. We receive from that community such services as food and materials for clothes, shelter, and fuel. We are not stewards of the place managing a piece of property for sustained yield or highest profit in the short time frame. We are attentive to the needs of the whole community. We are students of our place.

We are mindful of serving the vital needs of humans and all living beings. Many atrocities have been committed against humans by other humans, against other species, against the wilderness, against native plants and animals in the name of serving the needs of the human community. We engage only in necessary killing. We are aware that grand solutions most usually create more problems.

Nothing is forced, nothing demanded.

We honor each other. We realize ourselves through each other.

Notes

[1] There are many legal and customary principles which can be used to protect natural diversity. For the U.S.A. see *The Preservation of Natural Diversity: A Survey and Recommendations,* prepared for the U.S. Department of Interior by the Nature Conservancy, 1975. This study provides a state-by-state review of laws designed to protect natural diversity.

[2] For examples, see Ecology, Management and Utilization of California Oaks, symposium, June 26-28, 1979, Claremont, California, PSW-44, General Technical Report, US Forest Service; Selection, Management and Utilization of Biosphere Reserves Symposium on Biosphere Reserves, U.S.A., and U.S.S.R., Moscow, May, 1976, General Technical Report PNW-82, US Forest Service; California Wildlife and Their Habitats: Western Sierra Nevada, technical coordinators, Jared Verner, Allan S. Boss, 1980, PSW Forest and Range Experimental Station, US Forest Service. These are examples of the type of technical reports which provide some information on habitat needs and suggestions and guidelines which would restrain human activities that intrude on the habitat requirements of other species.

Epilogue

To study the Way is to study the self."
Dōgen *Genjō Kōan*

A small group of Native Americans and Earth First!ers are standing at the end of a paved road in the Siskiyou Mountains of northwestern California, looking over to the other side, into the high country. It is a bright day in late autumn, but a swift-moving storm of the previous night has left a light dusting of new snow on the trees and rocks—Doctor Rock, Peak Eight. Those aren't their authentic names but their map names given by government surveyors.

The diverse group is contemplating setting up a blockade along this road should the U.S. Forest Service grant a contract to build the Chimney Rock section, the last segment of the so-called GO (Gasquet-Orleans) Road.

The Forest Service has surveyed and mapped these wild lands. Now they want to build a paved road through the last eight miles of the high country—a land sacred to three Native American nations, the Tolowa, Yurok, and Karok, who believe the high country is not the property of humans. It is the place where shamans in training go to pray. For centuries their medicine men have listened to the "other side" of the high country. Native Americans and environmentalists have presented their case against the road through all administrative appeals and through federal courts. After the U.S. Court of Appeals forbid the Forest Service from building the Chimney Rock section, the Department of Justice appealed the decision to the U.S. Supreme Court. The Forest Service wants to develop the last wilderness in the name of public recreation and timber extraction.

Environmentalists say that the high country is the homeland of brewers spruce, wolverine, black bear, cascade lilies, and numerous other species of plants and animals, some of them rare. They respect the will-of-the-land as well as the Native American attachment to the high country as sacred space. Religious and environmental qualities are married in the high country. The quality of religious experience depends, in part, on land undisturbed by chainsaws and recreational vehicles. I cannot help but think of Aldo Leopold's statement, "Recreation development is not a job of building roads into lovely country, but of building receptivity into the still unlovely human mind" (Leopold 1949, 176).

Poet William Everson called the decision to build the Hetch Hetchy Dam in Yosemite National Park the "spiritual watershed" of the twentieth century for Americans. The issue of the GO road is a spiritual watershed in my bioregion for the late twentieth century. Will we who have spent three hundred years building hundreds of thousands of miles of roads, railroads and canals across the American continent respect the will-of-the-land for the last remaining wilderness? Or will we search out and attempt to bring the last sanctuaries under our control? How can we cross the metaphysical chasm which divides materialistic views of nature and reclaim our authentic place as humans listening to voices from the other side of the mountain?

"I went to the woods because I wished to live deliberately, to front only the essential facts of life," Thoreau said over a century ago. It requires the skill of a warrior to live so today. Living deliberately in the late twentieth century means fronting up to facts which were unheard of in Thoreau's time—nuclear war, mass extinction and new diseases. What is required is a new type of warrior—a person who is intense, centered, persistent, gentle, strong, sincere, attentive, and alert.

A warrior trained in Aikido advances and controls the center, the teacher says. Never retreat; draw your attacker into your own space; be receptive to life. And in the center of life is a great mystery. The new warrior is reconciling conflict, blending with the onrushing energy of the attacker. How does the new warrior blend with the onrushing energy of the technological juggernaut? How does the new warrior blend with the fanaticism of the Forest Service when the bureaucrats impose their doctrine of timber harvesting on the sacred high country?

Practice, keep practicing, the Aikido teacher says. Practice each day as if it were "nothing special," but paradoxically, realize that every day is special, every day is extraordinary.

Will practice help defend the high country from road building? Certainly all the tactics used by reform environmentalists have produced only short-term success. Perhaps, in the ultimate sense, the high country cannot be defended. But it can be entered with prayers and an open heart, listening, waiting, but not expecting miracles.

In an everyday sense, the new warrior can defend the integrity of all places, with arguments, affirmations, appeals to decision makers, and when necessary, nonviolent direct action.

For the new warrior, practicing deep ecology requires simple but steady discipline. Aikido talks of *shugyo*—austere training—and of *misogi*—purification of spirit in a place of mystery. The very word *mystery* is in disrepute in the English language. Frequently it is confused with superstition or evil or occult. All ultimate questions, however, are mysteries, and mystery is part of primal existence. Mystery includes a sense of wonder, letting go of efforts to manage, manipulate and manhandle the self-in-environment. And that is the difference between deep ecology and the ideologies which attempt to justify bringing the last wildernesses under control. The mystery of wilderness requires one to enter it thinking—not just at the analytical level of a surveyor, but with openness and a window of vulnerability.

The new warrior does not ask ultimate questions in daily practice because asking the question entangles the warrior in framing the question and interferes with the answer. But those questions permeate practicing like rain permeates the soil.

Bodies remember being, even if over-civilized minds have buried being-in-the-world beneath a thin layer of concepts and ideas. The new warrior does not separate thinking and action. Practicing deep ecology is physical. Perfect practice cannot be neatly spelled out in techniques described in a book. Bodies will resonate with meaning when minds are a mush of faddish theories. Standing in front of a bulldozer to affirm the integrity of wilderness, kayaking down a wild river, cross-country skiing—these are actions of affirmation, of the warrior dance. In all actions, the new warrior dances a great dance of reconciliation.

It matters not, in a certain sense, if the GO road is built, because no armed vehicles, no logging trucks, no workers surveying with the latest technology can really penetrate the mysterious existence of the high country.

The high country is entered authentically only by first accepting that one is ignorant; then affirming a faith in life that is free and flexible and equal to emergencies and broad enough to include death.

The warrior who truly believes in life does not fight, in the usual sense. Winning through the usual kind of fighting is actually losing because the world has then been defined by the old worldview, not by the deep ecology worldview.

Life is a war dance and in the dance there is meaning. Practicing is the end in itself. If through practicing one comes to a kind of deep ecology philosophical position from exploring the broad and deep self, then well and good. If not, then keep practicing.

Becoming a Warrior

The prospect of nuclear holocaust frightens most people. The prospect of loved ones and beloved places being completely destroyed in an instant brings up death images and grave anxiety. But nuclear holocaust is only one logical outcome of the social dynamics of our civilization. A state of war already exists and nuclear holocaust, as terrible as it would be, is only a continuation of that war. Mother Earth has been raped. The rain forests have been raped. Rape, an ugly, violent, abusive crime, is a shocking metaphor to use to describe the situation, but a most appropriate one.

Warriors have been raped. All are victims, but not humiliated and shamed. Warriors don't have to be filled with self hatred or pity. Fully accepting their situation, new warriors remain sensuous, erotic, touching their place, active, fully committed, alive to possibilities. Bells and drums announce the warriors' presence. They are not passive, sullen, or cynical.

Greenpeace tells the prophecy of an old Cree grandmother more than two hundred years ago—a mother with the name Eyes of Fire. She prophesied a time when fish would be poisoned in their streams and birds would fall from the sky and the seas would be "blackened"—all due to white man's technology and greed. Native American peoples would almost completely lose their spirit, but some would find it and teach some white people to have reverence for the body of the earth. Using the symbol of the rainbow, the races of the world would band together to bring an end to desecration and destruction of earth—Warriors of the Rainbow.

Warriors are not necessarily pure, in this society. Gary Snyder says they "must realize that these are abnormal times and there's no way that any of us can keep ourselves pure" (Snyder 1980, 88). All people carry a portion of the world's poisons.

Warriors are aware of the dangers. One great danger is the tendency to be too abstract, too intellectual. Some warriors want to build elaborate arguments for deep ecology, but in the context of the dominant mind-set of western society, the intuition of deep ecology cannot be completely justified. It is also dangerous to hold too much attachment. Many feel attached—ego involved—in winning and losing. Non-attachment is practiced by Buddhists through several methods. Warriors can learn this practice.

New warriors also face the temptation of desiring to be heroes. Today's heroes are usually media figures, or extraordinary individuals. In contrast, heroes in deep ecology are all those involved in the real work. Warriors may become heroes, but not of their own choosing, not from their own desire. New warriors seek transformation of self but *not* egotistical growth, not what some critics call "spiritual materialism." Social and political transformation are part of Self-realization.

New warriors train themselves with two weapons, one being the insight that they are connected with the net of life, that everything is connected and intermingled with everything else. The other weapon is compassion. Warriors take on the suffering of the world, feeling immense compassion. They also act effectively in politics. Persons who intellectually understand environmental problems and develop complex mathematical models of ecosystems or rivers yet never *know* the forest or the river as part of their "body," have not fully experienced the joy of the warrior.

Warriors do not deny their situation or its painfulness. While denial is a useful psychological mechanism in certain circumstances, denying the human impact on the Earth or evolution might tempt warriors to yield to an arcadian fantasy. Deep ecology warriors create ecotopian visions against which they compare the present situation; ecotopia is not a fantasy but rather a statement of an ecological and ethical ideal toward which all can strive.

Neither do warriors retreat into a private cave attempting through spiritual practice to avoid the pollution and dangers of this world. They are engaged in live blade practice in everyday affairs.

Warriors with deep self-identification with a territory, a place or another species of animals, defend it. There is nothing passive or boring or nihilistic about deep ecology warriors. They have affective, erotic relationships with bioregion, river, mountain, and they are passionate, aroused—sometimes even angry.

Most of all the deep ecology warriors live fully, rightly and deeply with the dilemmas and paradoxes of post-modern civilization. They live in the midst of a war zone, recognizing peril. Even when filled with suffering, they are calm. If even one person is calm in the midst of the terror, others are also. If warriors panic in the war, if they feel there is too much challenge and are overwhelmed with fear, then they become incompetent and their energies are scattered.

If warriors are uncommitted or too arrogant, if they feel they have control over the situation or are overconfident or lethargic, they will become boring to themselves and will never be able to act effectively.

Clear thinking, commitment, confidence, calmness. These are attributes which engage minds and bodies in the real work with centered charity.

New warriors are morally bound not to shrink from responsibility. "For if we shrink we close our eyes to reality, and therefore become as guilty of causing the earth's demise as those who produce the weapons and push the buttons," says the Beyond War Woman's Convocation.

Some people see the new warriors as dangerous, because they are serious about their real work. But they continue to practice, are practicing, diligently, and that is affirmation. Ordinary people in extraordinary times expand their capacity for suffering and become warriors.

For the warrior, every campaign may be his or her last, therefore it is the one most real. Warriors feel alive in the midst of the campaign—alive to possibilities in what Buddhists call the great emptiness.

Warriors recognize and accept the suffering, the wounds of the world. They take on the suffering of the rapist and the humiliation of the rape. Even under the best circumstances it is highly likely that they will witness massive human-induced destruction. They do not despair. They simply live.

The simple life is not easy. But warriors are not seduced by the comfortable life, the easy compromises with the dominant worldview. Nor are they seduced by romanticism, idealism, or sentimentalism. Ecological realism is a profoundly objective spiritual *way*.

They are exploring many possibilities for a graceful civilization. What a challenge. What a rich opportunity.

They are settling into *practicing.* In the midst of this war they are searching for ways of dwelling richly and complexly.

There is no opponent, no enemy, in this war. All action comes from the center of a great empty circle full of possibilities. Do nothing. Accept everything. Warriors have no great part to play in the mountain's destiny. Absorb the mountain. Listen to the mountain. Settle onto the mountain.

Perhaps a more mature person, one dwelling in a mixed community, is settling into a space not yet discovered. Some will say our destiny is in the stars. They plan great voyages to other planets. But many supporters of deep ecology say, "well and good. Plan your trips to other planets. That may be a great adventure. But we hardly know this earth. We are just learning ways of dwelling here. In this lifetime it is better to know this earth as a friend, not to dream of escaping to a distant planet."

So warriors stay in their homelands, thrilling to the adventures here. This work requires strength, but not the strength of a weight lifter. No search for perfection, no great achievements. Practice speaking for the rat, the wolf, the kangaroo. Practice mindfulness. Practice nothing. Nothing forced. No heroic gestures. Practice diving deeper into the river, dwelling now here, now there, now here again.

All data is in a sense ambiguous and most statements made (if they are interesting) are paradoxical.

What then are warriors to do? If they agree that most human-induced changes during the past three hundred years have been destructive, that the dominant worldview is anthropocentric, what must they do?

Paradoxically they must attempt to change everything in the culture that is anthropocentric and human-centered, and do nothing.

Warriors withdraw from the most violent and destructive elements in society. They withdraw support from political regimes which encourage warfare, development of nuclear weapons, and massive, destructive projects in the name of economic development. They actively avoid taking sides between capitalism and Marxism, between the U.S.A. and the U.S.S.R., between science and religion. They are neither left nor right. They are affirming the inherent worth of rain forests and grizzly bears. They are encouraging broader identification and solidarity.

Warriors work in political campaigns which are congenial with principles of deep ecology—restoring the Damaged Lands, protecting habitat, protecting biological diversity, helping people to richly experience their place. But they make no great plans, build no great monuments, do not encourage more mega-technology.

They are most active when affirming with their bodies what is not fully expressed in words.

Aikido's method of defense is seeing the openings in the attacker and filling them. It is a method for protecting both the attackee and the attacker. It is also an art. Each person practicing Aikido develops his or her own style within the general principles. Each person who is a supporter of deep ecology develops his or her own style within those deep ecology principles.

Warriors are constantly advised, "Work only on yourself, not on your opponent. . . . When you try to force, throw, take down or defeat your opponent you are using your will power and not your power. Keep to your own center. Let the action occur."

When they feel tired, depressed, defeated, discouraged, without hope of ever really learning Aikido, "keep practicing."

Of course warriors will at times feel frustrated, irritated, despairing. To say that they must feel good all times is to deny the full range of emotional response. In the context of the "great emptiness," emotions are part of the greatness.

Practicing diligently and precisely is challenging, engrossing, vital, and energizing.

Practicing, warriors can take on great suffering with dignity.

Practicing means sharing insights with others, but it also means realizing that those others must discover the insights of deep ecology for themselves, in their own place.

Practicing simply.

Practicing deep ecology means cultivating a sense of the wild center in a civilization out of balance. Action comes from the center of the circle where all is condemned, potential energy.

Practicing deep ecology is a win-win game. Engage the process and the process will continue to engage us. The more cooperation, the more living beings gain realization.

Practicing is subtle.

Practicing is simple.

Practicing is just practicing.

Nothing forced, nothing violent, just settling into our place.

Further Reading

Aitken, Robert. *The Mind of Clover: Essays in Zen Buddhist Ethics.* San Francisco: North Point Press, 1984. See Chapter 21, "Gandhi, Dōgen, and Deep Ecology."

Bennett, David and Richard Sylvan. "Deep Ecology and Green Politics." *The Trumpeter* 4 (Spring 1987): 16-18.

Bunyard, Peter and Fern Morgan-Grenville, eds. *The Green Alternative: Guide to Good Living.* London: Methuen, 1987.

Callicott, J. Baird. "Intrinsic Value, Quantum Theory, and Environmental Ethics." *Environmental Ethics* 7 (Fall 1985): 257-276.

Capra, Fritjof. *The Turning Point: Science, Society, and the Rising Culture.* New York: Simon and Schuster, 1982.

Cheney, Jim. "Eco-feminism and Deep Ecology." *Environmental Ethics* 9 (Summer 1987): 115-146.

Davis, Donald. "Ecosophy: The Seduction of Sophia?" *Environmental Ethics*, 8 (Summer 1986): 151-162. Also in *The Trumpeter* 4 (Summer 1987): 14-17.

Devall, Bill. "Deep Ecology and Its Critics." *Earth First! Journal.* Yule ed. (22 December 1987): 18-20.

_____. "The Deep Ecology Movement." *Natural Resources Journal* 20 (April 1980): 299-322.

_____. "John Muir as Deep Ecologist." *Environmental Review* 6 (Spring 1982): 63-86.

_____. "Reformist Environmentalism." *Humboldt Journal of Social Relations* 6 (Spring 1979): 129-158.

Devall, Bill and George Sessions. *Deep Ecology: Living as if Nature Mattered.* Salt Lake City, UT: Peregrine Smith, 1985.

_____. "The Development of Nature Resources and the Integrity of Nature." *Environmental Ethics* 6 (Winter 1984): 293-322.

Drengson, Alan. "Aikido and Harmony with the Universe." *Heartwood* 5 (Winter 1987): 14, 20.

_____. "Aikido in Daily Life." *Heartwood* 6 (Spring 1987): 17-20.

_____. "Applied Philosophy of Technology: Reflections on Forms of Life and The Practice of Technology." *The International Journal of Applied Philosophy* 3 (Spring 1986): 1-13.

_____. "Art and Imagination in Technological Society." *Research in Philosophy and Technology* 6 (Fall 1983): 77-91.

_____. "Being a Mountain, Astride a Horse. The Warlord Faces South: Reflections on the Art of Ruling." *Philosophy East and West* 33 (January 1983): 35-48.

_____. "Compassion and Transcendence of Duty and Inclination." *Philosophy Today* 25 (Spring 1981): 34-45.

_____. "Critique of Deep Ecology? A Response to Gray." *Journal of Applied Philosophy* 4 (October 1987): 223-227.

_____. "Developing Concepts of Environmental Relationships." *Philosophical Inquiry* 8 (1986): 50-65.

_____. "Ecological Agriculture." In an anthology titled, *After Bennett: A New Politics for British Columbia.* Edited by C. Doyle, R.B.J. Walker, W. Magnusson, and John DeMoreo. Vancouver, B.C.: New Star Books 1986: 134-149.

_____. "Ecosophy: Philosophical Reflections." *Pan Ecology* 3 (Fall 1987).

_____. "Four Philosophies of Technology." *Philosophy Today* 26 (Summer 1982): 103-117.

_____. "Masters and Mastery." *Philosophy Today* 27 (Fall 1983): 230-246.

_____. "Nature, Community and Self." *Communities Magazine* (Fall 1987).

_____. "Paganism, Nature and Deep Ecology." *Nerthus* (Spring 1988).

_____. "The Relevance of Humanities to Environmental Studies." *Journal of Thought* 13 (July 1978): 196-204.

_____. "The Sacred and the Limits of the Technological Fix." *Zygon* 19 (September 1984): 259-275.

_____. *Shifting Paradigms: From Technocrat to Planetary Person.* Victoria, BC: Lightstar, 1983.

_____. "Shifting Paradigms: From the Technocratic to the Person-Planetary." *Environmental Ethics* 3 (1980): 221-240.

_____. "Social and Psychological Implications of Human Attitudes Towards Animals." *The Journal of Transpersonal Psychology* 112 (1980): 63-74.

_____. "Toward a Philosophy of Appropriate Technology." *Humboldt Journal of Social Relations* 9 (Spring 1982): 161-176.

_____. "What is Appropriate Technology?" *Journal of Social Philosophy* 14 (1983).

_____. "What Means this Experience?" *Journal of Experiential Education* 3 (Spring 1982): 14-21.

_____. "Wilderness Travel as an Art and as a Paradigm for Outdoor Education." *Quest* 32 (1980): 110-120.

_____. "Wisdom, Mysticism and the Passions." *Religious Humanism* (Autumn 1978): 161-168.

Evernden, Neil. *The Natural Alien: Humankind and Environment.* Toronto: University of Toronto Press, 1985.

Fox, Stephen. *The American Conservation Movement: John Muir and His Legacy.* Boston: Little, Brown and Co., 1981.

Fox, Warwick. *Approaching Deep Ecology: A Response to Richard Sylvan's Critique of Deep Ecology.* Discussion Papers in Environmental Studies. Environmental Studies Occasional Paper No. 20. Hobart, Tasmania. Centre for Environmental Studies, University of Tasmania, 1986.

_____. Postscript on "Deep Ecology and Intrinsic Value." *The Trumpeter* 2 (Fall 1985): 20-23.

_____. "The Deep Ecology—Ecofeminism Debate and Its Parallels: A Defence of Deep Ecology's Concern with Anthropocentrism." University of Tasmania, 1988.

_____. "Deep Ecology: A New Philosophy of Our Time?" *The Ecologist* 14 (1984): 194-200.

_____. "Further Notes in Response to Skolimowski." *The Trumpeter* 4 (Fall 1987): 32-34.

_____. "On Guiding Stars to Deep Ecology." *The Ecologist* 14 (1984): 203-204.

_____. "Post-Skolimowski Reflections on Deep Ecology." *The Trumpeter* 3 (1986): 16-18.

_____. "Towards a Deeper Ecology." *Habitat Australia* (August 1985): 26-28.

Golley, Frank B. "Deep Ecology From The Perspective of Environmental Science." *Environmental Ethics* (Spring 1987): 45-55.

Grange, Joseph. "Being, Feeling and Environment." *Environmental Ethics* 7 (Winter 1985): 351-364.

Grey, William. "A Critique of Deep Ecology." *Journal of Applied Philosophy* 3 (1986): 211-216.

Jones, Alvyn. "The Violence of Materialism in Advanced Industrial Society: An Eco-Sociological Approach." *The Sociological Review* (February 1987): 19-47.

Kohak, Erazim. *The Embers and the Stars: A Philosophical*

Inquiry Into the Moral Sense of Nature. Chicago: University of Chicago Press, 1984.

LaChapelle, Dolores. *Earth Wisdom*. Los Angeles: Guild of Tudor Press, 1978.

_____. "Sacred Land, Sacred Sex." In *Deep Ecology*. Edited by Michael Tobias. San Diego: Avant Books, 1985: 102-121.

_____. *Sacred Lands, Sacred Sex: The Rapture of the Deep*. Silverton, CO, 1988.

_____. "Systemic Thinking and Deep Ecology." In *Ecological Consciousness*. Edited by Robert C. Schultz. Washington: University Press of America, 1981: 295-323.

Livingstone, John. *The Fallacy of Wildlife Conservation*. Toronto: University of Toronto Press, 1981.

Lombardi, Louis. "Inherent Worth, Respect, and Rights." *Environmental Ethics* 5 (Fall 1983): 257-270.

Manes, Christopher. "Deep Ecology as Revolutionary Thought (Action)." *The Trumpeter* 4 (Spring 1987): 12-14.

McLaughlin, Andrew. "Images and Ethics of Nature." *Environmental Ethics* 7 (Winter 1985): 293-320.

Naess, Arne. "The Arrogance of Anti-Humanism?" *Ecophilosophy* 6 (May 1984): 3-7.

_____. "Deep Ecology and Life Style." *The Paradox of Environmentalism*. Edited by Neil Evernden. Downview,

Ontario: York University, Faculty of Environmental Studies (June 1984): 57-59.

_____. "Deep Ecology in Good Conceptual Health." *The Trumpeter* 3 (1986): 18-22.

_____. "The Deep Ecology Movement: Some Philosophical Aspects." In *Philosophical Inquiry* 8 (1986): 10-31.

_____. "A Defense of the Deep Ecology Movement." *Environmental Ethics* 6 (1984): 265-270.

_____. "The Ecopolitical Frontier: A Case Study." *Intercollegiate Bulletin* 5 (1974): 18-26.

_____. "Environmental Ethics and Spinoza's Ethics. Comments on Genevieve Lloyd's Article." *Inquiry* 23 (1980): 313-325.

_____. "An Example of *Place*: Tvergastein." Manuscript. University of Oslo, 1987.

_____. "For Its Own Sake." *The Trumpeter* 4 (Spring 1987): 28-29.

_____. *Gandhi and Group Conflict: An Exploration of Satyagraha Theoretical Background*. Oslo: Universitets-forlaget, 1974.

_____. "Identification as a Source of Deep Ecology Attitudes." In *Deep Ecology*. Edited by Michael Tobias. San Diego: Avant Books, 1985.

_____. "Intrinsic Value: Will the Defenders fo Nature Please Rise?" In *Conservation Biology*. Edited by Michael E.

Soulé. Sunderland: Sinauer, 1986: 504-515.

_____. "Intuition, Intrinsic Value and Deep Ecology. Comments on an Article by Warwick Fox." *The Ecologist* 14 (1984): 201-203.

_____. "Modesty and the Conquest of Mountains." *The Mountain Spirit.* Edited by Michael Charles Tobias & Narold Drasdo. New York: The Overlook Press, 1979: 13-16.

_____. "Norway" In *Handbook of World Philosophy.* Edited by J. R. Burr. Westport, CT.: Greenwood Press, 1980: 159-171.

_____. "Notes on the Methodology of Normative Systems." *Methodology and Science* 10 (1977): 64-79.

_____. "Population Reduction. An Ecosophical View." University of Oslo: Manuscript, 1987.

_____. "The Primacy of the Whole." In *Holism and Ecology.* The United Nations University, HSDRGPID-61/UNEP-326, 1981: 1-10.

_____. *Self-realization. An Ecological Approach to Being in the World.* Keith Memorial Lecture, Murdoch University, 12 March 1986. In *The Trumpeter* 4 (Summer 1987): 35-41.

_____. "Self-realization in Mixed Communities of Humans, Bears, Sheep, and Wolves." *Inquiry* 22 (1979): 231-241.

_____. "The Shallow and the Deep, Long-Range Ecology Movement." *Inquiry* 16 (1973): 95-100.

_____. "Simple in Means, Rich in Ends: A Conversation with Arne Naess." *The Ten Directions* (Summer/Fall 1982): 7-12.

_____. "Spinoza and Attitudes Towards Nature." In *Spinoza—His Thought and Work.* Jerusalem: The Israel Academy of Sciences and Humanities, 1983: 160-175.

_____. "Spinoza and Ecology." *Speculum Spinozanum* 1677-1977. Edited by S. Hessing. London: Routledge, 1978.

_____. "Through Spinoza to Mahāyāna Buddhism, or through Mahāyāna Buddhism to Spinoza?" In *Spinoza's Philosophy of Man. Proceedings of the Scandinavian Spinoza Symposium 1977.* Edited by Jon Wetlesen. Oslo: Universitetsforlaget, 1978.

_____. "The World of Concrete Contents." *Inquiry* 28 (1985): 417-428.

Rifkin, Jeremy. *Time Wars: The Primary Conflict in Human History.* New York: Henry Holt and Co., 1987.

Rodman, John. "The Dolphin Papers." *North American Review* 259 (1974): 3-26.

_____. "Four Forms of Ecological Consciousness Reconsidered." In *Ethics and the Environment.* Edited by T. Attig and D. Scherer. Englewood Cliffs, N.J.: Prentice-Hall, 1983: 82-92.

_____. "The Liberation of Nature?" *Inquiry* 20 (1977): 83-131.

_____. "Paradigm Change in Political Science." *American Behavioral Scientist* 24 (1980): 49-78.

_____. "Theory and Practice in the Environmental Movement." In *The Search for Absolute Values in a Changing World.* New York: 1978.

Roszak, Theodore. *Person/Planet: The Creative Disintegration of Industrial Society.* Garden City, NY: Anchor Press/Doubleday, 1978.

_____. *Where the Wasteland Ends: Politics and Transcendence in Postindustrial Society.* Garden City, NY: Doubleday, 1972.

Schumacher, E.F. *Small is Beautiful.* New York: Harper and Row, 1973.

Seed, John. "Rainforest and Psyche." Lismore, New South Wales: Rainforest Information Centre, 1985.

_____. "Anthropocentrism." In *Deep Ecology.* Salt Lake City, UT: Peregrine Smith, 1985: 243-246.

Sessions, George. "Anthropocentricism and the Environmental Crisis." *Humboldt Journal of Social Relations* 2 (Fall 1974): 71-81.

_____. "The Deep Ecology Movement: A Review." *Environmental Review* 11 (Summer 1987): 105-126.

_____. "Ecological Consciousness and Paradigm Change." In *Deep Ecology.* Edited by Michael Tobias. San Diego: Avant, 1985.

_____. "Shallow and Deep Ecology: A Review of the Philosophical Literature." In *Ecological Consciousness: Essays from the Earthday X Colloquium.* University of Denver, April 21-24, 1980. Edited by Robert Schultz and J. Donald Hughes. (Washington, D.C.: University Press Sof America, 1981): 391-462.

Shepard, Paul and Daniel McKinley, eds. *The Subversive Science: Essays Toward an Ecology of Man.* Boston: Houghton Mifflin, 1967.

Spitler, Gene. "Justifying a Respect for Nature." *Environmental Ethics* 4 (Fall 1982): 255-260.

Sylvan, Richard (formerly Routley.) *A Critique of Deep Ecology.* Discussion Papers in Environmental Philosophy 17, Philosophy Department: Australian National University, 1985.

Taylor, Paul W. "In Defense of Biocentrism." *Environmental Ethics* 5 (Fall 1982): 237-244.

_____. "The Ethics of Respect for Nature." *Environmental Ethics* 3 (Fall 1981): 197-218.

_____. "Are Humans Superior to Animals and Plants?" *Environmental Ethics* 6 (Summer 1984): 149-160.

_____. *Respect for Nature: A Theory of Environmental Ethics*. Princeton: Princeton University Press, 1986.

Watson, Richard. "A Critique of Anti-Anthropocentric Biocentrism." *Environmental Ethics* 5 (Fall 1983): 245-256.

Watts, Alan. *Nature, Man and Woman*. New York: Vintage Books, 1970.

Wittbecker, Alan E. "Deep Anthropology: Ecology and Human Order." *Environmental Ethics* 8 (Fall 1986): 261-270.

Zimmerman, Michael. "Anthropocentric Humanism and the Arms Race." In *Nuclear War: Philosophical Perspectives*. Edited by Michael Fox and Leo Groarke. New York: Peter Lang Publishers, 1985.

_____. "Beyond Humanism: Heidegger's Understanding of Technology." *Listening* 12 (Fall 1977): 74-83.

_____. "The Crisis of Natural Rights and the Search for a Non-Anthropocentric Basis for Moral Behavior." *The Journal of Value Inquiry* 19 (1985): 43-53.

_____. "Ecofeminism and Deep Ecology: The Emerging Dialogue." From *Ecofeminist Perspectives* conference held at University of Southern California, March 1987. Volume edited by Irene Diamond.

_____. "Feminism, Environmental Ethics, and Deep Ecology." *Environmental Ethics* 9 (Spring 1987): 21-44.

_____. "Feminism, Heidegger, and the Technological Domination of Nature." To appear in *Research in Philosophy and Technology*.

_____. "Heidegger and Marcuse: Technology as Ideology." *Research in Philosophy and Technology* 2 (1977): 245-261.

_____. "Heidegger and Marx on the Technological Domination of Nature." *Philosophy Today* 23 (Summer 1979): 99-112.

_____. "Humanism, Ontology, and the Nuclear Arms Race." *Research in Philosophy and Technology* 6 (1983): 157-172.

_____. "Implications of Heidegger's Thought for Deep Ecology." *The Modern Schoolman* 64 (November 1986): 19-53.

_____. "The Role of Spiritual Discipline in Learning to Dwell on Earth." In *Dwelling, Place, and Environment*. Edited by David Seamons and Robert Mugerauer. The Hague: Martinus Nijhoff Publishers, 1985.

_____. "Toward a Heideggerean *Ethos* for Radical Environmentalism." *Environmental Ethics* 5 (Summer 1983): 99-131.

Deep Ecology Soundings

These recordings were reviewed by Lone Wolf Circles (P.O. Box 652, Reserve, NM 87830), in various issues of *Earth First!* journals in 1985-1987.

Brouk, Joanna. *Sounds of the Sea.*

Crichton, Scott. *Take Me Back to Old Montana.* Helena, MT: Milwaukee Road Productions, 1986.

Dakota Sid. *For the Birds.* Tucson: Earth First! Music, 1987.

Evenson, Dean. *Desert Dawn Song.*

_____. *Whistling Woodhearts.*

Horn, Paul. *Inside the Powers of Nature.* Golden Flute.

_____. *Magic of Findhorn.*

Keeler, Greg. *Songs of Fishing, Sheep and Guns in Montana.* Cassette. Tucson, AZ: Earth First! Music.

Koga, Masayukix. *The Distant Cry of Deer.* Fortuna Records, 1975.

Lee, Katie. *Fenced.* Cassette. Jerome, AZ: Katydid Records.

Lone Wolf Circles. *Full Circle.* Tucson: Earth First! Music, 1986.

_____. *Tierra Primera! The Deep Ecology Medicine Show.* Reserve, NM: 1987.

Naegle, David. *Rainforest Music.*

Nollman, Jim. *Orca Greatest Hits.* Friday Harbor, WA: Interspecies Communication, 1987.

Ortega, A. Paul. *Two Worlds.* Phoenix: Canyon Records.

Oliver, Bill. *Texas Oasis: Environmental Songs for Texas and the World.* 1982.

St. Marie, Buffy. *Sweet America.* ABC #ABCD-929.

Trapezoid. *Another Country.* Flying Fish 287, 1982.

Trundell, John. *Tribal Voice.*

Winter, Paul. *Ancient Future.*

_____. *Callings.* Cassette. Sausilito, CA: Living Music Records, 1980.

_____. *Canyon.* Sausilito, CA: Living Music Records.

_____. *Common Ground.* Cassette. A and M Records, 1978. CS-4698.

_____. *Missa Gaia.* Cassette. Sausilito, CA: Living Music Records, 1985. LMRC-5.

Bibliography

Abbey, Edward. *The Journey Home: Some Words in Defense of the American West.* New York: E. P. Dutton, 1977.

_____. *Desert Solitaire.* Salt Lake City, UT: Peregrine Smith Inc., 1981.

Aitken, Robert. *The Mind of Clover: Essays in Zen Buddhist Ethics.* San Francisco: North Point Press, 1984.

Allin, Craig W. *The Politics of Wilderness Preservation.* Westport, CT: Greenwood Press, 1982.

Anderson, Walter Truett. *To Govern Evolution: Further Adventures of the Political Animal.* New York: Harcourt, Brace, Jovanovich, 1987.

Arendt, Hannah. *Eichmann in Jerusalem: A Report on the Banality of Evil.* New York: Viking Press, 1963.

Bahro, Rudolf. *Socialism and Survival.* London: Heretic Books, 1982.

_____. *From Red to Green.* London: Verso, 1984.

_____. *Building the Green Movement.* London: Heretic Books, 1986.

Bahuguna, Sunderlal. *Forest and People.* Chipko, India, 1982.

Bailey, Jane. *Sea Otter: Core of Conflict, Loved or Loathed.* Morro Bay, CA: El Morro Publications, 1979.

Bandyopadhyay, Jayanta and Vandana Shiva. "Chipko: Rekindling India's Forest Culture." *The Ecologist* 17 (1987): 26-34.

Barlett, Richard. *Yellowstone: A Wilderness Besieged.* Tucson: University of Arizona Press, 1985.

Berger, John. *Restoring The Earth: How Americans are

Working to Renew Our Damaged Earth. New York: Alfred Knopf, 1985.

Berman, Morris. *The Reenchantment of the World.* Ithaca: Cornell University Press, 1981.

Bernard, Jessie. *The Female World.* New York: Free Press, 1981.

Bly, Robert. *News of the Universe: Poems of Twofold Consciousness.* San Francisco: Sierra Club Books, 1980.

Bookchin, Murray. "Social Ecology Versus 'Deep Ecology.'" *Green Perspectives* nos. 4 and 5 (Summer 1987).

_____. *The Ecology of Freedom: The Emergence and Dissolution of Heirarchy.* Palo Alto, CA: Cheshire Books, 1982.

Boer, Ben. "Social Ecology and Environmental Law." *Environment and Planning Law Journal* (September 1984): 241-249.

Brown, Lester and Jodi L. Jacobson. "The Future of Urbanization: Facing the Ecological and Economic Constraints." Worldwatch Paper 77. Washington, D.C.: Worldwatch Institute, 1987.

Bruntland Report. *Our Common Future: The World Commission on Environmental and Development.* New York: Oxford University Press, 1987.

Cahn, Robert, ed. *Environmental Agenda for the Future.* Washington, DC: Island Press, 1985.

Callicott, J. Baird, ed. *Companion to A Sand County Almanac.* Madison: University of Wisconsin Press, 1987.

_____. "Intrinsic Value, Quantum Theory, and Environmental Ethics." *Environmental Ethics* 7 (Fall 1985): 257-276.

_____. "The Metaphysical Implications of Ecology." *Environmental Ethics* 8 (Winter 1986): 301-316.

Campbell, Angus. *The Sense of Well-Being in America: Recent Patterns and Trends.* New York: McGraw-Hill, 1981.

Carson, Rachel. *Silent Spring.* Boston: Houghton Mifflin Co., 1962.

Capra, Fritjof. *The Turning Point: Science, Society and the Rising Culture.* New York: Simon and Schuster, 1982.

Catton, William R., Jr. "The World's Most Polymorphic Species." *BioScience* 37 (June 1987): 413-419.

Caufield, Catherine. *In the Rainforest: A Report from a Strange, Beautiful, Imperiled World.* New York: Alfred Knopf, 1985.

Chase, Alston. *Playing God in Yellowstone: The Destruction of America's First National Park.* Boston: Atlantic Monthly Press, 1986.

Cheney, Jim. "Eco-Feminism and Deep Ecology." *Environmental Ethics* 9 (Summer 1987): 115-146.

Chung-ying Cheng. "On the Environmental Ethics of the Tao and The Ch'i." *Environmental Ethics* 8 (Winter 1986): 351-370.

Cobb, Edith. *The Ecology of Imagination in Childhood.* New York: Columbia University Press, 1977.

Cohen, Jean and Andrew Arato. "The German Green Party: A Movement Between Fundamentalism and Modernism." *Dissent* 31 (1984): 327-332.

Cohen, Michael. *The Pathless Way: John Muir and American Wilderness.* Madison: University of Wisconsin Press, 1984.

Cohen, Michael J. *Prejudice Against Nature: A Guidebook for the Liberation of Self and Planet.* Freeport, ME: Cobblesmith, 1983.

Cooney, Robert and Helen Michalowski, eds. *The Power of the People: Active Nonviolence in the United States.* Philadelphia: New Society Publishers, 1987.

Coppinger, Raymond P. and Charles Kay Smith. "The Domestication of Evolution." *Environmental Conservation* 10 (Winter 1983): 283-291.

Crosby, Alfred W. *Ecological Imperialism: The Biological Expansion of Europe 900-1900.* Cambridge, Eng.: Cambridge University Press, 1986.

d'Aquilli, Eugene, Charles Laughlin Jr. and John McManus, eds. *The Spectrum of Ritual: A Biogenetic Structural Analysis.* New York: Columbia University Press, 1979.

Daly, Mary. *Gyn/Ecology: The Meta-Ethics of Radical Feminism.* Boston: Beacon Press, 1978.

Darlington, David. *In Condor Country.* Boston: Houghton Mifflin, 1987.

Day, David. *The Whale War.* San Francisco: Sierra Club Books, 1987.

Davidson, Nickolas. *The Failure of Feminism.* Buffalo, NY: Prometheus Books, 1987.

Diamond, Cora. "Eating Meats and Eating People." *Philosophy* 53 (1978): 465-479.

Diamond, Stanley. *In Search of the Primitive: A Critique of Civilization.* New Brunswick, NJ: Transaction, Inc., 1974.

Dodge, Jim. "Living by Life: Some Bioregional Theory and Practice." *CoEvolution Quarterly* (Winter 1981): 6-12.

Douglas, William O. *A Wilderness Bill of Rights.* Boston: Little, Brown, 1965.

Drengson, Alan. "Ecoagriculture." *The Trumpeter* (Spring 1985): 18.

_____. "Wilderness Travel as an Art and as a Paradigm for Outdoor Education." *Quest* 32 (1980): 110-120.

Durrell, Lawrence. *Spirit of Place: Letters and Essays on Travel.* Edited by Alan Thomas. New York: E. P. Dutton, 1971.

Ebenreck, Sarah. "A Partnership Farmland Ethic." *Environmental Ethics* 5 (Spring 1983): 33-46.

Ehrlich, Paul R. *The Machinery of Nature: The Living World Around Us—And How It Works.*

New York: Simon and Schuster, 1986.

Ehrlich, Paul R. and Anne. *Extinction: The Causes and Consequences of The Disappearance of Species.* New York: Random House, 1981.

Elder, John. *Imagining the Earth: Poetry and the Vision of Nature.* Urbana: University of Illinois Press, 1985.

Elgin, Duane. *Voluntary Simplicity: Toward a Way of Life That is Outwardly Simple, Inwardly Rich.* New York: William Morrow and Company, 1981.

Elkington, John. *Gene Factory: Inside the Genetic and Biotechnology Business Revolution.* New York: Carroll and Graff, 1985.

Evernden, Neil. *The Natural Alien: Humankind and Environment.* Toronto: University of Toronto Press, 1985.

Feldman, Saul D. and Gerald Thielbar, eds. *Lifestyles: Diversity in American Society.* Boston: Little, Brown and Co., 1972.

Fisher, Frank. "Deep Ecology Lifestyle." *The Deep Ecologist* 20 (April 1986).

Flader, Susan. *Thinking Like a Mountain: Aldo Leopold and the Evolution of an Ecological Attitude Toward Deer, Wolves, and Forests.* Columbia: University of Missouri Press, 1974.

Forbes, Jack D. "The Native American Experience in California History." *California Historical Quarterly* 50 (1971): 234-242.

Foreman, David, ed. *Ecodefense: A Field Guide to Monkeywrenching.* Tucson, AZ: Ned Ludd Books, 1985.

_____. "A Modest Proposal for a Wilderness Preserve System." *Whole Earth Review* 53 (Winter 1986): 42-45.

Foster, Thomas W. "The Taoist and the Amish: Kindred Expressions of Eco-Anarchism." *The Ecologist* 17 (1987): 9-14.

Fox, Michael W. "Nature Conservation, Animal Patenting and Biotechnology." *The Trumpeter* 4 (Fall 1987): 20-24.

Fox, Stephen. *John Muir and His Legacy.* Boston: Little, Brown, 1981.

Fox, Warwick. "Deep Ecology: A New Philosophy of Our Time?" *The Ecologist* 14 (1984): 194-200.

Franklin, Kay and Norma Schaeffer. *Duel for the Dunes: Land Use Conflict on the Shores of Lake Michigan.* Urbana: University of Illinois Press, 1983.

French, Marilyn. *Beyond Power: Women, Men and Morality.* New York: Summit Books, 1985.

Garreau, Joel. *The Nine Nations of North America.* Boston: Houghton Mifflin, 1981.

Gilligan, Carol. *In a Different Voice.* Cambridge, Eng.: Cambridge University Press, 1982.

Goffman, Erving. *The Presentation of Self in Everyday Life.*

Garden City, NY: Doubleday, 1959.

Goldean, Silas. "The Principle of Extended Identity." *The Trumpeter* 3 (Fall 1986): 22-24.

Goldsmith, Edward. "Ecological Succession Rehabilitated." *The Ecologist* 15 (1985): 104-112.

Goldsmith, Edward, ed. "The World Bank: Global Financing of Impoverishment and Famine." *The Ecologist* 15 (1985): whole issue.

Gray, David, ed. *Ecological Beliefs and Behavior: Assessment and Change.* Westport, CT: Greenwood Press, 1985.

Hallen, Patsy. "Making Peace with the Environment: or Why Ecology Needs Feminism." Unpublished paper. Murdoch, Western Australia: School of Social Inquiry, Murdoch University, 1987.

Halpin, Margorie, ed. *Manlike Monsters on Trial: Early Records and Modern Evidence.* Vancouver: University of British Columbia Press, 1980.

Hargrove, Eugene C. "Foundations of Wildlife Protection Attitudes." *Inquiry* 30 (1987): 3-31.

Hargrove, Eugene C. ed. *Religion and Environmental Crisis.* Athens, GA: University of Georgia Press, 1986.

Harris, Larry D. *The Fragmented Forest: Island Biogeography Theory and the Preservation of Biotic Diversity.* Chicago: University of Chicago Press, 1984.

Hays, Samuel P. *Beauty, Health, and Permanence: Environmental Politics in the United States, 1955-1985.* Cambridge, Eng.: Cambridge University Press, 1987.

Heckler, Richard, ed. *Aikido and the New Warrior.* Berkeley: North Atlantic Books, 1985.

Heidegger, Martin. *Basic Writings.* New York: Harper and Row, 1977.

Hemenway, Dan. "Eight Principles for Designing Natural Systems." *Whole Earth Review* 48 (Fall 1985): 72-73.

Herrero, Stephen. *Bear Attacks: Their Causes and Avoidance.* Piscataway, NJ: Einchester Press, 1985.

Holdgate, Martin W., Mohamed Kassas, Gilbert F. White, eds. *World Environmental Trends Between 1972 and 1982.* Dublin, Ireland: Tycooly International Publishing Co., 1982.

Hughes, J. Donald. *American Indian Ecology.* El Paso, TX: Texas Western Press, 1983.

Hwa Yol Jung. "The Orphic Voice and Ecology." *Environmental Ethics* 3 (Winter 1981): 329-340.

Ice Nucleation Minus Research Field Test, DEIS, University of California, Division of Agriculture and Natural Resources, December 1986.

Irwin, John. *Scenes.* Beverly Hills, CA: Sage Publications, 1977.

Jackson, Wes, Wendell Berry and Bruce Coleman, eds. *Meeting the Expectations of the Land: Essays in Sustainable Agriculture and Stewardship*. San Francisco: North Point Press, 1985.

Jeffers, Robinson. *Not Man Apart, Lines from Robinson Jeffers*. Edited by David Brower. San Francisco: Sierra Club Books, 1965.

Kammeyer, Kenneth C. W. and Helen L. Ginn. *An Introduction to Population*. Chicago: Dorsey Press, 1986.

Katz, Eric. "Organism, Community, and the 'Substitution Problem.'" *Environmental Ethics* 7 (Fall 1985): 241-257.

Kellert, Stephen. "Assessing Wildlife and Environmental Values in Cost-benefit Analysis." *Journal of Environmental Management* 18 (1984): 355-363.

Kheel, Marti. "Ecofeminism and Deep Ecology: Reflections on Identity and Difference." Paper read at Conference on Ecofeminism Perspectives: Culture, Nature, Theory. University of Southern California, March 1987.

Koopowitz, Harold and Hilary Kaye. *Plant Extinction*. Washington, D.C.: Stone Wall Press, 1983.

Krieger, Martin H. "What's Wrong with the Trees?" *Science* 179 (February 1973): 451.

LaChapelle, Dolores and Janet Bourque. *Earth Festivals: Seasonal Celebrations for Everyone Young and Old*. Silverton, CO: Way of the Mountain Center, 1976.

Lasch, Christopher. *The Minimal Self: Psychic Survival in Troubled Times*. New York: W. W. Norton, 1984.

LeGuin, Ursula. *Always Coming Home*. New York: Harper and Row, 1985.

Leopold, Aldo. *A Sand County Almanac*. New York: Oxford University Press, 1949.

Levin, David Michael. *Body's Recollection of Being: Phenomenological Psychology and the Deconstruction of Nihilism*. London: Routledge and Kegan, 1985.

London, Julius and Gilbert White, eds. *The Environmental Effects of Nuclear War*. AAAS Selected Symposium. Boulder, CO: Westview Press, 1984.

Love, Sam and David Obst. *Ecotage!* New York: Pocket Books, 1972.

Lovelock, J. *Gaia: A New Look at Life on Earth*. New York: Oxford University Press, 1979.

Lutts, Ralph H. "Chemical Fallout: Rachel Carson's *Silent Spring,* Radioactive Fallout, and the Environmental Movement." *Environmental Review* 9 (1985): 210-225.

Mackay, Donald. *Heritage Lost: The Crisis in Canada's Forest*. Toronto: MacMillan of Canada, 1985.

M'Gonigle, R. Michael. "The Tribune and the Tribe: Toward a Natural Law of the Market/Legal

State." *Ecology Law Quarterly* 13 (1986): 233-310.

McLaughlin, Andrew. "Images and Ethics of Nature." *Environmental Ethics* 7 (Winter 1985): 293-320.

McLaughlin, Corinne and Gordon Davidson. *Builders of the Dawn: Conmmunity Lifestyles in a Changing World.* Walpole, NH: Stillpoint Publishing Company, 1985.

McLuhan, T.C., comp. *Touch the Earth: A Self-Portrait of Indian Existence.* New York: E. P. Dutton, 1971.

McMillan, Carol. *Women, Reason and Nature.* Princeton: Princeton University Press, 1982.

Marco, Gino J., Robert M. Hollingworth and William Durham, eds. *Silent Spring Revisited.* Washington, D.C.: American Chemical Society, 1987.

Marcuse, Herbert. *Eros and Civilization.* Boston: Beacon Press, 1955.

Margolin, Malcolm. *The Ohlone Way.* Berkeley: Heydey Books, 1978.

Martin, Brian. "The Scientific Straightjacket: The Power Structure of Science and the Suppression of Environmental Scholarship." *The Ecologist* 11 (January 1981): 33-43.

Meine, Curt. *Aldo Leopold: His Life and Work.* Madison: University of Wisconsin Press, 1988.

Merchant, Carolyn. *The Death of Nature: Women, Ecology and the Scientific Revolution.* San Francisco: Harper and Row, 1980.

Midgley, Mary. *Heart and Mind.* New York: St. Martin's Press, 1981.

Milbrath, Lester W. *Environmentalists: Vanguard for a New Society.* Albany: State University of New York Press, 1984.

Miller, G. Tyler, Jr. *Living In the Environment.* 5th ed. Belmont, CA: Wadsworth Publishing Co., 1988, chapter 26, "Environmental Ethics."

Mische, Patricia. "Women and Power." *New Age* 4 (November 1978): 38-48.

Morris, Betsy. "As a Favored Pastime, Shopping Ranks High With Most Americans." *Wall Street Journal* (30 July 1987): 1.

Mosley, Geoff, ed. *Australia's Wilderness: Proceedings of the First National Wilderness Congress, October 21-23, 1977.* Hawthorn, Victoria: Australian Conservation Foundation, 1978.

Mowat, Farley. *Woman in the Mists.* New York: Warner, 1987.

Myers, Norman. *The Primary Source: Tropical Forests and our Future.* New York: W. W. Norton, 1984.

Naess, Arne. "Deep Ecology and Lifestyle." In *The Paradox of Environmentalism.* Edited by Neil Evernden. Downview, Ontario: York University, 1984.

_____. *Gandhi and Group Conflict: An Exploration of Satyagraha Theoretical Background.* Oslo: Universitetsforlaget, 1974.

_____. "Identification as a Source of Deep Ecology Attitudes." *Deep Ecology*. Edited by Michael Tobias. San Diego: Avant Books, 1985.

_____. "Modesty and the Conquest of Mountains." In *The Mountain Spirit*. Edited by Michael Tobias and Harold Drasdo. Woodstock, NY: Overlook Press, 1979: 13-16.

_____. "Self-realization: An Ecological Approach to Being in the World." Murdoch University, 12 March 1986.

_____. "Self-realization in Mixed Communities of Humans, Bears, Sheep and Wolves." *Inquiry* 22 (1979): 231-241.

_____. "The Shallow and the Deep, Long-Range Ecology Movement." *Inquiry* 16 (1973): 95-100.

_____. "The World of Concrete Contents." *Inquiry* 28 (1985): 417-428.

Nash, Roderick. *Wilderness and the American Mind*. 3rd ed. New Haven: Yale University Press, 1984.

National Research Council, Committee on Population Growth and Economic Development: Policy Questions. Washington, D.C.: National Academy Press, 1986.

Nelson, Richard. *Make Prayers to the Raven: A Koyukon View of the Northern Forest*. Chicago: University of Chicago Press, 1983.

Nollman, Jim. *Animal Dreaming: The Art and Science of Interspecies Communication*. New York: Bantam Books, 1987.

Norwood, Vera L. "The Nature of Knowing: Rachel Carson and the American Environment." *Signs* 12 (Summer 1987): 740-760.

Ortner, Sherry. "Is Female to Male as Nature is to Culture?" In *Women, Culture and Society*. Edited by Michelle Rosaldo and Louise Lampshere. Palo Alto: Stanford University Press, 1974.

Palmer, Tim. *Stanislaus: The Struggle for a River*. Berkeley: University of California Press, 1982.

Parsons, James J. "On 'Bioregionalism' and 'Watershed Consciousness'." *The Professional Geographer* 37 (February 1985): 1-6.

Pawlick, Thomas. *A Killing Rain: the Global Threat of Acid Precipitation*. San Francisco: Sierra Club Books, 1984.

Perera, Victor and Robert D. Bruce. *The Last Lords of Palenque: The Lacandon Mayas of the Mexican Rain Forest*. Berkeley: University of California Press, 1982.

Phillips, David and Hugh Nash, eds. *The Condor Question: Captive or Forever Free?* San Francisco: Friends of the Earth, 1981.

Plumwood, Val. "Ecofeminism: An Overview and Discussion of Positions and Arguments in Women and Philosophy." Supplement to vol. 64.

Australian Journal of Philosophy. 1986.

Polanyi, Karl. *The Great Transformation.* Boston: Beacon Press, 1944.

Poniewaz, Jeff. *Dolphin Leaping in the Milky Way.* Milwaukee: Inland Ocean Books, 1986.

Porritt, Jonathon. *Seeing Green: The Politics of Ecology Explained.* New York: Basil Blackwell, 1984.

Postel, Sandra. "Defusing the Toxics Threat: Controlling Pesticides and Industrial Waste." Worldwatch Paper 79. Washington, D.C.: Worldwatch Institute, September 1987.

Rappaport, Roy. "Restructuring the Ecology of Cities." *Raise the Stakes* no. 11 (Summer 1986): 4-5.

Repetto, Robert. "Population, Resources, Environment: An Uncertain Future." *Population Bulletin* 42 (July 1987).

Rich, Bruce. "The Multidevelopment Banks, Environmental Policy and the United States." *Ecology Law Review* 12 (1985): 681-746.

Robbins, William G., Robert J. Frank and Richard E. Ross, eds. *Regionalism and the Pacific Northwest.* Corvallis: Oregon State University Press, 1983.

Roszak, Theodore. *Person/Planet: The Creative Disintegration of Industrial Society.* Garden City, NY: Anchor Press/Doubleday, 1978.

_____. *Where the Wasteland Ends: Politics and Transcendence in Postindustrial Society.* Garden City, NY: Anchor Press/Doubleday, 1972.

Ruether, Rosemary Radford. *New Woman/New Earth: Sexist Ideologies and Human Liberation.* New York: The Seabury Press, 1975.

Rusho, W. L., comp. *Everett Ruess: A Vagabond For Beauty.* Layton, UT: Gibbs M. Smith, Inc., 1983.

Sagoff, Mark. "Process or Product? Ethical Priorities in Environmental Management." *Environmental Ethics* 8 (Summer 1986): 121-138.

Sale, Kirkpatrick. *Dwellers in the Land: The Bioregional Vision.* San Francisco: Sierra Club Books, 1985.

_____. "The Forest for the Trees: Can Today's Environmentalists Tell the Difference?" *Mother Jones* (November 1986): 23-29.

Sax, Joseph. *Mountains Without Handrails.* Ann Arbor: University of Michigan Press, 1980.

Schafer, R. M. *The Tuning of the World.* New York: Alfred Knopf, 1977.

Schrepfer, Susan. *The Fight to Save the Redwoods: A History of Environmental Reform, 1917-1978.* Madison: University of Wisconsin Press, 1983.

Schumacher, E. F. *Small is Beautiful: Economics as if People Mattered.* New York: Harper and Row, 1973.

Scitovsky, Tibor. *The Joyless Economy: An Inquiry into*

Human Satisfaction and Consumer Dissatisfaction. New York: Oxford University Press, 1976.

Scully, Vincent. *Mountain, Village, Dance.* New York: Viking Press, 1975.

Seamon, David. "Emotional Experience of the Environment." *American Behavioral Scientist* 27 (August 1984): 757-770.

_____. *A Geography of the Lifeworld: Movement, Rest, and Encounter.* New York: St. Martin's Press, 1979.

_____. "The Phenomenological Contribution to Environmental Psychology." *Journal of Environmental Psychology* (1982): 119-140.

Seamon, David and Robert Mugerauer, eds. *Dwelling, Place and Environment: Towards a Phenomenology of Person and World.* Martinus Nijhoff Publishers, 1985.

Seed, John. "Anthropocentrism!" in Devall, *Deep Ecology.* Salt Lake City, UT: Peregrine Smith, 1985: 243-246.

Shepard, Paul. "Introduction—Ecology and Man—a Viewpoint." In *The Subversive Science: Essays Toward an Ecology of Man.* Edited by Paul Shepard and Daniel McKinley. Boston: Houghton Mifflin, 1969: 1-10.

_____. *Thinking Animals: Animals and the Development of Human Intelligence.* New York: Viking Press, 1978.

Shepard, Paul and Barry Sanders. *The Sacred Paw: The Bear in Nature, Myth, and Literature.* New York: Viking Press, 1985.

Sheridan, David. *Off-Road Vehicles on Public Land.* Washington, D.C.: Council on Environmental Quality, 1979.

Snyder, Gary. *The Real Work: Interviews and Talks—1964-1979.* Edited with an introduction by William Scott McLean. New York: New Directions, 1980.

_____. *Turtle Island.* New York: New Directions, 1974.

_____. "Wild, Sacred, Good Land." *Resurgence* no. 38 (May/June 1983): 10-15.

Sorenson, Steve. "The Fine Art of Recreating Meadows." *Whole Earth Review* (March 1985): 28-32.

Soulé, Michael E., ed. *Conservation Biology: The Science of Scarcity and Diversity.* Sunderland, MA: Sinauer Associates, 1986.

_____. "What is Conservation Biology?" *Bioscience* 35 (December 1985): 727-734.

Spretnak, Charlene. *The Spiritual Dimension of Green Politics.* Santa Fe, NM: Bear and Company, 1986.

Spretnak, Charlene and Fritjof Capra. *Green Politics: The Global Promise.* Santa Fe, NM: Bear and Company, 1984.

Starhawk. *Dreaming the Dark: Magic, Sex and Politics.* Boston: Beacon Press, 1982.

Stegner, Wallace and Page Stegner. *American Places.* New York: E. P. Dutton, 1981.

Swan, Jim. "Sacred Places in Nature." *Journal of Environmental Education* 14 (Summer 1983): 32-37.

Sylvan, Richard and David H. Bennett. "Deep Ecology and Green Politics." *The Deep Ecologist* 20 (April 1986).

Taylor, Paul W. *Respect for Nature: A Theory of Environmental Ethics.* Princeton, NJ: Princeton University Press, 1986.

Thich Nhat Hanh. *Being Peace.* Berkeley, Parallax Press, 1987.

_____. *A Guide to Walking Meditation.* Translated by Jenny Hoany and Nguyen Ann Huong. Berkeley: The Fellowship of Reconciliation, 1985.

Thomas, William, Jr., ed. *Man's Role in Changing the Face of the Earth.* Chicago: University of Chicago Press, 1956.

Thompson, Mark. *Gay Spirit: Myth and Meaning.* New York: St. Martin's Press, 1987.

Tobias, Michael, ed. *Deep Ecology.* San Diego, CA: Avant Books, 1985.

Tronto, Joan C. "Beyond Gender Difference To A Theory of Care." *Signs* 12 (Summer 1987): 644-663.

Tuan, Yi-fu. *Segmented Worlds and Self.* Minneapolis: University of Minnesota Press, 1982.

_____. *Topophilia: A Study of Environmental Perception, Attitudes and Values.* Englewood Cliffs, NJ: Prentice Hall, 1974.

Udall, Stewart. *The Quiet Crisis.* New York: Holt, Rinehart and Winston, 1963.

Uusitalo, Lisa. *Environmental Impacts of Consumption Patterns.* New York: St. Martin's Press, 1986.

van de Kaa, Dirk J. "Europe's Second Demographic Transition." *Population Bulletin* 42 (March 1987).

van der Post, Laurens. *Testament to the Bushmen.* New York: Viking Press, 1985.

Van Newkirk, Allen. "Bioregions: Towards Bioregional Strategy for Human Cultures." *Environmental Conservation* 2 (1975): 108-109.

Vaughan, Frances. *The Inward Arc: Healing and Wholeness in Psychotherapy and Spirituality.* Shambhala Press, 1986.

Vernadsky, V. I. "The Biosphere and the Noosphere." *American Scientist* (January 1945): 1-11.

Vogt, Per. *Fridtjof Nansen: Explorer, Scientist, Humanitarian.* Oslo: Dreyers Forlag, 1961.

Wade, Nicholas. "Sahelian Dought: No Victory for Western Aid." *Science* (July 1974): 236.

Wallace, David Rains. *The Klamath Knot.* San Francisco: Sierra Club Books, 1984.

Warren, Karen J. "Feminism and Ecology: Making Connections." *Environmental Ethics* 9 (Spring 1987): 3-20.

Watts, Alan W. *Nature, Man and Woman.* New York: Vintage Books, 1970.

Weil, Robert. "In Human Bondage." *Omni* (November 1986).

Weir, David. *The Bhopal Syndrome: Pesticides, Environment*

and Health. San Francisco: Sierra Club Books, 1987.

Welch, Lew. *Ring of Bone: Collected Poems, 1950-71*. Edited by Donald Allen. Bolinas, CA: Grey Fox Press, 1973.

Weston, Joe, ed. *Red and Green: A New Politics of The Environment*. London: Pluto Publishers, 1986.

White, Lynn, Jr. "The Historical Roots of Our Ecologic Crisis." *Science* 155 (1967): 1203-1207.

Wilbur, Ken. *The Spectrum of Consciousness*. Wheaton, IL: Theosophical Publishing House, 1980.

_____. *No Boundary*. Boulder, CO: Shambhola, 1981.

Willamette National Forest. "Ecotage From Our Perspective: An Explanation of the Willamette National Forest's Policy on Environmental Sabotage Known as 'Ecotage.' " Eugene, OR: September 1985.

Williams, Walter. *The Spirit and the Flesh: Sexual Diversity in American Indian Cultures*. Boston: Beacon Press, 1986.

Wilson, Edward O. *Biodiversity*. Washington, D.C.: National Academy Press, 1988.

_____. *Biophilia*. Cambridge, MA: Harvard University Press, 1984.

Wilson, Roger. *From Manapouri to Aramoana: The Battle for New Zealand's Environment*. Auckland, New Zealand: Earthworks Press, 1982.

Wolf, Edward C. "On the Brink of Extinction: Conserving the Diversity of Life." Worldwatch Paper 78. Washington, D.C.: Worldwatch Institute, June 1987.

Wood, Harold W., Jr. "The United Nations World Charter for Nature: The Developing Nations' Initiative to Establish Protections for the Environment." *Ecology Law Quarterly* 12 (1985): 977-996.

Wordsworth, William. *Selected Poems and Prefaces*. Edited by Jack Stillinger. Boston: Houghton Mifflin, 1965.

Worldwatch Institute. *State of the World*. Annual. New York: W. W. Norton and Co., 1984, 1985, 1986, 1987.

Worster, Donald. *Nature's Economy*. San Francisco: Sierra Club Books, 1977.

Yett, Jane. "Women and Their Environment: A Bibliography for Research and Teaching." *Environmental Review* 8 (1984): 86-94.

Zimmerman, Michael E. "Feminism, Deep Ecology and Environmental Ethics." *Environmental Ethics* 9 (Spring 1987): 21-44.

Zupan, Borut. "The Green Movement: A New Political Factor in the Industrialized Society." *Review of International Affairs* 34 (5 July 1983): 30-32.